Lecture Notes in Computer Science 8822

Commenced Publication in 1973
Founding and Former Series Editors:
Gerhard Goos, Juris Hartmanis, and Jan van Leeuwen

Frank Ortmeier   Antoine Rauzy (Eds.)

Model-Based Safety and Assessment

4th International Symposium, IMBSA 2014
Munich, Germany, October 27-29, 2014
Proceedings

 Springer

Volume Editors

Frank Ortmeier
Otto von Guericke-University Magdeburg
Faculty of Computer Systems
Chair of Software Engineering
Universitätsplatz 2, 39106 Magdeburg, Germany
E-mail: frank.ortmeier@ovgu.de

Antoine Rauzy
École Polytechnique, Laboratoire d'Informatique (LIX)
Route de Saclay, 91128 Palaiseau Cedex, France
E-mail: antoine.rauzy@lix.polytechnique.fr

ISSN 0302-9743   e-ISSN 1611-3349
ISBN 978-3-319-12213-7   e-ISBN 978-3-319-12214-4
DOI 10.1007/978-3-319-12214-4
Springer Cham Heidelberg New York Dordrecht London

Library of Congress Control Number: 2014950397

LNCS Sublibrary: SL 2 – Programming and Software Engineering

Typesetting: Camera-ready by author, data conversion by Scientific Publishing Services, Chennai, India

Printed on acid-free paper

Springer is part of Springer Science+Business Media (www.springer.com)

Preface

The International Symposium on Model-Based Safety and Assessment (IMBSA) has now been held for the fourth time. Since the first edition in Toulouse 2011, the workshop has evolved to a forum where brand new ideas from academia, leading-edge technology, and industrial experiences are brought together. The objectives are to present experiences and tools, to share ideas, and to federate the community. To foster academic and industrial collaboration, the program is split into three main parts: an academic part presenting new research, a tools and tutorials part presenting leading-edge development support, and an industrial part reporting on experiences and challenges in industrial practice.

The last conferences in Bordeaux (2012) and Versailles (2013) showed an increasing interest in practical demonstrations of model-based safety analysis techniques and tools. As a consequence, tool and tutorial demonstrations are now an important part in the event's program. We believe that a mixture of conventional talks about the newest achievements, presentation of practical experiences, and interactive learning allows for fruitful discussions, exchange of information, as well as future cooperation. Therefore, the focus of this year's edition in Munich, Germany, was placed on the tools and tutorials session, which, as a premiere, was given a full-day time slot.

Nevertheless, the main scientific and industrial contributions were presented in traditional talks and are published in this special volume of LNCS. For IMBSA 2014, we received 31 submission from authors of 12 countries. The best 15 of these papers where selected by an international Program Committee to be published in this volume. In addition to this LNCS volume, IMBSA 2014 also published separate tutorial and tool proceedings. These are aimed at an industrial audience and focus on recapitulating the practical demonstrations.

As program chairs, we want to extend a very warm thank you to all 24 members of the international Program Committee. The comprehensive review guaranteed the high quality of the accepted papers. We also want to thank the local organization team at the Otto von Guericke University of Magdeburg (OvGU), the chairs Martin Bott, Jürgen Mottok, and Christel Seguin, the Zühle Engineering Group, and the Gesellschaft für Informatik (GI).

Finally, we wish you pleasant reading of the articles in this volume. On behalf of everyone involved in this year's International Symposium on Model-Based Safety Assessment, we hope you will be joining us at the 2015 IMBSA edition.

August 2014

Frank Ortmeier
Antoine Rauzy

Organization

Program Committee

Jean-Paul Blanquart	Astrium Satellites, France
Martin Bott	Züelke Engineering, Germany
Marco Bozzano	FBK-irst, Italy
Jean-Charles Chaudemar	ISAE, France
Jana Dittmann	Otto von Guericke University Magdeburg, Germany
Marielle Doche-Petit	Systerel, France
Lars Grunske	University of Stuttgart, Germany
Matthias Güdemann	Systerel, France
Michaela Huhn	Technical University of Clausthal, Germany
Kai Höfig	Siemens AG, Germany
Tim Kelly	University of York, UK
Leila Kloul	Université de Versailles, France
Agnes Lanusse	CEA LIST, France
Till Mossakowski	Otto von Guericke University of Magdeburg, Germany
Juergen Mottok	LaS, OTH Regensburg
Frank Ortmeier	Otto von Guericke University of Magdeburg, Germany
Yiannis Papadopoulos	University of Hull, UK
Antoine Rauzy	École Polytechnique, France
Wolfgang Reif	Augsburg University, Germany
Jean-Marc Roussel	LURPA, ENS Cachan, France
Christel Seguin	ONERA, France
Pascal Traverse	Airbus, France

Table of Contents

Modeling Paradigms

Validation and Testing

Fault Detection and Handling

Safety Assessment in the Automotive Domain

Case Studies

A Practicable MBSA Modeling Process Using Altarica

Shaojun Li* and Duo Su

Airworthiness and Safety Technology Research Center
China Aero-ploy Technology Establishment, AVIC
Beijing, China
jinerli@126.com

Abstract. With the increasing system scale and complexity, safety analysis based on formal models has been widely used in the development of aircraft products. However, it's quite difficult to build a complete, accurate and consistent safety model, especially for dynamic complex systems. To solve these problems, a practical safety modeling methodology based on Altarica, which contains three phases like information collection, model construction and model V&V, is proposed to establish a more structured, systematic and efficiency way in this paper. Detailed processes are declared for each phase. At last, a hydraulic system is taken as an example to show how to apply the safety modeling methodology in practical.

Keywords: Safety, model based safety analysis, formal modeling, modeling process, Altairca.

1 Introduction

With the increasing system scale and complexity, safety analysis based on formal models is developed with more advanced model description capacity and automated analysis process, and has been highly accepted by safety-critical industries in different areas [1], such as aviation, railway transport and nuclear power, etc. However, with the wide use of formal models in the development of aircraft products, lots of problems on model construction arise [2][3][4], especially when multiple departments or suppliers participate within the process together. These problems could be summarized as follows.

First of all, modeling a safety model needs large amounts of information, such as interfaces, system architectures, function flows and failure data, etc. Insufficient information collection could not only increase modeling difficulties but also delay safety assessment progress. For example, references [4] [5] introduce the modeling process of the electronic system, hydraulic system and transmission system, but not fully define the information that should be collected before modeling (such as system configuration in different phases). No detailed researches provide reasonable, ordered and limited steps to gather sufficient information for a complete model. Second, with lack of well-defined procedures, many man-made errors are introduced in the

---

* Corresponding author.

F. Ortmeier and A. Rauzy (Eds.): IMBSA 2014, LNCS 8822, pp. 1–13, 2014.

disordered modeling process. Finally, after modeling, model verification and validation may be ignored to check the consistency between the model and the real system.

To solve the problems above, a practicable safety modeling process using Altarica
is proposed in this paper. First, the whole framework of safety modeling is divided
into three phases as information collection, model building and model V&V. And
then, the sub-processes contained in each phase are depicted as well as their rationali-
ty. Finally, one of safety assessment cases which this modeling process is applied to is
chosen to prove the validity of this process.

2   Fundamental Principles

2.1   Static Safety Models

Static safety models describe the propagation of the effects of failure modes, also we
could say that they model on failure logic. The failure logic modeling (FLM) approach emerged in the 1990s. FLM comes from traditional safety analysis method
such as FTA and FMEA, but it overcomes the problems of great difficulty to modify
, reuse and application to large systems. A component's failure logic describes how
deviations of component inputs (input failure modes) combine with each other and
with internal abnormal phenomena (internal failures) to cause particular deviations of
behavior of component outputs (output failure modes) as shown in Fig.1.The system's
FL are composed from the FL of individual components. Altarica could be used to
model failure logics as well as FPTN[6], FPTC[7], Hip-Hops[8],etc.

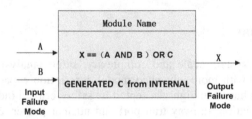

Fig. 1. Failure logic of a component

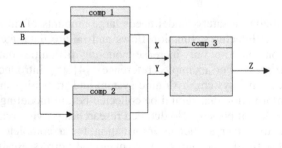

Fig. 2. FPTN notion of a system

According to connectives in the design models, a failure logic model of the system can be composed from the characterizations of individual components by connecting output failure modes of the component to input failure modes of other components, as shown in Fig. 2. Boxes can be seen a set of fault trees. Causes of output failure modes (such as Z in Fig. 2) can be deduced through the graphs and fault trees could be built in that way.

2.2 Dynamic Safety Models Using Altarica

Altarica is a formal language that has been widely used in the aviation areas[9]. Altarica could not only be used to model static failure logic, but also build a dynamic safety mode automaton. The characters of Altarica are introduced as follows.

AltaRica language is hierarchical and compositional. Each component is described by a mode automaton [10]. The basic unit to model a system component is called a "node" and is composed with three different parts: 1) the declaration of variables and events; 2) the definition of transitions; 3) the definition of assertions.

Each component has a finite number of flow variables and state variables. Flow variables are the inputs and the outputs of the node: they are the links between the node and its environment. State variables are internal variables which are able to memorize current or previous functioning mode (for example, failure mode). In our models, these variables (flow and state) are either Boolean or enumerated. Then, each node owns also events which modify the value of state variables. These events are phenomenon such as a failure, a human action or a reaction to a change of one input value. The transitions describe how the state variables are modified. They are written such as "G(s,v) |- E ->s_" where G(s,v) is a Boolean condition on state s and input variables v, E is the event and s_ is the effect of the transition on state variables. If the condition G is true, then event E can be triggered and state variables are modified as described in s_. The assertions describe how output variables are constrained by the input and state variables.

2.3 Simifa

Many tools have been developed to support building and analyzing Altarica models. In this paper , we adopted tool Simfia™ EADS APSYS which provides a graphical interface to design models and allow analyzing them by different ways such as simulation, automatic generation of minimal cuts (i.e. shortest scenarios leading to the failure condition) or sequences (i.e. ordered cuts).

3 The Modeling Process

Safety models are usually used to take safety assessment of identified risks or hazards which exist for reasons of endogenous and exogenous causes. Therefore, before describing the modeling process, we have to stress that identification of risks in a structured and systematic way is the basis of normalized, systematic and structured safety modeling process. After finishing identification of risks or hazards, the modeling process could start.

The modeling process contains three phase: information collection, model construction and model verification and validation. Each phase owns different sub-processes as shown in Figure 3.

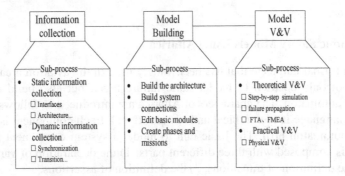

Fig. 3. Modeling phases and relevant processes

3.1   Information Collection

Complete information collection is quite necessary before constructing a model. Incomplete information would lead to an incorrect model, which means more efforts to modify the model later. The information used to build static and dynamic modes is concluded as follows.

3.1.1   Static Information Collection

The static information collection process is shown in Fig.4.

1. Specify the system architecture, external entities and external interfaces

The system architecture, external entities and external interfaces should be specified first. The architecture is the basis for the model. External entities contain origin producers of model input, target consumers of system output, and other entities representing technological exchanges or measures with external environments. External entities could be used to specify model inputs and outputs.

There exist three kinds of model inputs: (1) fluids like energy or supplied flows; (2) command and control flows issued by the operator or pilot; (3) configuration transmitted manually or automatically to the system and referring to the state of the architecture in different flight phases and missions.

According to the hierarchical level of the modeling system, the model may be later used to be integrated into a much higher level model. Meanwhile, the modeling system may have a quite high hierarchical level itself, which means it needs to assemble sub-system models (or supplier models) for this system. Therefore, in order to successfully assemble supplier models later, it's necessary to specify the interfaces among different sub-models.

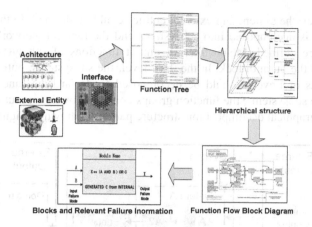

Fig. 4. Information collection process

2. Build the function tree to specify the functions and services to model

Build the function tree, and specify the safety-relevant functions and services to model according to the aircraft FHA and system FHA results. The system architecture is hierarchical. In order to be consistent with the hierarchical architecture, the system fiction should be hierarchical also, which could be reflected by the function tree.

3. Specify system breakdown structure

The function chains and relevant blocks/entities (blocks/entities refer to the subjects that output relevant functions which could be system, sub-system, components with different breakdown levels) could be determined after specifying the functions to model. Some entities could be regrouped to reach a proper level of precision. In order to build a hierarchical and readable model, the break down structure should be then specified. The regroupment and the structure should be validated by designers to ensure correctness.

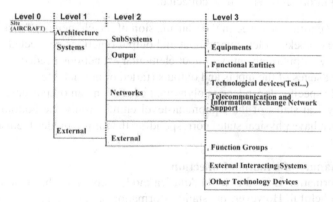

Fig. 5. Model decomposition level

In the first level, the system and external entities could be defined. In the second level, the system is decomposed into subsystems and the function networks formed by sub-systems are defined. Meanwhile, all output functions of sub-systems could be integrated into the output block. In the third level, the subsystems, output blocks and external blocks of Level 2 could be decomposed to declare the functional entities composing the subsystems, the function groups contained by the output block of Level 2, etc. The graphical decomposition structure pattern is shown in Figure 6.

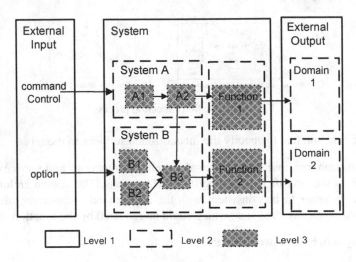

Fig. 6. Structured Model Pattern

4. Analysis the functions and services to be modeled

After Process 3, internal functional analysis (such as building function flow diagrams) has to be prepared to identify all functional chains contributing to the functions. List the elementary functions and relevant entities contributing to the main functions, and the following information should be collected:

(a) blocks / entities involved in the transmission of the elementary functions
(b) for every blocks, elementary input and output functions connected
(c) for every output of an entity, input elementary functions needed
(d) relevant states of the inputs and outputs (failed or normal, etc.)
(e) possible specific dependency polynomial concerning an output state
(f) the physical states of the equipment-level entities (only the bottom-level entities must have physical states corresponding the failure modes themselves)

3.1.2 Dynamic Information Collection
Dynamic information is used to build Altarica mode automata. The static information above is also helpful. However, the static information should be processed. Since the dynamic model is based on the theory of mode automata, a state diagram is quite useful to gather the necessary dynamic information.

A state diagram could state the dynamic information as follows:

o inputs and outputs of the object
o states that the object owns
o the polynomials of outputs, inputs and self-states
o the way that one state transformed to another
o the synchronized transition events happened to a system
o the initial state

State explosion is a problem that maybe introduced by the dynamic models. In order to reduce the states and simply the models, the states of certain object should be determined by its function failure modes instead of hardware failure modes. Hardware failure modes are usually much more than function failure modes, and it is difficult to determine its output when hardware failure mode occurs.

3.2   Model Construction

After collection of information, it's time to start model construction and build a hierarchical model like Fig.6. The precise process is as follows.

1. Build the architecture

According to the architecture and system breakdown structure, build a hierarchical architectural model. Determine the constituent blocks of different level models. It starts from the system level, and then the sub-system level until the bottom item level.

2. Build the connection among different levels and different blocks

According to the function flow charts, the connection among different blocks of different levels could be built. There is no need to clearly define the characters of connection, which could be detailed in the following steps. However, the pre-defined connection could avoid missing input information when editing the blocks in the next step. It would be much more reasonable to connect the blocks from the top level to the bottom level.

There are two ways to connect the blocks with the main functions and services to be provided by the system. For dynamic models, only is the first is allowed since dynamic models represent actual operation situations.

— Connect according to the topological structuration of the functional network. Describe all elementary functional flows exchanged by the different entities, and identify those logical and functional chains constituting at the end the different contributions to the main service provided.
— Connect according to system composition. Determine the elementary entities contributing to the main function, and connect these entities with functions issued from the supporting entities directly to the main entity.

3. Edit the bottom blocks

For static models, there are three steps to edit the elementary blocks or bottom blocks. First, define the input and output of the blocks. Then, define the states of the each block. At last, define the logic relations among outputs, inputs and states.

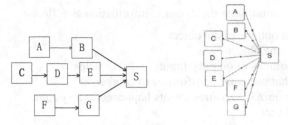

Fig. 7. (a) Modeling according to the topological structuration; (b) Modeling according to the composition

For dynamic models, more work needs to do except for the above three steps. The forth step is define the state transitions. Some transitions may happen at the same time. After editing the elementary blocks, the synchronous transition should be defined in the block of the corresponding higher level.

4. Create missions and phases

Create missions and phases to declare the initial state. When safety analysts try to build static models, this step is necessary if the system has different configurations during different phases. For dynamic model, it is always necessary to define the initial state.

3.3   Model Verification and Validation

Model V&V is to ensure the correctness and completeness of models.

1. Theoretical V&V

V&V checklists, FMEA/FTA/Reliability diagrams could be used to support V&V process. FMEA/FTA/Reliability diagrams could be used to check if the results are consistent with the previously known causes of failure conditions. V&V checklists should contain as many requirements as possible to guarantee the correctness and completeness.

Step-by-step simulation is supported by lots of analysis toolsets today. For static models, it is possible to choose a failure state, and observe how it influences other items. Similarly, after setting up a trigger event (or transition), it is possible to observe how the system operates. In that way, we could verify if the model is built correct.

2. Practical V&V

Practical V&V is valid only if a physical model or real sample of the model can be used. Practical V&V works through producing real failures on the real system, and check if there is a coherency between the real effects produced and those predicted by the FMECA generated from the model.

4   Case Study

The modeling process is applied to a hydraulic system of a helicopter with the detailed results described as follows.

4.1   Information Collection

1. Specify the system architecture, external entities and external interfaces

The hydraulic system contains two main hydraulic subsystems (named A and B) and a cold backup C. Subsystem A and C provide pressure and flow for the left cavity of the rotor booster. B is designed for the right. When A failed, C starts working. Subsystem A and B are powered by the engine. However, C relies on an electric machine. The system architecture, external entities, and interfaces are shown in Fig.8. Since C doesn't work at first, its initial state is spare (configuration information).

2. Build the function tree to specify the functions and services to model

The function tree is translated into Table1. According to the FHA results, A, B and C failed to provide hydraulic pressure and flow are a catastrophic event. That's, all functions in Tables 2 have to be modeled.

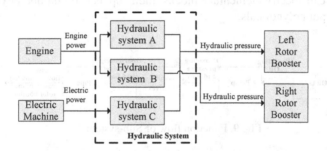

Fig. 8. Hydraulic systems Architecture

Table 1. Function tree of the hydraulic system

Function of Level 1	Functions of Level 2	Functions of Level 3
providing pressure and flow for the rotor booster	providing pressure and flow for the left cavity of the rotor booster	providing pressure and flow from A
		providing pressure and flow from C
	providing pressure and flow for the right cavity of the rotor booster	providing pressure and flow from B

3. Specify system breakdown structure

According to the decomposition method in Chapter 3, the hydraulic system is decomposed as shown in Table 2.

Table 2. The breakdown level of the hydraulic system

Level 1	Level 2	Level 3
Hydraulic system	Sub-system A	Oil tank Pump Assembled valves Pipe …
	Sub-system B Sub-system C	….
	Providing pressure and flow for the rotor booster	Providing pressure and flow for the left cavity of the rotor booster Providing pressure and flow for the right cavity of the rotor booster
External power source	Engine Electric machine	Engine Electric machine
Rotor booster	Left cavity of the rotor booster Right cavity of the rotor booster	Left cavity of the rotor booster Right cavity of the rotor booster

4. Analysis the functions and services to be modeled

Taking providing pressure and flow for the left cavity of the rotor booster from A as an example, the function flow diagram is built in Fig.9. Through function and failure analysis, one can specify elementary blocks, their inputs and outputs, physical failure states and output polynomials.

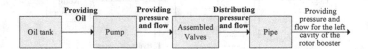

Fig. 9. Function flow of Sub-system A

Table 3. Function analysis and failure analysis results

Elementary block	Physical state itself	Input function (and state)	Output function (and state)	Output polynomial
Tank	Leak	——	Providing oil (normal, failed)	And
Pump	Stuck Cracked	Providing oil (normal, failed)	Providing hydraulic pressure and flow (normal, no-pressure, low-pressure, high-temperature, etc.)	The polynomial should be described for each abnormal output function state.
…	…	…	…	...

5. State diagram analysis

Take the pump of sub-system B as an example to show how to determine the dynamic information. In order to take a complete description of state charts of the pump, we need to specify its inputs and outputs, states, asserts, transitions, synchronism, and initial states one by one.   As talked in 3.1.2, to reduce the number of states, it is sensible to simply the states. Therefore, for the pump, its dynamic information could be assumed as follows:

• two states of inputs: normal(with oil providing by the tank), and failed (without oil providing)
• two states of outputs: normal (providing oil with certain pressure and flow), and failed (disabled to provide oil with certain pressure of flow)
• two self-states: normal and failed
• asserts: when the pump works normal and its input is normal, then its output is normal; If its input is failed or the pump is failed, its output is failed
• Transition: when the pump failed, its state transformed from normal to fail.
• Synchronism: when the pump's state converts to failed, the state of pump of subsystem C turns to working from waiting.
• initial state: normal

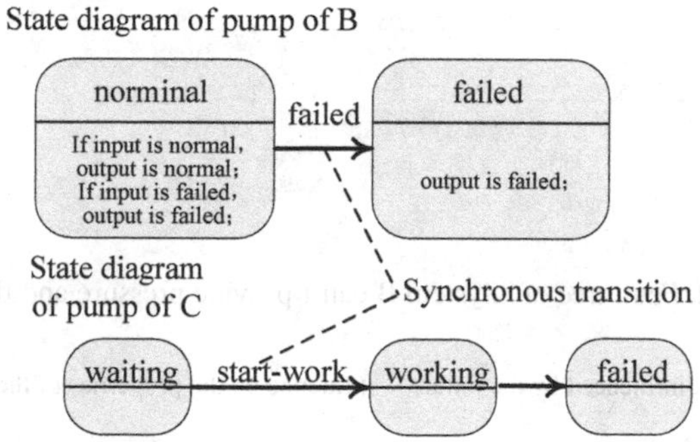

Fig. 10. State diagram of pump of B

4.2   Model Construction

Construct the model according to the procedures talked in 3.1. In this case, the Simfia toolsets provided by EADS APSYS were adopted. The partial model is shown in Fig.11.

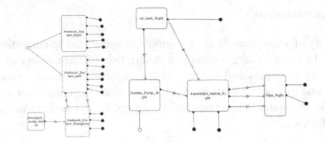

Fig. 11. (a) System level model; (b) Sub-system level model

4.3   Model V&V

In this case, "Sub-system B can't provide pressure and flow" was taken as a top event to generate a fault tree as shown in Fig.12. Through validation the correctness of this fault tree by relevant system designers, the correctness of this model is verified correct partially.

Fig. 12. Fault tree of "System B can't provide pressure and flow"

block influenced by the failure   influence on the properties of the block

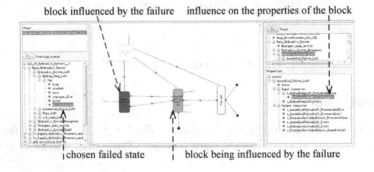

chosen failed state   block being influenced by the failure

Fig. 13. Step by step simulation

Step-by-step simulation could help to verify the correctness of models. Choose the failure state of one block, and check its influence on other blocks step by step.

In Figure 13, the "No-operation" state of pump of A is chosen, the red block (the left block in the Fig.12 which is displayed in red color in the toolset) stands for the block that has been influenced by the failure, and the blue block (the right block in the Fig.12 which is displayed in blue color in the toolset) stands for the block being influenced right now. The detailed influence is shown on the value of the properties on the lower right corner of the figure.

5 Conclusion

A practicable safety modeling process using Altarica is proposed in this paper. The methodology could normalize the safety modeling process and enhance the model readability, correctness and completeness, and avoid unnecessary modeling errors.

References

1. Joshi, A., Whalen, M., Heimdahl, M.: Model-based safety analysis final report, NASA contractor report, NASA/CR-2006-213953 (2006)
2. Bieber, P., Bougnol, C., Castel, C., Heckmann, J.-P., Kehren, C., Metge, S., Seguin, C.: Safety Assessment with AltaRica - Lessons learnt based on two aircraft system studies. In: 18th IFIP World Computer Congress, Topical Day on New Methods for Avionics Certification. IFIP-AICT, vol. 155, pp. 505–510. Springer, Heidelberg (2004)
3. Humbert, S., Seguin, C., Castel, C., Bosc, J.-M.: Deriving Safety Software Requirements from an AltaRica System Model. In: Harrison, M.D., Sujan, M.-A. (eds.) SAFECOMP 2008. LNCS, vol. 5219, pp. 320–331. Springer, Heidelberg (2008)
4. Adeline, R., Cardoso, J., Darfeuil, P., Humbert, S., Seguin, C.: Toward a methodology for the AltaRica modeling of multi-physical systems. In: ESREL 2010, Rhodes, Greece (2010)
5. Kehren, C., et al.: Advanced Multi-System Simulation Capabilities with AltaRica. In: Proceedings of the International System Safety Conference (2004)
6. Fenelon, P., McDermid, J.A.: An Integrated Toolset for Software Safety Analysis. Journal of Systems and Software (1993)
7. Paige, R., et al.: FPTC: Automated Safety Analysis for Domain-Specific Languages. Models in Software Engineering, 229–242 (2009)
8. Papadopoulos, Y., Walker, M.: Engineering failure analysis and design optimisation with HiP-HOPS. Engineering Failure Analysis, 590–608 (2011)
9. Point, G., Rauzy, A.: Altarica - constraint automata as a description language. European Journal on Automation (1999)
10. Rauzy, A.: Mode Automata and their compilation into fault trees. Reliability Engineering and System Safety 78, 1–12 (2002)

On Efficiently Specifying Models
for Model Checking

Mykhaylo Nykolaychuk, Michael Lipaczewski,
Tino Liebusch, and Frank Ortmeier

Chair of Software Engineering,
Otto-von-Guericke University of Magdeburg,
Germany
https://cse.cs.ovgu.de

Abstract. Using formal methods for quality assurance is recommended
in many standards for safety critical applications. In most industrial
contexts, model checking is the only viable option for formal verification,
as interactive approaches often require very highly specialized experts.
However, model checking typically suffers from the well-known state-
space explosion problem. Due to this problem, engineers typically have
to decide on a trade-off between readability and completeness of the
model on one side, and the state space size, and thus, computational
feasibility on the other. In this paper, we propose a method for reducing
the state space by restructuring models. The core idea is to introduce as
few additional states as possible by model design making state transitions
more complex. To avoid unreadability and infeasible model sizes, we
introduce a concept for hierarchical boolean formulas to efficiently specify
state transitions. For evaluation purposes, we applied this approach to
a case study using the VECS toolkit. In this exemplary case study, we
were able to reduce the state space size significantly and make verification
time feasible.

Keywords: design for verification, state-space explosion, formal verification, stateless transitions, SAML.

1 Introduction

More and more elements of our daily lives are automated using better and faster
processing units. This holds also for safety critical applications, which dramat-
ically increased over the past ten years. At the same time, these systems are
increasing in complexity due to the usage of software components. Formal methods became a useful and important tool to verify this kind of systems.

In recent years, model checkers, modelling languages and modelling environments have been improved to allow for easier and more flexible verification of
complex systems. Unfortunately, even though it is now possible to model almost
every kind of system, it is still not possible to verify their behavior using model
checkers. This is due to the very well-known state-space explosion problem [8,22],

F. Ortmeier and A. Rauzy (Eds.): IMBSA 2014, LNCS 8822, pp. 14–27, 2014.

an exponential increase in memory usage and computation time with increasing model size.

The core challenge in modelling and checking safety critical systems is to find a compromise between level of abstraction (granularity) and size of the model (state space). Fine and exact modelling of complex systems often make model checking infeasible due to the state-space explosion. On the other hand, too abstract models may omit important aspects relevant to the system's safety [11].

This paper describes an approach to make excessive use of stateless elements to model major parts of a system. The automata that not depend on its own internal state are redundant and will be replaced with boolean *formulas*. This allows to balance the trade-off between state space size and efficiency of model checking. We demonstrate this approach on a case study of a landing gear system [4]. Note that this approach can (of course) not circumvent the state space explosion problem. It is rather a suggestion of trading state space against complexity of the state transition matrix.

The reminder of the paper is structured as follows: After a description of the case study in Section 2, the modelling approach is presented and discussed in

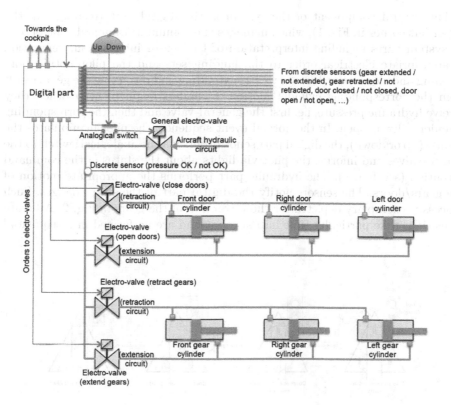

Fig. 1. Global landing gear system architecture [4]

Section 3. Section 4 introduces the SAML language with its core capabilities, which is then used to create the case study model. Proposed modelling paradigm is used for the modelling of landing gear system in Section 5. An evaluation of the model checking is given in Section 6. In Section 7 we refer to the relevant literature on automated safety analysis and conclude our work with a summary in Section 8.

2   Case Study

The landing gear system specification [4] is a proposed benchmark for comparing and evaluating different formal model checking approaches. The Landing gear system is the safety critical part of an aircraft and have to maneuver the gears and associated doors. The system consists of three major parts (see Fig. 1):

- a mechanical part including all devices of three landing sets (front, left, right) as well as a set of sensors monitoring the different devices,
- a digital part including the control software,
- a pilot interface consisting of an up/down handle and a set of lights to illustrate the current health state of the system.

The central component of the system is the digital part (rectangle in the upper left corner in Fig. 1), which manages the communication and control over all system parts including interpretation of the sensor information, generation of appropriate electrical order to the landing sets and the pilot notification. Opening and closing the doors as well as extending and retracting the gears result from the corresponding cylinder motion. Cylinders begin to move when they receive hydraulic pressure, i.e. first the general-valve and then the corresponding cylinder valve is open. In the normal event sequence, the pilot manipulates the handle (up or down), the digital part sends orders via the analogical switch to the electro-valves and informs the pilot via lights about the status of the command execution (see Fig. 1). The hydraulic part performs the appropriate motion of the gears/doors. The sensors notify the digital part of the state changes. Such process is exemplary depicted for the retraction of the gears in Fig. 2. All state transitions take particular time into account and are performed in a sequential

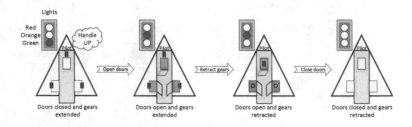

Fig. 2. The landing gear retraction sequence overview

way. Only after finishing previous transitions, the next one can fire. At any time, one or more system components can fail. Only permanent failures are considered.

The expected behavior of the system equipment has to satisfy several temporal constraints. Requirement R_{31} demands that in normal mode, the stimulation of the gear-extending or retracting electro-valves can only happen when the three doors are locked open. The fourth requirement demands that in normal mode the electro-valves for opening and closing the doors as well as for extending and retracting the gears are not stimulated simultaneously. R_5 requires that it is not possible to stimulate the maneuvering electro-valve (opening, closure, retracting, extending) without stimulating the general electro-valve. The computed results of these requirements against our system model are presented in Section 6. For more detailed information on the landing gear system as well as the functional and safety-related requirements, we refer to Boniol et al. [4].

3   New Modelling Approach

A functional model of software-intensive systems includes components of software, hardware and environment in which the system is embedded. Typically derived from system architecture, these model parts will be designed as state machines. If the system is large, i.e. it consists of many (sub)components, or a high level of detail is needed, a state-space explosion is likely.

For building a model, most modelling languages allow for some sort of operator parallel composition. Although the semantics of such operators may vary, their main intention is to enable compact specifications of large models (e.g., three parallel components/automata of 20 states each together describe a product automat with state space of 20^3). For verification, these parallel components are unfolded and an automatic reduction (typically in the form of binary decision diagrams (BDDs) [1]) is done.

In this paper, we propose to replace specific automata by boolean *formulas* (stateless, parameter-free expressions that can refer to any state or combination of states) as often as possible during the modelling process. This can be done for all components that just forward/process some information but do not depend on an internal state. The core advantage of replacing particular automata with *formulas* is a smaller state space. Note that modelling with *formulas* has a slightly different semantic than modelling with (synchronous) parallel composition: While *formulas* are re-evaluated instantaneously, state machine changes have effect only in the next time step. In such a way we change the semantic of the time-dependent system behavior, i.e. the *formula* becomes *true* immediately as soon as direct dependencies are in desired state. So we save one time step compared with automata, which becomes *true* in the next step.

Further, some disadvantages are possible: This approach may easily lead to huge and complicated boolean expressions due to the internal representation of frequently-used nested *formulas* (in our example a simple specification file would become at least 100.000 lines huge). Thus, reading, understanding and maintaining the model can be hard. To deal with this problem, clear naming conventions, hierarchical nesting and modelling practices must be followed.

While using nested *formulas* is very beneficial, it brings the danger of creating cyclic dependencies. Our Eclipse-based tool called Verification Environment for Critical Systems (VECS) [15] has implemented features that detect possible infinite dependency loops automatically during the modelling process.

Summarizing, we propose to replace automata with *formulas* whenever it is possible. To keep models readable, elaborate tool support for namespaces as well as for nested formulas is required. In addition, translation into input languages of specification tools is also required. This support technology has been implemented in the VECS specification environment. The core difference to (automatic) state-space reduction (which every modern model checker employs) is that our approach leads engineers to build semantically "smaller" models. The key aspect is to provide tools and technology that enable an engineer to specify such a model as easily as a "simple" automata model. In Section 5, we model the landing gear system using the proposed approach. Before, we will briefly introduce the specification language we used.

4   SAML - Safety Analysis Modelling Language

The Safety Analysis Modelling Language (SAML) [13] is intended to allow for two different kinds of formal analysis techniques based on one unified model. In general, system analysis is divided into *qualitative* analysis with two-valued logic, and *quantitative* analysis where probabilities are computed.

For safety critical systems, both qualitative and quantitative analyses are of interest. This is typically done by building two separate models for these two kinds of analysis. In addition to the huge effort of manual building, maintaining and verifying the correctness of these independent models, this technique is error-prone and time-consuming. To unify the modelling process and to bring the advantages of model checking to safety engineers, we proposed the SAML modelling language as well as the VECS development environment [15]. SAML is a formal tool-independent language that allows the specification of both, qualitative and quantitative aspects of a system in a single model.

To that end, the language was designed in such a way that a more general model can be created that is expressive enough to model all types of software and hardware systems, but at the same time it is simple enough for automatic translation into the input languages of verification engines of both types.

For verification, numerous excellent verification tools are available and proven in use. The idea of SAML is to provide a single tool-independent model that can be verified by these already existing tools. This is done by transforming SAML models on a syntactical level into the input language of the desired analysis tool. Currently, there exist converters to NuSMV[1] (for qualitative analysis) and to PRISM[2] (for quantitative analysis). Additionally, there are a number of prototypes for other model checkers (such as MRMC, UPPAAL and Z3). The output

---

[1] http://nusmv.fbk.eu/

[2] http://www.prismmodelchecker.org/

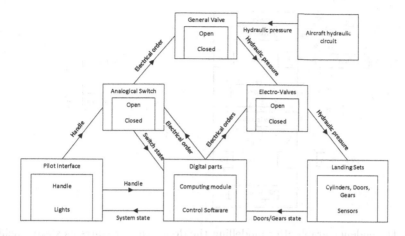

Fig. 3. Architecture of the landing gear system model in SAML

of this transformation is a semantically equivalent model expressed in the input language of the chosen verification tool. A formal proof of the semantic equivalence of the transformed models may be found in Güdemann et al. [13].

The use of automatic model transformations offers two big benefits: first, the separation allows switching between different verification engines without touching the model. This allows for the integration of more advanced (bigger/better/faster) verification engines. Second, it is guaranteed that all analyses are done on the same model. Therefore, since the same model is used, all results are consistent with each other.

5   Efficient Modelling of the Case Study

This section describes the formal modelling of the landing gear system in SAML using the proposed formula-centric approach. In SAML, a synchronous discrete time model (i.e. all parallel finite state machines of the model in each time unit execute an update rule) is used. Note that duration of all movements in the landing gear system is assumed to be always the same and does not deviate from corresponding mean values.

Based on the given mean operation durations of the landing gear system, we defined the temporal resolution of the model as $\Delta t = 200ms$. The reasons are that $\Delta t = 200ms$ is the biggest common denominator of all given timing constraints. Within this time period no significant safety critical state changes can happen. Each time-dependent physical behavior of the system is then modelled according to Δt as a counter automaton. For example, the action "unlock front gear cylinder in down position", which takes about $0.4s$, will be performed in our model in 2 time steps. The gears state "locked down" ($counter < 2$) switches to "unlocked down" ($counter = 2$) according to the time steps counter. Here, at each time step we need to know the intern (previous) state of the counter and

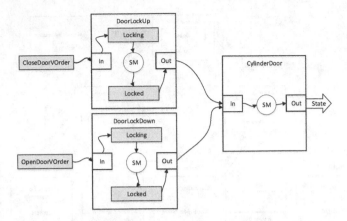

Fig. 4. Dependency graph after modelling the door cylinder states as state machine

consequently cannot model this component with *formulas* only. The landing gear system components (e.g. pilot interface; left, right and front landing sets) that have no timing constraints, but exhibit non-deterministic behavior (like the pilot handle) must be modelled as state machines as well. So far, our model consists of the following components (state machines): pilot interface, analogical switch, electro-valves, three landing sets containing hydraulic cylinders for moving doors and gears, and the computing module. Fig. 3 presents all modelled components with their corresponding dependencies: Arrows visualize the information flow direction (like system state transfer from the digital part to the pilot interface) or directed physical phenomena transmission (like electrical order or hydraulic pressure) between the components. Note that Fig. 3 is not a state machine but depict only the information / physical phenomena flow direction between system components modelled as state machines. This corresponds very well to the case study specification in Fig. 1.

Exemplary, without loss of generality, we show how to design the appropriate system behavior using our approach described in Sec. 3 on the door cylinders within the landing set model. We concentrate on the cylinders that are responsible for moving the doors.

The dependency graph as a result of the naïve modelling approach (the cylinder is modelled as finite state machine) is shown in Fig. 4. These graphs can be generated automatically with VECS. The components (state machines) are visualized as white rectangles (e.g., *CylinderDoor*). The *formulas* are represented with grey rectangles (e.g., *locked, locking*). The state variables are expressed as circles within the corresponding components. The arrows of the resulting graph represent the direct dependencies of the sink vertices from the sources.

The *formulas OpenDoorV Order* and *CloseDoorV Order* serve as input from the corresponding electro-valves and inform about the current state (open or closed) of the valves. These *formulas* trigger the locking operation of the doors in the down or up position respectively. Between the three cylinder states (down,

```
enum cylinder := [down , high , intermediate];
component CylinderDoor
        cylinderState : cylinder init down;
        component DoorLockUp

                ...

        endcomponent
        component DoorLockDown

                ...

        endcomponent
        !DoorLockUp.locked & !DoorLockDown.locked ->
                choice: ((cylinderState'= cylinder.intermediate));
        DoorLockUp.locked & !DoorLockDown.locked ->
                choice: ((cylinderState'= cylinder.high));
        !DoorLockUp.locked & DoorLockDown.locked ->
                choice: ((cylinderState'= cylinder.down));
endcomponent
```

Fig. 5. SAML model of the door cylinder expressed as a state machine

high, intermediate), a certain amount of time elapses. To control these timing constraints, the state machines *DoorLockUp* and *DoorLockDown* are used. Note that the missing timing constraints for the actions "door unlock up", "door move up" and "door move down" are present in the model, but are not visualized for the sake of clarity. Depending on their state, the *CylinderDoor* component derives the door cylinder's state. This state serves as an output to the computing module (i.e., as sensor information). In Fig. 5, the simplified SAML model of the door cylinders is shown. The transitions of the cylinder state machine within the *CylinderDoor* component depend on the current state of the *DoorLockUp* and *DoorLockDown* state machines.

The straightforward modelling approach where each hardware and software component of the system was modelled as a state machine is modified to the extent that stateless constructs such as *formulas* are used in certain cases. The resulting SAML model (after restructuring according to our approach) is shown in Fig. 6. The state machine *CylinderDoor* with three states (down, high, intermediate) is replaced with three *formulas DoorOpen*, *DoorClosed* and *DoorIntermediate*. Such substitution is feasible, if a state machine (in our case *CylinderDoor*) depends on other state machines only, but not on itself. In such a way we change the semantic of the time-dependent system behavior. Before replacement the state changes in *DoorLockUp* and *DoorLockDown* take effect in the next time step. Such delay could cause in some cases the incorrectly modelled system behavior due to timing constraints violation and subsequently dissatisfaction of requirements. After replacement the *CylinderDoor* dependent system components are affected immediately. In our case study the timing constraints are defined with particular tolerance so that both models (before and after replacement) satisfy the system requirements. Now the current cylinder state can be requested via the corresponding *formula*.

```
component DoorLockUp
      ...
endcomponent
component DoorLockDown
      ...
endcomponent

formula DoorIntermediate := !DoorClosed & !DoorOpen;
formula DoorClosed := DoorLockUp.locked & !DoorLockDown.locked;
formula DoorOpen := !DoorLockUp.locked & DoorLockDown.locked;
```

Fig. 6. SAML model of door cylinder expressed as *formulas*

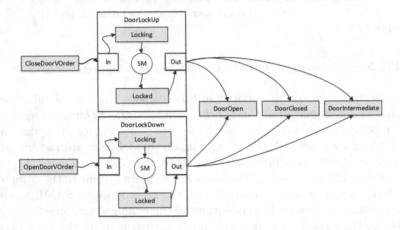

Fig. 7. Dependency graph after modelling the door cylinder states as *formulas* using our approach

Thus, the state machines for the cylinder states are avoided (Fig. 7) and consequently the system state space is smaller and the landing gear system model is verifiable in shorter time (see detailed analysis in Section 6).

Furthermore, the technical and behavioral similarity of three landing sets allows for the usage of the *template* design pattern: This allows modelling a state machine that can be instantiated several times. This improves not only the readability of the model, but also allows for reusing parts of the model in other projects. Once defined, three instances of front, right and left landing sets can be created.

To model the failure performance in SAML, *failure* components are used. In our model, for all failure components the occurrences are set to *nondet* (nondeterministic) and *recovering* to *never*. During the analysis, we are able to check the failure state of the desired component as a normal boolean expression (e.g. !*AnalogicalSwitchFail*). Further details about formal failure modelling and failure patterns in SAML can be found in our previous work [18].

6   Evaluation

The safety analysis of the landing gear system model containing normal and possible failure modes was performed on a 6 core 3.2 GHz computer with 16GB of RAM. To check the correctness of the model, its appropriate internal representation in NuSMV has to be built. The performance of this task is one of the crucial criteria for the modelling quality in SAML.

The evaluation was done on two landing gear models that only differ in the modelling of the landing sets. The first model was created using the naïve approach, here called the *standard* model. The second model was created using our approach and is here called the *restructured* model. The rest of the landing gear model is identical in both cases.

Translation of the landing gear system model (including failure components) from SAML to NuSMV takes in VECS about $30s$ for both, the *standard* and *restructured* model. The output file sizes of the NuSMV model are about $280kB$ and $570kB$, respectively. This difference is due to the substitution of formula names by their defining expressions in the NuSMV model, which are always set in parentheses to ensure an execution order. The creation of the internal BDD representation of the landing gear model in NuSMV takes $14.2s$ for the *standard* model and $0.2s$ for the *restructured* model. Here, we can see the first significant difference between the modelling approaches. Partially such big time difference can be explained by the fact that three landing sets form the significant part of the whole system model. Our model satisfies all requirements defined in specification [4], which indicates the correctness of the modelled landing gear system. Note, that the failure mode requirements R_6, R_7 and R_8 of the landing gear system are not evaluated in our work due to the similarity with system health monitoring which is part of the computing module. Beside model correctness, the goal of this work was to show the performance benefit due to our model restructuring approach. The comparison of the BDD-based model checking performance of the *standard* and *restructured* model is presented in Table 1.

Table 1. Results of the model checking on the *standard* (white row) and *restructured* (grey row) model

Req.	time step, ms	all states	reachable states	BDD nodes	time, s	used RAM, MB
R_{11}	200	2^{273}	2^{79}	3830081	20.053	181
		2^{263}	2^{68}	806275	0.388	64
R_{12}	200	2^{273}	2^{79}	3830078	20.109	181
		2^{263}	2^{68}	806275	0.408	65
R_{31}	200	2^{273}	2^{79}	3599284	17.325	181
		2^{263}	2^{68}	806158	0.396	74
R_{32}	200	2^{273}	2^{79}	3599284	17.297	189
		2^{263}	2^{68}	806158	0.372	51
R_{41}	200	2^{273}	2^{79}	3599284	17.213	171
		2^{263}	2^{68}	806154	0.372	62
R_{51}	200	2^{273}	2^{79}	3599284	17.229	194
		2^{263}	2^{68}	806154	0.364	47

The first two columns in Table 1 display the requirement ID and temporal resolution (in milliseconds) of the SAML model. Values in these two columns are identical for both checked model types: the *standard* model in the first line and the *restructured* model as in the second line with grey background. The values of the remaining columns (all states, reachable states, BDD nodes, time in seconds, used RAM in MB) differ depending on model type and requirement ID. The first requirement R_{11} to be proven means that all gears will be locked and all doors will be closed within $15s$ of the handle state change. The number of all and reachable states differs between the two modelling approaches by 2^{10} and 2^{11} respectively (these values are constant for all checked requirements). The BDD size of the *restructured* model is smaller by a factor of 4.75. The model checking time was faster by a factor of 50. That is the second great difference between the two models, and the one that clearly demonstrates the advantages of restructuring the *standard* model. The performance differences for the other requirements are of similar magnitude. Again, the better performance in terms of BDD size (by an average factor of 4.5) and model checking time (by a factor of 43) was achieved by restructuring the *standard* model.

7   Related Work

The way to design verifiable system models is a poor addressed issue [11]. Most research activities are concerned with the question of how to analyze given models well. In practice, the analysis to verify safety aspects of software-intensive systems is mostly done manually. Existing safety analysis tools focus on a specific class of problems with a corresponding specification language.

Safety analysis tools can be separated into two classes regarding the goals of modelling and checking: *qualitative analysis* to find out, if something can cause a system failure. This is mostly solved by formal verification and model checking techniques [5,17,19] and *quantitative analysis* to estimate the probability of a system failure. This is done with stochastic models and quantitative approximations [3,12,16].

The most known example of a formal language used for the development of safety critical applications is the SCADE suite, developed by Esterel Technologies. SCADE is based on the synchronous data-flow language LUSTRE. However, the included model-checker is not well suited for more complex safety analysis [14]. It also does not allow probabilistic analysis.

The open source project TopCased built a modelling framework for software and systems modelling. Their approach is described by Vernadat et al. [23]. Target input languages are SysML, UML and the architecture analysis and design language (AADL) [20]. The goal of TopCased is to allow for the formal analysis of these models. Models specified in the modelling framework are then transformed into the FIACRE [9] intermediate language. From there, models are transformed into the input language of different analysis tools (e.g. CADP [10], TINA [2]). The resulting FIACRE models are often too complex for the analysis so that only very small models can be analyzed efficiently. Also, only qualitative analyses are possible.

A framework for the specification of safety-critical systems and model-based safety analysis is developed in the Correctness, Modelling and Performance of Aerospace Systems (COMPASS) project [7]. It combines both qualitative and quantitative modelling capabilities by using a formalization of a subset of AADL [20] and its error annex [21]. This combination allows analyzing models specified in the SLIM language [6]. Nevertheless, the design is very much tool-dependent and exchanging the model-checking tools is not possible.

The purpose of our work is to provide a method and tools for the design of efficiently checkable system models. We propose a combination of the advantages of SAML and the benefits of a user-friendly design environment (VECS) for model-based analysis along with the proposal of design guidelines that address the problem of state space explosion already at the engineering level.

8 Conclusions and Further Work

Our work paid attention to the question of making behavioral systems analyzable. We presented a method for reducing state spaces by restructuring models. Our idea is to limit the state space already at the engineering level by making state transitions more complex. For this purpose, we substitute all replaceable state machines of the model with stateless boolean expressions. Once defined in the system model scope, the *formulas* are accessible for an arbitrary number of times and at arbitrary places in the model. To deal with possible unreadability or infeasible length of the model, we use a concept of hierarchical boolean *formulas*. The nesting of the *formulas* allows for efficient specification of the state transitions.

For evaluation purposes, we used this approach for modelling of the landing gear system in the VECS toolkit. In this case study, we were able to reduce the state space size by a factor of 2^{11}. The size of the internal binary decision diagram (BDD) could be minimized by an average factor of 4.5. The verification time of the *restructured* model compared to the *standard* model was reduced by a factor of 43. In general, significant differences between two checked models regarding state space size, number of BDD nodes and verification time show that our approach can reduce the state space, allowing to model and check more complex systems. We also admit, that we cannot completely solve the problem of state space explosion with our approach, but we still created a new directive for making larger models verifiable.

Further, we want to examine whether very large models can be made verifiable by means of our approach. Besides BDD-based model checker, we plan to investigate the effect of our approach using *satisfiability (SAT)*-based techniques. With the proposed approach, we hope that our tool VECS will be more feasible in practical applications such as the certification of safety critical systems. Implementing appropriate heuristics, that automatically identify state machine candidates for substitution with *formulas*, could be an useful feature of VECS tool.

Acknowledgments. Mykhaylo Nykolaychuk is funded by the German Ministry of Education and Science (BMBF) in the VIP-MoBaSA project (project-Nr.: 16V0360).

References

1. Akers, S.: Binary Decision Diagrams. IEEE Transactions on Computers C-27(6) , 509–516 (1978)
2. Berthomieu, B., Ribet, P.O., Vernadat, F.: The Tool TINA - Construction of abstract state spaces for Petri Nets and Time Petri Nets. International Journal of Production Research 42, 2741–2756 (2004)
3. Böde, E., Peikenkamp, T., Rakow, J., Wischmeyer, S.: Model based importance analysis for minimal cut sets. Reports of SFB/TR 14 AVACS 29, SFB/TR 14 AVACS, ISSN: 1860-9821 (April 2008)
4. Boniol, F., Wiels, V.: Landing gear system (2013), http://www.irit.fr/ABZ2014/landing_system.pdf (accessed on August 5, 2014)
5. Bozzano, M., Villafiorita, A.: Improving system reliability via model checking: The FSAP/NuSMV-SA safety analysis platform. In: Anderson, S., Felici, M., Littlewood, B. (eds.) SAFECOMP 2003. LNCS, vol. 2788, pp. 49–62. Springer, Heidelberg (2003)
6. Bozzano, M., Cimatti, A., Katoen, J.P., Nguyen, V.Y., Noll, T., Roveri, M.: Model-based codesign of critical embedded systems. In: Proceedings of the 2nd International Workshop on Model Based Architecting and Construction of Embedded Systems (ACES-MB 2009), vol. 507, pp. 87–91. CEUR Workshop Proceedings (2009)
7. Bozzano, M., Cimatti, A., Katoen, J.P., Nguyen, V.Y., Noll, T., Roveri, M.: Safety, dependability, and performance analysis of extended AADL models. The Computer Journal (2010)
8. Clarke, E., Grumberg, O., Peled, D.: Model Checking. MIT Press (2008)
9. Farail, P., Gaufillet, P., Peres, F., Bodeveix, J.P., Filali, M., Berthomieu, B., Rodrigo, S., Vernadat, F., Garavel, H., Lang, F.: FIACRE: an intermediate language for model verification in the TOPCASED environment. In: European Congress on Embedded Real-Time Software (ERTS 2008). SEE (January 2008), http://www.see.asso.fr
10. Fernandez, J.C., Garavel, H., Kerbrat, A., Mounier, L., Mateescu, R., Sighireanu, M.: CADP - a protocol validation and verification toolbox (1996)
11. Groote, J.F., Kouters, T.W.D.M., Osaiweran, A.: Specification guidelines to avoid the state space explosion problem. In: Arbab, F., Sirjani, M. (eds.) FSEN 2011. LNCS, vol. 7141, pp. 112–127. Springer, Heidelberg (2012)
12. Grunske, L., Colvin, R., Winter, K.: Probabilistic model-checking support for FMEA. In: Proceedings of the 4th International Conference on Quantitative Evaluation of Systems (QEST 2007). IEEE (2007)
13. Güdemann, M., Ortmeier, F.: A framework for qualitative and quantitative model-based safety analysis. In: Proceedings of the 12th High Assurance System Engineering Symposium (HASE 2010), pp. 132–141 (2010)
14. Güdemann, M., Ortmeier, F., Reif, W.: Using deductive cause-consequence analysis (DCCA) with SCADE. In: Saglietti, F., Oster, N. (eds.) SAFECOMP 2007. LNCS, vol. 4680, pp. 465–478. Springer, Heidelberg (2007)

15. Lipaczewski, M., Struck, S., Ortmeier, F.: Using tool-supported model based safety analysis - progress and experiences in SAML development. In: Winter, V., Gandhi, R., Parakh, A. (eds.) IEEE 14th International Symposium on High-Assurance Systems Engineering, HASE 2012 (2012)
16. Ortmeier, F., Reif, W.: Safety optimization: A combination of fault tree analysis and optimization techniques. In: Proceedings of the Conference on Dependable Systems and Networks (DSN 2004). IEEE Computer Society Press, Florence (2004)
17. Ortmeier, F., Thums, A., Schellhorn, G., Reif, W.: Combining formal methods and safety analysis – the ForMoSA approach. In: Ehrig, H., Damm, W., Desel, J., Große-Rhode, M., Reif, W., Schnieder, E., Westkämper, E. (eds.) INT 2004. LNCS, vol. 3147, pp. 474–493. Springer, Heidelberg (2004)
18. Ortmeier, F., Güdemann, M., Reif, W.: Formal failure models. In: Proceedings of the 1st IFAC Workshop on Dependable Control of Discrete Systems (DCDS 2007). Elsevier (2007)
19. Åkerlund, O., Bieber, P., Boede, E., Bozzano, M., Bretschneider, M., Castel, C., Cavallo, A., Cifaldi, M., Gauthier, J., Griffault, A., Lisagor, O., Luedtke, A., Metge, S., Papadopoulos, C., Peikenkamp, T., Sagaspe, L., Seguin, C., Trivedi, H., Valacca, L.: ISAAC, A framework for integrated safety analysis of functional, geometrical and human aspects. In: Proceedings of 2nd European Congress on Embedded Real Time Software, ERTS 2006 (2006)
20. SAE-AS5506: Architecture analysis and design language, AADL (2004)
21. SAE-AS5506/1: Architecture analysis and design language (AADL) Annex E: Error Model Annex (2006)
22. Valmari, A.: The state explosion problem. In: Reisig, W., Rozenberg, G. (eds.) APN 1998. LNCS, vol. 1491, pp. 429–528. Springer, Heidelberg (1998)
23. Vernadat, F., Percebois, C., Farail, P., Vingerhoeds, R., Rossignol, A., Talpin, J.P., Chemouil, D.: The TOPCASED project - a toolkit in open-source for critical applications and system development. In: Data Systems in Aerospace (DASIA), European Space Agency. ESA Publications (2006)

A Model-Based Methodology to Formalize Specifications of Railway Systems

Melissa Issad[1,3], Leïla Kloul[2], and Antoine Rauzy[1]

[1] LGI, Ecole Centrale de Paris, Grande Voie des Vignes,
92290 Châtenay-Malabry, France
[2] PRiSM, Université de Versailles, 45 Avenue des États-Unis, 78000 Versailles, France
[3] Siemens SAS, 150 avenue de la République, 92320 Châtillon, France

Abstract. In this article, we propose a modeling methodology for the formalization of the specifications of railway systems. Most of the railway systems are actually still specified in natural language. It results lengthly and ambiguous descriptions, which is obviously a concern regarding safety and security. Hence the current trend to move to the model based approach, i.e. to translate textual specifications into models. To achieve this goal, the choice of a suitable modeling formalism and modeling methodology is of paramount importance. The modeling formalism should be close enough to the practitioners way of thinking so to facilitate the acceptance of the approach. It should be also formal enough to avoid ambiguity. We discuss here these issues based on experiments we made on railway automation solution Trainguard©Mass Transit Communication Based Train Control of Siemens.

1   Introduction

In this article, we report the preliminary work we made for the formalization of the specifications of the railway automation solution Trainguard©Mass Transit Communication Based Train Control of Siemens. We present the domain specific modeling language we designed for that purpose and modeling methodology we adopted.

Most of the railway systems are still specified in natural language. It results lengthy and ambiguous descriptions. For instance, the Trainguard©MT CBTC specifications spread over about one thousand pages. Such specifications make the system hard to develop and even harder to verify, to validate and to maintain, not to speak about knowledge capitalization and stakeholders awareness. Hence the current trend to move to the model based approach, i.e. to translate textual specifications into models. However, if translating text into informal or semi-formal diagrams is certainly of some help to better understand the system under study, it cannot fully achieve the goal of removing ambiguity. We face actually two problems:

- How to extract the relevant information from huge textual descriptions that mix up different levels of details and abstraction and that involve lots of implicit knowledge?

F. Ortmeier and A. Rauzy (Eds.): IMBSA 2014, LNCS 8822, pp. 28–42, 2014.

– How to cross the bridge between informal and formal while staying close enough to the practitioners way of thinking so to facilitate the adoption of the approach?

To handle these two problems, we decided to determine first what are the concepts at stake and how these concepts are linked together. Eventually, this process ended up into a small domain specific modeling language. We are convinced that some general lessons can be drawn from this experience (which is still ongoing at the time we write these lines).

The remainder of the article is organized as follows. Section 2 describes the Trainguard©MT CBTC. Section 3 provides architectural views of this system. Section 4 presents the domain specific modeling language we designed. Section 6 explains the methodology for formalizing textual specifications. Section 7 discusses some related works. Finally, section 8 concludes the paper and outlines directions for future works.

2   Running Example: Trainguard Mass Transit CBTC

The Trainguard©MT CBTC[10] system is a solution for railway automation(see figure1). It represents the operating system of a train. It is composed of two subsystems, the on-board and the wayside.

The on-board subsystem controls the train doors, the braking, the train position, its speed and the stop with the information to the passengers. The wayside mainly determines the train movement authority according to its speed and position.

In order to test and verify our methodology, and to enhance our modeling language, we chose some scenarios of the Trainguard©MT. Let's take as an example the arrival at station of a train: The wayside must select a stopping point for the train to activate the braking system. After the train stop, the platform and the doors can be opened by the wayside and the train. $OBCU$, ATS, WCU_ATP

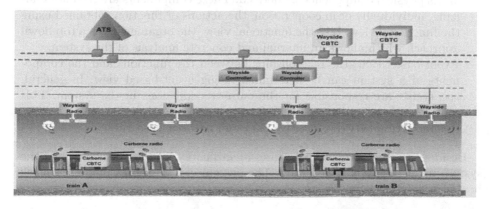

Fig. 1. Trainguard Mass Transit CBTC[1]

and HMI are system components. In the functional specification, it is initially described this way in the system specification:

1. ATS selection
2. the ATS selects the stopping point
3. the ATS sends the stopping point to the WCU_ATP
4. The WCU_ATP sends the stopping point to the on-board
5. Arrival of the information to the $OBCU$ that triggers the braking
6. the $OBCU$ detects that the train is at the stopping point and informs the HMI
7. After the train stop, the $OBCU$ maintains the braking system
8. the $OBCU$ sends the braking data to the HMI

In the following sections, we will explain how, starting from this informal and complex specification, we build a formal model able to be understood by all the stakeholders of the system engineering and used for formal analysis.

3   The System Architecture

A system architecture provides a description of the different parts of the system. It aims at simulating their behaviors and the way they interact. In order to understand the behavior of a complex system, different views of its architecture have to be investigated. These are the following:

- *Functional view:* the behavior of a complex system can be described through the *actions* or the *functions* the system has to realize in order to achieve its operational missions. The functional view aims at developing a breakdown structure of the system behavior in order to derive all its actions (main and subsidiaries) and all the relationships between them.
- *Organic view:* using this view, one can describe the system by defining its physical *components*. From the main component, which is the system itself, all its physical components are derived. These components are the ones realizing, individually or in cooperation, the actions or functions obtained using the functional view. Like the functional view, the organic view is a top-down approach which allows an internal and concrete analysis of the system.
- *Event-based view:* the relationships between the functions and the components of a system can be determined using event-based view. In general, the *events* are responsible for the data transmissions in the system. This representation is very useful for further system analysis because it allows differentiating between sensitive data and non-sensitive ones.

Besides the three previous views, an identification of the stakeholders of the system under analysis is necessary. The system can be represented as a black box with different connections:

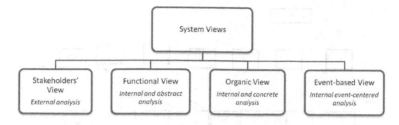

Fig. 2. The System Architecture Definition

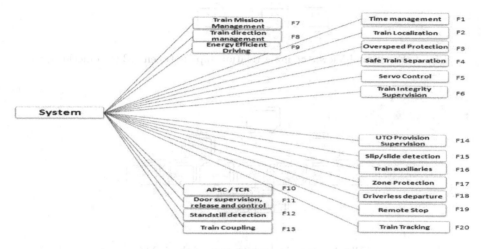

Fig. 3. Functional View: the CBTC architecture

- The inputs: they are the variables that interfere in the system behavior;
- The outputs: they are the data and the results of the system's deployment;
- The supports: they are all the external stakeholders of the system.

Consider the CBTC example. In order to identify all the actions, the components, and the events of this system, we investigate the corresponding views. The *functional view* of the CBTC provides the functions hierarchy in Fig. 3, which allows us to identify a total of twenty functions or actions. The functional view provides also the relationships between these functions in Fig. 4. This figure shows a strong correlation between these functions as most of them require data from others in order to be achieved. These data are sent periodically or by broadcast. Only three functions (F13, F15, F16) are completely independent.

As the CBTC is a complex system, the *organic view* provides a multi-level structure, each corresponding to a different level of abstraction of the system (see Fig. 5). Among the system components is the *environment*, which is also a stakeholder that has an impact on the safety of the actual components of the system, and as a such, must be taken into account. Investigating the relationship between the components and the functions they realize, we have a {n, n}

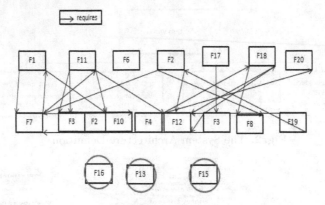

Fig. 4. Functional View: the main relationships between CBTC functions

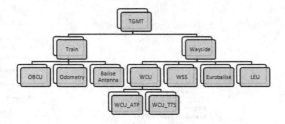

Fig. 5. Organic Architecture of the CBTC

relationship between them (see Fig. 6). A component realizes several functions while a function requires several components to be completed.

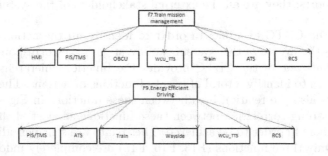

Fig. 6. Relationship between the Components and the Functions

The *event-based view* of the CBCT provides a partial view of the system, but with another type of relevant information. It also helped understand how important events are in the communication part of the system (see figure7).

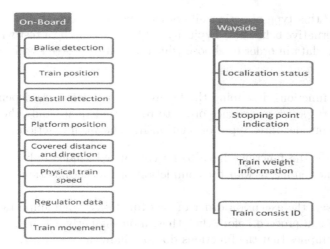

Fig. 7. High level event-based view of the CBTC

4   SDLg: The Description Language for Complex Systems

SDLg is the System Description Language we have developed for the modeling of complex systems architectures. This language relies on the information provided by the different views of the system, that is, the functional, the organic, and the event-based views. This information is then translated into a graphical representation of the system, using SDLg operators. In the following, we present the elements of the language and show how a system like the CBTC can be modeled using this language.

Using the information provided by the different views, we can define a system as a set of components $\mathcal{C}$ which execute functions, either individually or in cooperation. Let $\mathcal{F}$ be the set of all the functions in the system, and $\mathcal{F}(C)$ the set of functions in which component C, $C \in \mathcal{C}$, is involved. Assuming that each component in $\mathcal{C}$ has its own resource to execute a function, a shared function f, $f \in \mathcal{F}$, between two components C_1 and C_2 in the system is a function that requires the resources of both components to be completed, that is $f \in \mathcal{F}(C_1) \cap \mathcal{F}(C_2)$. However, if f requires the resource of component C_1 solely, then f is not a shared function. Moreover, as a function can be defined as an action which may requires input data, which may produce results that may, or may not, be useful for other functions, we consider that a function may be of one of the following types:

- S_action: this is a simple action that requires the resources of a single component to be completed. This type of action may require input data, that may be provided by one or several other actions. The input data, if there are any, are analyzed in order to generate an output result, after some process and calculation.
- T_action: this is a shared action between two or more components. Such an action can be a data transmission between two components of the system, and thus requires the cooperation of both components.

- *Q_action*: this type of action allows the system to choose between two or more alternative behaviors. Typically, a *Q_action* can be a test which has to be run on data in order to choose which action to proceed with in the next step.

Often the functions describing the behavior of a system are dependent, and thus have to respect a precedence order to receive adequate and coherent information. We consider three types of relationships between functions:

- *Precedence*: the functions have to be completed sequentially. This implies that a function has to wait the completion of another function, before starting.
- *Parallelism*: the execution order of two functions is not important. In this case, one can proceed before the other, independently. Clearly, such a relationship implies that the functions do not share the resources.
- *Preemption*: after a *Q_action*, a function among a set of two or more is chosen to proceed. In this case, the other functions are discarded.

Because the different views of the system architecture may provide too detailed functions (functional view), components (organic view) and events (event-based view), it becomes necessary, during the system engineering process, to structure this information and introduce a certain hierarchy between them. For that, we introduce the notion of abstraction *level* as one of our main language elements. This notion allows distinguishing between a high-level function with just enough details to understand the part of the system behavior it represents, and an atomic function which results from successive refinements of a high-level function into smaller functions of lower level. In order to progress from one level to another, SDLg relies on the information provided by the different views of the system and its operational scenarios.

SDLg provides a small but efficient set of operators, which allow expressing the behavior of the system's components, the relationships between them, and the relationships between the functions they realize.

- **Precedence** $f_1 \rightarrow f_2$: as the corresponding relationship has been defined above, this operator models a certain order in which two functions f_1 and f_2 have to be realized. In this case, function f_1 has to completed before f_2.
- **Parallelism** $f_1 \rightleftharpoons f_2$: this operator implies that functions f_1 and f_2 are independent and the order in which they are completed is not important. It models the independency between the two functions.
- **Choice** $f_1 \vee f_2$: the system has the choice between two functions to complete. The selection of a function will discard the other.
- **Cooperation** $C_1 \curvearrowright C_2$: it expresses the cooperation between two components C_1 and C_2 on a function completion.
- **Assignment** $C_1 \equiv C_2$: this models the assignment of the behavior of component C_2 to component C_1.

- **Refinement** $L_n \downarrow L_{n+1}$: this models the transition from one abstraction level n to a lower abstraction level $n + 1$. This transition implies a further step in the refinement of the system description. The refinement does not concern T_Actions when it is about components

As SDLg uses a graphical representation of the system, it also provides the following idiomatic representations:

- $\boxed{f}$: f is an atomic or complex function.

- $\bigcirc\!\!\!C$: C is a component of the system.

- $\boxed{f} \atop \bigcirc\!\!\!C$: component C realizes function f.

Because of the paper size constraint, we omit the presentation of SDLg grammar.

5 Modeling the Operational Scenarios

The objective of the SDLg is modeling the behavior of a system. The behavior of any system is provided by its operational scenarios. A scenario is a set of functions of the highest abstraction level $Level_0$ that are realized by the components of the system in order to achieve an ultimate goal. Each of these functions, which are executed following one of the relationships defined earlier (*Precedence, Parallelism, Preemption*), can be detailed and decomposed into a set of functions of lower level ($Level_1$). This process continues as long as the targeted abstraction level is not reached. Clearly, the lower is the abstraction level (detailed), the better will be the understanding of the system behavior system.

The concept of level improves substantially the comprehension of a system because it allows a structured, and thus better, system formalization. Moreover it allows linking the different views of the system architecture. For example, consider the CBTC system. After deriving the different views of the system, we investigate its operational scenarios. In this example, we consider $Scenario_1$, an operational scenario in which only two components of the system are involved: the *train* itself and the *wayside*.

$Scenario_1$: The entrance of the train to the station.

For this scenario to occur, according to the information provided by the functional view, a sequence of ten functions must be realized:

- $f_{0,1}$: The **wayside** selects the stopping point
- $f_{0,2}$: The **wayside** sends the stopping point to the **train**
- $f_{0,3}$: The **train** triggers the braking system
- $f_{0,4}$: The **train** informs the **wayside** of the doors opening
- $f_{0,5}$: The **wayside** opens the platform doors

- $f_{0,6}$: The **wayside** informs the **train** of the platform doors opening
- $f_{0,7}$: The **train** opens the doors
- $f_{0,8}$: The **train** informs the passengers of the next stop station
- $f_{0,9}$: The **wayside** triggers a timer at the train stop
- $f_{0,10}$: The **train** triggers the propulsion system

We denote by $f_{l,k}$, the kth function of $Level_l$, $l = 0, \ldots, L-1$, L being the number of abstraction levels in the model. Functions $f_{0,k}$, $k = 1, \ldots, 10$, constitute the highest abstraction level ($Level_0$) in the model. Using the SDLg notation, Fig.8 shows which components are involved in the realization of each function, and on which function these components have to interact (cooperate).

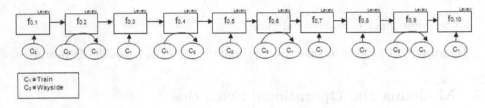

Fig. 8. $Scenario_1$: *The entrance of the train to the station*

The refinement of $Level_0$ functions allows investigating the internal components of the system that are actually involved in their realization, and thus have an impact on the system reliability. For example, consider function $f_{0,3}$. Thanks to the information provided by the functional view, we know that this function can be decomposed in the following four sub-functions:

- $f_{1,1}$: *The train detects that it is at the stopping point.* This S_action is realized by internal component $OBCU$.
- $f_{1,2}$: *The train informs the driver that it is at the stopping point.* This T_action requires the cooperation between components $OBCU$ and HMI to be completed. Thus $OBCU \curvearrowright HMI$.
- $f_{1,3}$: *The train triggers the braking system.* This S_action is also realized by component $OBCU$.
- $f_{1,4}$: *The train sends the braking information to the driver.* This T_action requires also the cooperation between components $OBCU$ and HMI to be completed. Thus $OBCU \curvearrowright HMI$.

As shown in Fig. 9, functions $F_{1,k}$, $k = 1, \ldots, 4$, are part of the function set of $Level_1$.

The refinement of abstraction $Level_2$ is not possible as the functions of this level are either S_action or T_action, thus atomic. We can proceed similarly with all the functions of $Level_0$. The complete SDLg model of $Scenario_1$ is depicted in Fig. 10.

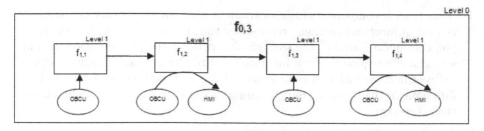

Fig. 9. Refinement of $Level_0$ function $f_{0,3}$

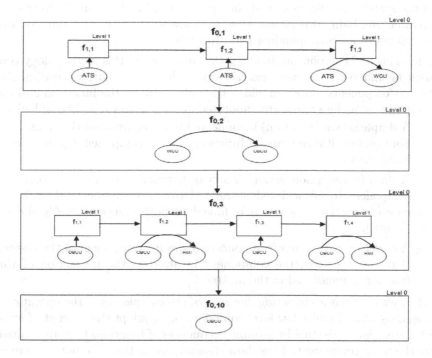

Fig. 10. SDLg model of the scenario1

6   From Informal Specifications to a Formal Model

In this section, we present the methodology that allows us to generate the SDLg model of a system architecture from its informal specifications. Once all the operational scenarios of the system are identified, this methodology consists of five steps to follow for each scenario: functions and components identification, linking the functions to the functional architecture, functions and components binding, abstraction levels architecting, and finally safety analysis. All the information collected during these steps are stored in a functions/components matrix.

1. *Functions & components identification:* in a system specification, a scenario is a set of functions (actions) realized by the system components. For example, consider $Scenario_1$, the scenario described in the previous section. This scenario is a sequence of ten functions realized by two components, individually or in cooperation. The objective of this step is the identification of the functions in the scenario and the components involved in the realization of these functions.

2. *Linking the functions to the functional architecture:* in this step, the functions in the operational scenarios are linked to those in the functional view and thus to the system requirements. Indeed, these requirements are part of the system specifications and thus part of the functions in the functional architecture. Using this information, each low level abstraction function can be related to its corresponding main function.

3. *Functions and components binding:* the third step in this methodology consists in understanding who exactly does what? For that, we use an Actions/Components matrix in which the links between the functions and the components in the system are annotated according to the following logic:

   – A simple action (S_action) is connected to the component that realizes it. For example, it is the case for function $f_{0,1}$ and component C_2 ($Wayside$) in $Scenario_1$.

   – A data transmission action (T_action), which requires more than one component to be achieved, is related to two components. This is the case of function $f_{0,2}$ which is linked to both components C_2 and C_1 ($Train$).

   – A Q_action may or may not concern a specific component of the system. If this is the case, the component involved in the realization of this function is annotated in the matrix.

4. *Abstraction levels architecting:* because of the complexity of the operational scenarios which involve low level components, we adopt the concept of *levels of abstractions*. We start by grouping sequences of functions that are realized by the same component. Thus data transmission actions are not concerned. For each group of functions, a function of a higher level of abstraction is created. Similarly, using the organic view, several components can be grouped in a macro-component, allowing a higher abstraction level of the system. By doing so, we are then able to, once again, group sequences of functions that are realized by the same macro-component. This process can continue until it is no more possible to obtain a higher level of abstraction of the system. Thus the objective of this step is to obtain multiple abstraction levels of the system representation.

5. *Safety analysis:* the objective of this step is to take into consideration the impact of the functions and the components on the safety of the system. The system requirements include also information on the safety relationship between the system elements. If a requirement is vital, its corresponding function will be vital. Similarly will be the component which is in charge

of achieving this function. With the information on the safety, we complete our matrix.

-Application of the methodology to the Trainguard$©$ MT CBTC

In this part, we look for a reverse-engineering technique to transform the initial system specification of the Trainguard$©$MT and obtain the main properties of the system. Our methodology as we explained relies on the grammar we developed. This technique start from the lowest level of abstraction and builds a formal abstract model with multiple views. Let's consider a step of a Trainguard$©$MT operational scenario:

The *ATS* selects a stopping point at the platform via *ATS_I_Select_Stopping_Point*. The *WCU_ATP* now uses the selected stopping point in the *WODs* to the on-board subsystem. The *WCU_ATP* reflects the information on the selected stopping point to the *ATS(ATS_O_Stopping_Point)*

Considering the train and the wayside as the main components of the system, the decomposition generates three(3) functions:

f_1: *ATS* selects a stopping point at the platform via *ATS_I_Select_Stopping_Point*.
f_2: *WCU_ATP* now uses the selected stopping point in the *WODs* to the on-board subsystem.
f_3: The *WCU_ATP* reflects the information on the selected stopping point to the *ATS(ATS_O_Stopping_Point)*.
Following the steps of the methodology, the result appears in the following matrix(see figure11). It details the functions decomposition into abstract levels and the connection with the system architecture(organic and functional view). Finally, we added the safety relation that helps enlighten the safety actions to minimize the duration of the safety analysis.

	Level	Functional Architecture	Train					Wayside			
Level 0	Level1	Function	OSUB	Platform	HMI	Train Control	PIS/TMS	WCU_ATP	WCU_TTS	ATS	Safety related
	The ATS selects a stopping point at the platform via ATS_I_Select_Stopping_Point	F7								X	No
The wayside selects the stopping point	The WCU_ATP now uses the selected stopping point in the WODs to the on-board subsystem	F7						X			No
	The WCU_ATP reflects the information on the selected stopping point to the ATS	F7						X		X	No

Fig. 11. Actor/Action matrix of an operational scenario of the Trainguard$©$MT CBTC

7   Related Work

In this section, we present the different existing studies that have been made in the model-driven system engineering. After the analysis of different papers, we first realized that the issue of correctly modeling a complete complex system[11] starting from a natural-language system specification have not been deeply addressed. However we found out works trying to model parts of the system or some views of it.

These approaches can be divided into two main methodologies, some are language-centric and others are system-centric. Language-centric methodologies rely on a modeling language, SysML[7] is the more often used in complex systems because it offers a panel of diagrams that allow the graphical representation of systems parts. This approach aims to use all or most of the language properties to express some system views. Thomas Krueger in[2] establishes a modeling methodology using SysML trying to represent the functional and organic views of an aerospace system. He uses activity diagrams to model the link between functions and components. This methodology realizes the link between simulation tools with the system for automatic code generation needs. The main advantage is that it represents structural and behavioral views. The inconvenient is the lack of interaction between components, the system is seen as an independent component which is rarely the case for complex systems. Claver et al.[3] also tried to model astronomical systems by representing the requirements, the logical and physical views with internal and block definition diagrams. The inconvenient is the lack of information, the behavior is forgotten.

Regarding the second approach, methodologies do not focus on the modeling language, they use it as a tool to represent all the information needed of the system, the language is extended or restrained. Wielkiens and Lamm in[4] focused on the functional behavior of a complex system. Soares et al.[5] focused on the requirements of the system, the advantage of these methodologies is that the language becomes specific to the system and is customized in order to respond to its properties. The inconvenient is that some views are incomplete. The system is too specific, it cannot be used for formal analysis with other tools.

The language-centric approaches give redundant information. SysML or any other modeling language proposes different diagrams for structure and behavior, the objective is to seek for the adequate diagram for the adequate view. Sometimes, we notice a lack of information because the language is not specific to the system. The system-centric approaches modify the language to fit the system, we do not notice redundancy. But, these changes make it difficult to use the system for other purposes. Another objective of the system modeling is to find a formalism able to be reused in all the steps of the system engineering.

Regarding the existing approaches, we can say that our methodology has the advantage of looking deeply into the system's concepts in order to obtain a formal modeling language that fits the system and its requirements and views. Unlike the existing methodologies, the architecture and the behavior are linked in order to enlighten the system properties. The problem of redundancy cannot occur since the language is complete. The aim of the methodology and the language is to be formal, so it can easily be reused for formal analysis.

8   Conclusion and Future Work

In this paper, we have presented a modeling methodology for the railway automation solution Trainguard MT CBTC of Siemens. We have addressed the recurrent issue of model-based engineering, that is the incompleteness and the redundancy of the models. Our approach is based on the necessity of identifying the different system's concepts and its relevant information. Different aspects of the system (functional, organic and event-based) have been considered, allowing us to enhance the operational scenarios of the system and their structural formalism. We also introduced the concept of abstraction levels which allows us to refine the functions and the components of the system, and thus to have multiple abstraction views of the system, that can be useful for the different system stakeholders. The objective of this modeling methodology is to ease the system design and development and to have the necessary data for the next steps of the system life-cycle (integration, V&V and safety). We are convinced that this approach will help saving a valuable time for engineers. Our next step is to enrich our models by taking into account the different types of data exchanged between components to check the safety relevance, and the duration of the functions to perform formal analysis on the system. We will also need to study the safety aspects of each component and each function and have a complete probabilistic analysis to measure the availability and the performances of the system.

References

1. F. Lagrange, V. Goumy, E. Rose, G. Yelloz, JM Gimenez, E. Dubois VignalTGMT CBTC Presentation, Siemens external presentation (2009)
2. Krueger, T.: Modeling of a complex system using sysml in a model based design approach. In: Proceeding of the ASTRA conference on Automation and Robotics, Noordwijk, The Netherlands (2011)
3. Claver, C.F., Debois Felsmann, G.P., Delgado, F., Hascall, P., Marshall, S., Nordby, M., Schumacher, G., Sebag, J.: The LSST: A System of Systems American Astronomical Society, AAS Meeting #217, #252.02, vol. 43, Bulletin of the American Astronomical Society (2011)
4. Lamm, J.G., Weilkiens, T.: Funktionale Architekturen in SysML. In: Maurer, M., Schulze, S.-O. (eds.) Tag des Systems Engineering, Carl Hanser Verlag, München, Germany, pp. 109–118 (November 2010); English translation by J. Lamm
5. Dos Santos Soares, M., Vrancken, J.: Requirements Specification and Modeling through SysML. In: Proceedings of the IEEE International Conference on Systems, Man, and Cybernetics (SMC), Montreal, Canada, pp. 1735–1740 (2010)
6. Krob, D.: Eléments de systémique - Architecture de systémes, in Complexité-Simplexité, Editions Odile Jacob (2012)
7. Friedenthal, S., Moore, A., Steiner, R.: A Practical Guide to SysML. The Systems Modeling Language. MK/OMG Press (2009), ISBN 978-0-12-378607-4

8. 1474.1-1999 - IEEE Standard for Communication Based Train Control Performance Requirements and Functional Requirements
9. Espinasse, B.: Méthodes fonctionnelles: SADT, Support de cours, Université Aix-Marseille
10. Trainguard MT CBTC: The moving block communications based train control solutions, Siemens Transportation Systems
11. Yaung, S.A.: Foundations of complex system theories. Cambridge University Press (1998)
12. Stollberg, M., Elvesæter, B.: A Customizable Methodology for the Model-driven Engineering of Service-based System Landscapes
13. Marca, D.A., McGowan, C.L.: SADT: structured analysis and design technique. McGraw-Hill, Inc., New York (1987) ISBN:0-07-040235-3
14. Pohl, K.: Requirements Engineering: Fundamentals, Principles, and Techniques. Springer Publishing Company (2010) (Incorporated) ISBN 978-3642125775

A Systematic Approach to Requirements Driven Test Generation for Safety Critical Systems*

Toby Wilkinson**, Michael Butler, and John Colley***

University of Southampton, UK
{stw08r,mjb,J.L.Colley}@ecs.soton.ac.uk

Abstract. We describe ongoing work into the generation of test cases for safety critical systems using Event-B and the Rodin toolset. Verification of software to DO-178C is a two stage process. First a suite of test cases must be validated against the system requirements (requirements coverage), and then the software implementation is verified using the validated test suite. During verification of the implementation structural coverage is also measured.

Our work focuses on the first step, the generation of test cases and their validation against the requirements. We construct closed-system models incorporating both the system to be tested and its environment. These models capture the system requirements, and describe the interactions between the system and its environment. In particular, safety constraints can be represented by invariants, and their preservation ensured through event guards. From these models test cases can be generated, and requirements coverage can be measured from model coverage.

Keywords: Event-B, STPA, Safety Critical Systems, Test Generation.

1 Introduction

Safety critical systems must be verified, and that means testing. Even systems developed using formal methods and automated code generation must be tested to confirm that no erroneous assumptions were made during the development process, though the expectation is that few, if any, faults will be found.

An important task during system development therefore, is the generation of a test suite for the system. This test suite must be able to distinguish an implementation that meets the system requirements, from an implementation

---

* This document is an overview of MOD sponsored research and is released to inform projects that include safety-critical or safety-related software. The information contained in this document should not be interpreted as representing the views of the MOD, nor should it be assumed that it reflects any current or future MOD policy. The information cannot supersede any statutory or contractual requirements or liabilities and is offered without prejudice or commitment.
** Supported by the Defence Science and Technology Laboratory (Dstl) project HASTE.
*** Supported by the FP7 project ADVANCE (http://www.advance-ict.eu).

F. Ortmeier and A. Rauzy (Eds.): IMBSA 2014, LNCS 8822, pp. 43–56, 2014.
© Springer International Publishing Switzerland 2014

that does not. However, it is unrealistic to expect a test suite to be able to detect all possible implementation errors. The reason for this is simple; for many systems the set of possible legitimate behaviours is huge, if not infinite, and testing can only explore a finite subset of these.

The best therefore that we can hope to do, is to create a test suite that both covers the requirements, and for which the test cases can be performed using a realistic amount of resources. The key is therefore to understand what it means for a test suite to cover the requirements, in particular, to answer the question "When is a test suite good enough?".

1.1   Civil Aviation Software Development Guidelines: DO-178B/C

In DO-178 (revisions B and C) [16,17] a test suite must be validated against the system requirements, both high level and low level, and must cover both normal range and robustness tests. This must happen before the test suite is applied to the implementation. Only once the test suite has been validated against the requirements, and the test cases traced to the requirements, can it be used to verify the implementation.

For the higher Software Levels[1,2] structural coverage of the implementation by the test suite is also required: Level C is required to achieve Statement Coverage (SC); Level B, Decision Coverage (DC); and Level A, Modified Condition/Decision Coverage (MC/DC). Structural coverage is assessed against Section 6.4.4.3 of DO-178B: Structural Coverage Analysis Resolution. Code that was not exercised during the testing is assigned to one of four categories, and the appropriate action taken (the following paraphrases DO-178B Section 6.4.4.3):

Poor Quality Test Cases: the test cases must be improved and the testing repeated. In addition, the process by which requirements coverage was measured should be examined.

Inadequate Requirements: the requirements must be revised and further test cases produced to cover the new requirements.

Dead Code: any code that cannot be reached by the test cases should be removed and testing repeated.

Deactivated Code: additional evidence should be produced to show that the code remains deactivated in the target environment.

1.2   COTS and Component Reuse

With the increasing complexity and sophistication of systems, and the increasing pressure of reduced timescales and budgets, there is a desire in many safety

---

[1] Under DO-178B/C software is assigned one of five Software Levels (A through E), where Level A is the most safety critical - failure may be catastrophic (loss of aircraft or loss of life).

[2] ARP4754A [18] introduces the terminology Functional Development Assurance Level (FDAL) and Item Development Assurance Level (IDAL), where the IDAL assigned to a software component is the corresponding Software Level [18, p.12].

critical industries to construct new bespoke systems form third party COTS (Commercial Off The Shelf) components, or to reuse proven components from previous systems in new developments.

The question that arises in such a situation is how to ensure the resulting (composite) system is safe. A proven component from a previous development may have been safe in the context of that development, but it may not be safe when incorporated into some other system. Indeed, it is a mistake to talk about the safety of components, it only makes sense to talk about the safety of a complete system, as many hazards arise from uncontrolled interactions between components [15].

Components therefore need to be tested to determine if they are safe in the context into which they will be deployed. Each reuse of a component will require a reassessment of the suitability and safety of the component, and if previous testing of the component did not cover all the circumstances of the new context, further testing must be performed.

1.3   Advancing the State of the Art for Software Testing

To facilitate the reuse of components, and the use of COTS components, we need to develop tools and techniques for verifying the suitability and safety of components in new contexts. The key point to note here, is that the context is key. The context will impose requirements upon the component, including safety constraints, and it is with respect to these requirements that the safety of the component must be assessed.

This leads to another question. What is the real purpose of measuring structural coverage? If we could test every possible interaction between a component and the context into which it is to be deployed, then provided the component passed all the tests, we would not need to care about the internal structure of the component. We could simply treat it as a black box that we plug into the rest of the system. However, such exhaustive testing is in general infeasible.

Measuring structural coverage therefore compensates for this inability to fully test all the behaviour allowed by the requirements. For example, whilst it is permissible under DO-178B/C to have deactivated code in an implementation (Section 1.1), this has to be explicitly justified. Therefore failure to achieve full structural coverage requires the validation of the test suite to be revisited, to determine if the test cases, or the requirements themselves, are inadequate.

The point is, that in a conventional development scenario, the requirements are presented informally, and therefore may be inconsistent or incomplete. Thus any test suite validated against such requirements may also be inconsistent or incomplete. The code itself, whilst developed from these same requirements, will typically have undergone informal, exploratory, testing by the developer. Therefore the code may be more correct than the requirements, at least in the case of nominal behaviour. Thus measuring structural coverage can potentially find faults in the test suite and the requirements.

Incomplete or inconsistent requirements also have obvious cost and safety implications. If mistakes in the requirements are found late on in the project, then the cost of fixing them can be high. Even worse is the possibility that the mistakes are not found, for then the system may be unsafe. Such a system may have passed all testing, and even achieved full structural coverage, whilst still remaining unsafe. Our aim therefore should be to improve the quality of the requirements, and if we can do this, and also if we can produce tests that cover these requirements, then perhaps we can do away with the need for also measuring structural coverage. The degree to which this is possible will depend upon the degree to which the test cases cover the requirements.

We believe that the only realistic way to significantly improve the quality of system requirements is through their formalisation in some mathematical language. Such a language must be expressive enough to cover realistic engineering scenarios, but also simple enough for regular engineers to use. Moreover, such a language should come with powerful tool support to automate the checking of the resultant specifications for inconsistencies, and tools to help validate the requirements against the engineer's mental concept of how the system should be. In our work we make use of the Event-B formal language and the Rodin toolset [3].

For safety critical systems however, it is not enough to have a formal language for writing down the requirements, we also need to be sure that we have identified all the requirements. In particular, we need to be certain that we have identified all the safety constraints required for the safe operation of the system in the context into which it will be deployed. For this we advocate the use of STPA (System-Theoretic Process Analysis), a hazard analysis technique developed by Leveson at MIT [15].

Our main contributions are the combining of the hazard analysis process of STPA with the formal method Event-B, and the systematic generation of test cases from the resulting models. STPA initiates the discovery of safety requirements, and Event-B helps detect inconsistencies and missing requirements. The resulting closed-system model of a system and its context is then used for the generation of test cases for the system.

2   Formal Modelling in Event-B

To create our formal model of a system in its context we use Event-B, which is a formal method for system-level modelling and analysis [2]. Event-B is an extension of the B-Method [1], and uses set theory as a modelling notation. Refinement is a key feature of Event-B, enabling systems to be represented at different abstraction levels, and mathematical proof is used to verify the consistency between refinement levels.

The B-Method has been successfully used in the development of many complex high integrity systems, including: the Driverless Train controller for Line 14 of the Paris Metro, the controllers for the Light Driverless Shuttle for Paris-Roissy airport, and Platform Screen-Door Controllers.

Event-B differs from traditional program verification methods like Hoare logic [12], in that it can be used for system level reasoning, rather than just reasoning about the correctness of programs. By this we mean reasoning about an overall system rather than just the software parts of a system. An initial abstract model is produced that describes the main purpose of the system, and this is then successively refined to layer in other features. Refinement enriches or modifies a model in order to augment the functionality being modelled, or explain how some purpose is achieved. The successive refinements form a chain, and this chain facilitates abstraction since it allows us to postpone treatment of some system features to later refinement steps. Abstraction and refinement together allow us to manage system complexity.

In Event-B a system is modelled in terms of state variables and guarded events that alter that state. Refinement in Event-B allows essential properties to be expressed at a very abstract (hence simple and clear) level and then progressive refinements allow more and more detail to be added until the full detail of the system has been described. At each refinement the consistency of the model has to be proven including the correctness of the refinement (i.e. that no new traces have been introduced and that the refined state has equivalence with the abstract state).

In Event-B, an abstract model comprises a *machine* that specifies the high-level behaviour and a *context*, made up of sets, constants and their properties, that represents the type environment for the high-level machine. The machine is represented as a set of *state variables*, v and a set of events, *guarded atomic actions*, which modify the state. If more than one action is enabled, then one is chosen non-deterministically for *execution*.

For example, here we define a context which declares the type SOME_TYPE to have two possible values, A or B.

CONTEXT abstract_context
SETS
    $SOME\_TYPE$
CONSTANTS
    A
    B
AXIOMS
    axm1 : $partition(SOME\_TYPE, \{A\}, \{B\})$
END

An example machine that sees this context could then be defined. It declares variable to be of type SOME_TYPE and initialises it to the value A. The event some_event takes a parameter v, and the guard grd1 ensures that this parameter has a different value from that stored in variable. The event body act1 then sets the value of variable to the value passed in v.

MACHINE abstract_machine
SEES abstract_context
VARIABLES
    $variable$
INVARIANTS
    inv1 : $variable \in SOME\_TYPE$

EVENTS
Initialisation
  begin
        act1 : $variable := A$
  end
Event $some\_event \mathrel{\widehat{=}}$
  any
        v
  where
        grd1 : $v \neq variable$
  then
        act1 : $variable := v$
  end
END

Event-B defines proof obligations to ensure that events preserve *invariants* on the variables. A more concrete representation of the machine may then be created which refines the abstract machine, and the abstract context may be extended to support the types required by the refinement. *Gluing invariants* are used to verify that the concrete machine is a correct *refinement*: any behaviour of the concrete machine must satisfy the abstract behaviour. Gluing invariants give rise to proof obligations for pairs of abstract and corresponding concrete events. Events may also have parameters which take, non-deterministically, the values that will make the guards in which they are referenced true.

The Rodin Platform is an Eclipse-based IDE for Event-B that provides effective support for refinement and mathematical proof [3]. The platform is open source, and can be extended with plug-ins that provide additional functionality. Rodin includes automatic tools to generate proof obligations of the models consistency, and provers that attempt to automatically discharge these obligations. ProB is a model checker and animator that is available as an extension to the Rodin toolset [14]. The UML-B plug-in supports modelling and refinement of class diagrams and state machines, and translates models into Event-B for animation, model checking, and proof [19].

The automated tools available in Rodin, such as model checkers and automated proof systems, play a key role in improving the quality of models through identification of errors, pin-pointing of required invariants, and proofs of consistency. We use proof to verify the consistency of a refinement step, while failing proof can help us identify inconsistencies.

The resulting models, and their invariants, increase our understanding of a problem and its proposed solution. In effect, during the modelling process, the model and the system requirements are co-validated, both against each other, and against the engineer's mental model of the system. This leads to improvements in the quality of requirements, as the requirements become a natural language explanation of the model, and the model itself is validated through animation and proof. All this can be achieved long before the system has been implemented, and is able to inform design decisions, and provide evidence of the extent to which a system is fit for purpose.

3   Hazard Analysis with STPA

Our aim is to verify safety critical systems, or their components. To do this we construct a closed-system model of the system, or component, and the context into which it will be deployed. The model thus contains the entire universe as far as the component, or system, is concerned.

To ensure the safety of the system, the model must constrain the behaviour of the system to allow only safe actions to be performed. The identification of these safety constraints is thus the key first step to ensuring system safety. To do this we employ a hazard analysis technique called STPA (System-Theoretic Process Analysis), that builds upon an accident causality model called STAMP (System-Theoretic Accident Model and Processes). Both were developed at MIT by Leveson [15].

3.1   STAMP

STAMP (System-Theoretic Accident Model and Processes) is an accident causality model based upon systems theory. It incorporates three main concepts, which are summarised here from [15, Chapter 4]:

Safety Constraints: Safety is an emergent property, and can only be achieved by constraining the behaviour of the interacting components of a system. Safety is thus a control problem.

Hierarchical Safety Control Structures: Systems are hierarchical structures, where the behaviour of each layer is constrained by the layer above it. Each layer controls the behaviour of the layer below it through information passed on a *reference channel*, and feedback is provided via a *measuring channel*, through which the layer above can monitor how successfully control is being achieved.

Process Models: Every controller must have a model of the process that it aims to control. Such a model should contain the current state, a description of how the process state can change, and the control laws that should be followed. Feedback from the process is used to update the process model, and this in turn is used to determine the necessary control actions. Accidents can occur when the controller's process model is incorrect, and the controller issues unsafe commands.

3.2   STPA

STPA (System-Theoretic Process Analysis) is a hazard analysis process based upon STAMP. It is a systematic way of examining a system to discover potential hazards, and their possible causes. The resulting analysis identifies safety constraints that must be imposed upon the system.

The STPA process has two main steps described in [15, Chapter 8], which we present here in a simplified form appropriate for our use:[3]

---

[3] The STPA process is applicable to any sociotechnical system, where controllers can also include individuals, as well as regulatory bodies and governments.

1. For each control action identify incorrect or inappropriate behaviour that could cause the system to enter a hazardous state:
   (a) The control action is not applied when it should be.
   (b) The control action is applied when it should not be.
   (c) The control action is applied at the incorrect time, or out of order.
   (d) The control action is terminated early or continued for longer than necessary.
2. For each potentially unsafe control action from Step 1, determine how it may arise:
   (a) Examine the controller for possible causes: actuator failures, sensor failures, lost messages etc.
   (b) Devise ways to eliminate or mitigate hazardous states: redundant sensors, enter safe mode, switch on warning light etc.
   (c) Identify possible coordination problems or conflicts between multiple controllers of the same plant.

3.3 STPA and Event-B

Formalising an STPA analysis, or incorporating STPA into an Event-B development, is straightforward. Firstly the state variables of the Event-B model are examined to make sure that the controller has a model of the process that it is attempting to control.

Then from the analysis of Step 1, safety constraints can be identified and represented in the model. For example, if a control action changes the state of an entity, the analysis of Step 1 may yield a safety constraint of the form *"The entity must be in state STATE_A when P is true"*. This can be represented in Event-B as the invariant

inv1 : $P = \text{TRUE} \Rightarrow entity\_state = STATE\_A$

The four cases considered in Step 1 (above) identify when application of the control action would violate this invariant. To prevent this, guards are added to the event(s) representing the control action, such that the event(s) is(are) disabled when applying the control action would be unsafe. For example

Event   *change_to_STATE_B* $\hat{=}$
   where
         grd1 : $P = \text{FALSE}$

A more detailed worked example of this process can be found in [7], or the ADVANCE project deliverable D5.2 [4].

Typically an abstract model of the system and its context (the environment) will be created first, and in this model actuate or sense events for the control actions and sensory feedback may be introduced. In subsequent refinements, the actuate and sense events may be refined by events corresponding to the different possible failure modes identified in Step 2. Similarly, refinements may introduce details of any communication medium and introduce events corresponding to lost messages from Step 2.

The hazard elimination and mitigation strategies from Step 2 must also be incorporated into the model, along with any mechanisms required to coordinate multiple controllers.

Throughout this process, formal proof is used to show that safety constraints introduced as event guards are sufficient to ensure the preservation of the safety constraints introduced as invariants. Proof is also used to show that any refinement of a safe abstract system remains safe.

4 Test Generation

Once we have created a model of the system, or component, and the context into which it will be deployed, we would like to generate a test suite for any possible implementation of the component or system.

In most cases the model will, like the real system, have an infinite number of possible behaviours – for example a controller that is intended to run indefinitely can exhibit arbitrarily long traces. Testing however, is necessarily finite, as tests cases must be of finite duration, and a test suite can only contain a finite number of test cases. The question therefore arises as to how we choose a finite subset of the behaviour of the model as the set of test cases against which we intend to test any implementation of the system.

The choice of the test suite must be justified. For example under DO-178B/C the test cases must be shown to cover the requirements, and this must be both justified and documented, with requirements traced to the corresponding test cases. Any process by which we generate test cases from a formal model must therefore provide this justification, and we must be able to validate the resulting test suite against the requirements.

A fully automated approach to test generation is therefore unacceptable. Instead we believe that test suite selection, whilst automated, must also be engineer guided. In this approach, rather than the tool automatically selecting some finite subset of the behaviour of the system, and then leaving the engineer the task of justifying why this subset is sufficient to ensure that any implementation that passes the corresponding tests is safe; instead, test generation should be directed by the engineer, with system behaviour excluded from that to be tested on the basis of testing hypotheses (Section 4.1). The resulting test suite is then much easier to justify and document.

Moreover, we hope that such an approach will produce test suites that are much better at finding faults. Our reasoning is based upon the idea that in making testing decisions, the engineer will be guided by previous experience of the sorts of mistakes and errors that occur during the implementation of a system of that type, and will attempt to create tests that will discover those sorts of defects.

4.1 Standard Testing Techniques

The idea of engineer guided test selection is not new. Indeed, in the absence of a machine readable model of the system it is the only possible approach, and the testing community has developed methods for identifying the sorts of tests required: equivalence partitioning, boundary value analysis etc. [13]. These testing techniques are typically applied in a manual process of test generation, and implicitly employ certain *testing hypotheses* that can be formalised [5,10]. We briefly describe two commonly used testing techniques.

Loops. Many safety critical systems consist of a controller responsible for the safe action of some plant. This controller typically has a control loop, where the environment is sensed, a control action performed, and then the loop repeated indefinitely. Obviously such a system has infinite behaviour as traces can be arbitrarily long, but for testing purposes the length of traces must be bound, otherwise testing becomes infeasible.

For functional testing of such a controller it is often enough to show that all the different possible ways in which a single action of the control loop could be performed have been covered, and that the controller can perform some predetermined (possibly quite small) number of cycles. It is then reasoned that this evidence is enough to conclude that it has been verified that the controller will repeatedly cycle through the loop, and any trace of the system will simply be the concatenation of the traces of the individual control cycles.

Input Partitioning. In many systems the parameters of the input events can take a large, possibly infinite, number of different values. Testing all these values is often hugely impractical, so traditional testing techniques aim to test a reasonably small subset of representative values. Two techniques employed are equivalence partitioning, and boundary value analysis.

The aim of equivalence partitioning is to partition the values of an input parameter into a set of classes, where for each class, any two values within the class should be processed in the same way by the system, i.e. will follow the same path through the code in the case of a software system. Test cases are then generated that cover these equivalence classes.

In boundary value analysis, the aim is to determine whether in the implemented system the boundaries between the equivalence classes are in the correct place. Test cases are generated that are on the boundary, and slightly to either side of the boundary.

Between them, boundary value analysis and equivalence partitioning aim to reduce to a manageable number, the number of test cases required to show that inputs are processed correctly.

4.2   Engineer Directed Test Generation Using Event-B

Our aim is to use ProB, a model checker and animator plug-in for Rodin, to generate abstract test cases from our closed-system models. ProB also has constraint solving capabilities, and our aim is to use ProB to extract paths from the model that satisfy certain conditions and constraints. These will be the abstract test cases. Concrete test cases will then be generated from the abstract test cases in a form in which they can be directly executed against a potential implementation of the system.[4]

At the moment, the conditions and constraints passed to ProB must be manually generated, but our long term goal is to develop support within Rodin to automate as much of the process as possible. It should also be possible in an automated tool to combine the test cases directed by the engineer, with those automatically generated according to some model structural coverage target.

Recall, we are interested in verifying the safety of a system or component in a particular context, a context that has been captured as part of our closed-system model. Moreover, during the STPA hazard analysis we discovered the possible actuator and sensor failures that could lead to hazardous states, and these were incorporated into our model as distinct events in the environment (Section 3.3). The test cases generated should at least cover all these plant failure events, and possibly certain sequences of them as well. The exact coverage required must be determined by the engineer, based upon their detailed knowledge of the domain.

In order to reduce the number of test cases in a test suite, whilst still covering enough of the behaviour in the model to ensure the test suite covers the requirements in accordance with DO-178B/C, we employ the testing techniques discussed in Section 4.1. To do this we introduce *ghost variables* into our model to aid with the generation of the conditions and constraints to be passed to ProB. Once again, at the moment this is a manual process, but the intention is for the tool to automate this process under the guidance of an engineer.

Loops. We can refine the model by adding a variable that counts the number of control loops that have been performed. This variable can then be used to bound the length of test cases produced, or force them to include a minimum number of control loops etc.

Input Partitioning. For the events that define the input interface between the surrounding context, and the system or component, we can take each input parameter, and introduce a ghost variable that records which equivalence class contained the value passed by the event. These ghost variables can then be used to ensure test cases are generated that cover all the equivalence classes.

Note: in order to perform boundary value analysis, equivalence classes can contain just single values.

Whether it is sufficient for the test suite to simply cover each of the input equivalence classes in at least one test case, i.e. for each equivalence class there exists a test case which covers that class, or whether it is necessary for combinations and sequences to be covered, is a judgement that can only be made by an engineer with knowledge of the system. However, in some cases it may be feasible to generate all possible test cases that cover the equivalence classes, up to a certain bound in length, where this bound is possibly determined by bounding the number of control loops performed.

---

[4] For the moment we are ignoring the *oracle problem* - deciding whether the result of a test execution is acceptable or not [5,10].

4.3 Case Studies

To help with the development of our approach, on the HASTE project we created a case study based upon a synthetic model of the FADEC (Full Authority Digital Engine Control) system of a hypothetical helicopter. For this case study we constructed an initial Event-B model for a subset of the functionality – an Anti-Ice Bleed Valve (AIBV).

STPA hazard analysis was performed on the AIBV, and safety constraints discovered and modelled in Event-B. The resulting closed-system model was then decomposed into two submodels: a model that embodies the actual AIBV valve, actuators, sensors, and the rest of the environment; and a model that describes the functionality required of the AIBV controller for the safe operation of the AIBV. The first of these models captures the assumptions made about the context into which the AIBV controller will be deployed, and the second forms the specification for the AIBV controller itself. That the specification is safe with respect to the intended context follows automatically from the closed-system model from which they were both derived.

Work is currently ongoing to use the closed-system model of the AIBV to generate test cases that can verify whether an implementation of the AIBV controller specification is safe (given the environmental assumptions). To determine the effectiveness of our test cases, we have used the code generation capabilities of the Rodin toolset to generate an implementation of the AIBV controller from the Event-B model of its specification.

To further validate our approach, we intend to expand the model to include a larger subset of the FADEC functionality. This will obviously create some challenges, as already mentioned in Section 4.2, we currently lack full tool support for the test generation.

In addition to the HASTE case study, on the ADVANCE project further cases studies were conducted into the use of STPA with Event-B [7,4].

5 Related Work

The generation of test suites from models is not a new idea, it is well known, and is commonly referred to as Model Based Testing (MBT). Indeed, previous work has been done on Model Based Testing of Event-B models [9], and there is an MBT plug-in for Rodin [8].

The problem with most automated approaches, and certainly that of the Rodin MBT plug-in, is that the generation of the test suite is automated in a way that makes it difficult to trace the requirements to the test cases. For example, the Rodin MBT plugin creates test cases by first constructing a finite state machine that approximates the Event-B model. The problem is, that in a development undertaken to DO-178B/C, an engineer will need to demonstrate that this finite state machine does not exclude important behaviour of the system. This is likely to be an error prone task, as it corresponds to tackling the problem the wrong way round.

Another issue with Model Based Testing is that it has been shown that test suites generated to meet certain structural coverage criteria of the model can have very poor fault finding power [11]. In particular in [11], the authors show that in their case study, state coverage, transition coverage, and decision coverage have poor fault finding power, and that random testing found more faults. MC/DC coverage of the model is not explicitly performed in their case study, but the authors speculate that whilst it may improve upon the performance of decision coverage, due to masking issues, it may still fall short of the standard required.

Again, this should not come as too much of a surprise, as such model structural coverage criteria do not refer to the requirements. Whilst a properly validated model **is** the requirements, test suite coverage of the requirements would correspond to full coverage of **all** the behaviour of the model. This is obviously not the same as state coverage, or transition coverage etc., and it is naive to assume that such crude criteria will always select an appropriate test suite from the possibly infinite behaviour of the model.

The standard testing techniques of Section 4.1 can be formalised as testing hypotheses [5,10], and in [6] a test generation tool that makes explicit use of such testing hypotheses is developed using the Isabelle theorem prover. This is an interesting idea, and more work needs to be done to see how this relates to our approach.

6 Conclusions and Future Work

Our work aims to develop a systematic approach to test generation, with a particular emphasis on test cases that are driven by the requirements, and in particular, safety requirements.

Our approach aims to use the formal method Event-B not only to model the requirements, but to help facilitate the discovery of the requirements. Specifically, the pairing of Event-B with STPA creates a powerful method by which the STPA leads an engineer to discover important safety requirements and constraints, and Event-B and the Rodin toolset bring the necessary tool support and automation to allow the reasoning about these safety concerns in complex systems.

The technique we are developing is applicable to whole systems, or components; and to new developments, or to the reuse of proven components in new contexts. From the constructed model, we propose a systematic method of test case generation driven by the requirements, and guided by an engineer. The resulting test suite is then an engineer chosen compromise between full coverage of the system behaviour, and a test suite that can be implemented in practice.

Future work includes further validation of our approach with a larger subset of the functionality from our FADEC case study, and the development of the necessary tooling to help automate the test generation. Such a tool would take the form of a Rodin plug-in, but work still remains to determine the correct interface for the engineer guiding the test generation.

References

1. Abrial, J.-R.: The B-Book: Assigning Programs to Meanings. Cambridge University Press (1996)
2. Abrial, J.-R.: Modeling in Event-B: System and Software Engineering. Cambridge University Press (2010)
3. Abrial, J.-R., Butler, M., Hallerstede, S., Hoang, T.S., Mehta, F., Voisin, L.: Rodin: an open toolset for modelling and reasoning in Event-B. International Journal on Software Tools for Technology Transfer 12(6), 447–466 (2010)
4. ADVANCE: D5.2 - ADVANCE Process Integration II (2013), http://www.advance-ict.eu/files/AdvanceD5.2.pdf
5. Bernot, G., Gaudel, M.-C., Marre, B.: Software testing based on formal specifications: a theory and a tool. Software Engineering Journal 6(6), 387–405 (1991)
6. Brucker, A., Wolff, B.: On theorem prover-based testing. Formal Aspects of Computing 25(5), 683–721 (2013)
7. Colley, J., Butler, M.: A formal, systematic approach to STPA using Event-B refinement and proof. In: Dale, C., Anderson, T. (eds.) Assuring the Safety of Systems: Proceedings of the 21st Safety-Critical Systems Symposium (2013)
8. Dinca, I., Ipate, F., Mierla, L., Stefanescu, A.: Learn and test for event-B – A rodin plugin. In: Derrick, J., Fitzgerald, J., Gnesi, S., Khurshid, S., Leuschel, M., Reeves, S., Riccobene, E. (eds.) ABZ 2012. LNCS, vol. 7316, pp. 361–364. Springer, Heidelberg (2012)
9. Dinca, I., Ipate, F., Stefanescu, A.: Model learning and test generation for Event-B decomposition. In: Margaria, T., Steffen, B. (eds.) ISoLA 2012, Part I. LNCS, vol. 7609, pp. 539–553. Springer, Heidelberg (2012)
10. Gaudel, M.-C.: Testing can be formal, too. In: Mosses, P.D., Nielsen, M., Schwartzbach, M.I. (eds.) CAAP 1995, FASE 1995, and TAPSOFT 1995. LNCS, vol. 915, pp. 82–96. Springer, Heidelberg (1995)
11. Heimdahl, M., George, D., Weber, R.: Specification test coverage adequacy criteria = specification test generation inadequacy criteria? In: Proceedings Eighth IEEE International Symposium on High Assurance Systems Engineering, pp. 178–186 (2004)
12. Hoare, C.A.R.: An axiomatic basis for computer programming. Commun. ACM 12(10), 576–580 (1969)
13. International Software Testing Qualifications Board: Advanced Level Syllabus: Test Analyst (2012)
14. Leuschel, M., Butler, M.: ProB: An automated analysis toolset for the B method. International Journal on Software Tools for Technology Transfer 10(2), 185–203 (2008)
15. Leveson, N.G.: Engineering a Safer World: Systems Thinking Applied to Safety. The MIT Press (2011)
16. RTCA, Inc.: DO-178B, Software Considerations in Airborne Systems and Equipment Certification (December 1992)
17. RTCA, Inc.: DO-178C, Software Considerations in Airborne Systems and Equipment Certification (December 2011)
18. SAE International: ARP4754A, Guidelines for Development of Civil Aircraft and Systems (December 2010)
19. Snook, C., Butler, M.: UML-B: Formal modeling and design aided by UML. ACM Transactions on Software Engineering and Methodology 15(1), 92–122 (2006)

Model-Based Safety Approach for Early Validation of Integrated and Modular Avionics Architectures

Marion Morel

THALES AVIONICS S.A.S., 31036 Toulouse, France
marion.morel@fr.thalesgroup.com

Abstract. Increasing complexity of avionics systems leads to reconsider methods that are used today to analyze them from a safety point of view.

This paper presents how the Model-based techniques can be used for safety assessment in early validation to support flexible and rapid prototyping of integrated systems (such as Integrated Modular Avionics and Cockpit Display), in order to evaluate and compare several envisaged architectures with their compliance to the safety objectives (under nominal and dispatch conditions).

Keywords: model-based, safety assessment, shared resources, modular avionics, safety architectural patterns.

1 Context and Problematic

Safety assessment process (as described in ARP4761 ref. [1] and ARP4754A ref. [2]) aims to identify safety hazards for an Aircraft and to demonstrate compliance of its design with safety objectives. These objectives are provided in Aircraft and system's Functional Hazard Analysis (FHA) which covers quantitative probabilistic requirements (probability of occurrences of Failure Conditions) and qualitative requirements (fail-safe criteria, items and functions Development Assurance Levels, no common modes between critical functions and items, etc.) under system's certified configuration.

Over the past few years, avionics systems have become more and more complex. For instance, not so far analysis ago, each avionics function was supported by a hardware unit. In these conditions, to perform the safety assessment according to aeronautics guidelines (ref. [1]) was quite natural. This is no more the case today. Above all, aircraft functions are more and more numerous and intricately designed, to alleviate pilot workload or ensure maximum traffic density while guarantying safety margins, resulting in upward trend of embedded avionics systems criticality due to their wider functional coverage. Meanwhile, software architecture become more and more complex (use of Operating Systems, middleware, etc.) ;, and functional integrations and interdependencies between systems are increasing, eased by the improving computing and communication performances of processors and Ethernet-based network communications. It is now common to use Avionics Data networks based on ARINC 664 standard or Integrated Modular Avionics (IMA) in avionics systems, which are good examples (see **Fig. 1**) of the way the avionics systems evolve towards resources sharing.

F. Ortmeier and A. Rauzy (Eds.): IMBSA 2014, LNCS 8822, pp. 57–69, 2014.

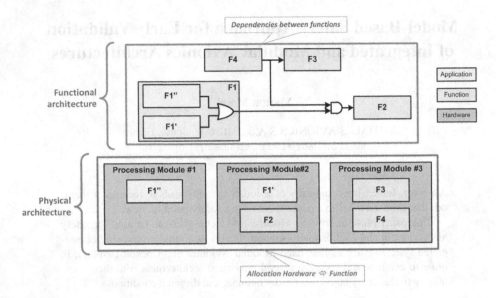

Fig. 1. Integrated Modular Avionics functional[1] and physical architectures

Moreover, as one hardware resource hosts several aircraft functions, the system Functional Hazard Analysis (FHA) established at the beginning of the design life cycle to assess functional failures may not covered all combinations of resource failures. A specific assessment of the effects of the cumulative functional failures at Aircraft level is then performed at the end of the design life cycle, when all functions are allocated to a hardware module.

Therefore, the Safety Validation and Verification activities result in a long and iterative process during the whole design life cycle, in order :

- to define specific safety objectives related to each resource system, depending on the allocation of aircraft functions to these resources,
- to verify the safety performances (in term of availability and integrity) of the resource system face to its objectives, in nominal cases and for all dispatch cases (aircraft flights with inoperative equipment, to improve its operational availability),
- to validate the functional allocation to hardware resource modules, by assessing the cumulative failures effects due to single or multiple resource failures face to aircraft safety objectives and impacts on the flight crew workload, taking into account potential common modes inside the resource system (errors impacting at the same time several hardware or software items),
- to determine alerts and pilot's abnormal procedures needed to mitigate effects of each resource failure.

---

[1] A function here is an end-to-end product which provides operational capability to an aircraft ; a function uses one or several application software resources, themselves hosted by different hardware resources (avionics computers, network, etc.).

In order to handle difficulties resulting from these functional and hardware dependencies in the safety assessment, a Model-based Approach has been deemed very fruitful. Indeed, this kind of approach, due to the necessity to formally describe items dependencies and behaviours (failures consequences, failures detection means and associated sanctions, etc.), helps to organize the assessment process in a structured and iterative way, aiming to master system complexity in the development process and then to improve level of confidence in the safety assessment results (ref. [7]).

The tool that we used is based on ALTARICA language formalized by the LaBRI (ref. [3]) ; this language, which uses constraint automata, supports modelling of dynamic systems thanks to a semantics more flexible than the Boolean formulae used in the Fault-Tree models. It provides also modular, pre-validated and re-usable bricks easier to re-arrange according to the different system architecture variants. Moreover, the graphical simulation of injected failures propagation offered by industrial tools (as CECILIA OCAS) reduces difficulties for design engineers to verify the safety model and helps to ensure completeness and correctness of the resulting analyses.

Then, Fault-Trees and associated minimal Cutsets, or research of all dynamic sequences of events, leading to each observed Failure Condition may be automatically computed from the ALTARICA model (ref. [4]), to demonstrate that the system architecture meets its safety objectives identified in the system Functional Hazard Analysis (FHA),as in any classical systems safety assessment. Modelling tool may be coupled to a classical Fault-Tree tool to compute probabilistic occurrences of feared events. In addition, a single failures assessment (such as "system's FMEA") may be automatically generated from the model, by triggering any event and observing its effects on the system (particularly used for the cumulative functional failures assessment).

The Model-based approach followed in early validation supports then flexible and rapid prototyping of integrated systems (such as IMA and Avionics Data network) in order to evaluate and compare several envisaged architectures with their compliance to the safety objectives (FHA under nominal and dispatch conditions). The model may be built in a modular and iterative way to manage the intrinsic complexity of avionics hardware architecture where targeted aircraft functions to be embedded in the hardware modules may be subsequently defined and may evolve all along the aircraft design and operational life.

This paper is structured as follows :

- First the objectives, the work-flow and the methodology of the Model-based approach applied to our case study are presented,
- The second part of this paper shows how the model of the Integrated Modular Avionics is built to answer to these objectives,
- Finally the conclusion provides some results and perspectives of future work related to the case study.

2   Modelling of Integrated and Modular Avionics Architectures in Early Validation

2.1   Objectives and Work-Flow

The objectives of the safety assessment are to benchmark and identify the weaknesses of the proposed IMA architectures(s) with regards to safety point of view and to determine an optimal allocation at three levels :

— Choice of the best suited fault-tolerant functional architecture (e.g. COM/MON, etc.) for the logical internal architecture of each aircraft function hosted by the IMA system, depending on the function's intrinsic FHA and of safety performances achieved by the IMA hardware modules, in term of integrity and availability,

— Specification of quantitative requirements (e.g. probability of occurrence of loss of availability or loss of integrity failure modes) for the items of the IMA hardware modules, taking into account potential hardware dependencies, redundancies or monitoring at IMA physical level, inside a hardware module or between different modules, and depending of safety objectives associated to each IMA hardware modules, resulting from embedded functions' FHAs.

— Choice of the best suited allocation of functions to Hardware resources, taking into account the number of IMA modules, design constraints such as number and types of IOs per module, segregation constraints due to Aircraft installation, and each function's logical architecture pre-requisite (e.g. functional COM/MON architecture split on two different IMA hardware modules), and depending on the comprehensive Aircraft FHA assessing potential combinations of different functions' Failure Conditions.

To resolve this problematic aiming to optimize three interdependent axes of the architectures, we decide to split off the assessment process in two main steps, as shown in **Fig. 2** :

— First, the different IMA architectures are compared each other's with standardized references of functional architectures, which will not depend on the definition of targeted functions hosted by IMA system and their functional allocation to IMA hardware modules : common Safety Architectural Patterns used in the design of safety critical embedded systems (see ref. [5] which provides an exhaustive list of these patterns). This step allows to benchmark the proposed IMA architectures, even eliminate architectures not complying with "state-of-the art" safety performances of Safety Patterns, help to determine specifications of quantitative requirements for hardware items, and provide quantitative criteria for the choice of best suited functional architecture for each embedded function on the IMA system,

— Secondly, when targeted embedded functions are known, and associated to a Safety Architectural Pattern, the foreseen allocations {functions on IMA hardware modules} may be assessed taking into account the best IMA architectures resulting from the benchmark performed during the first step.

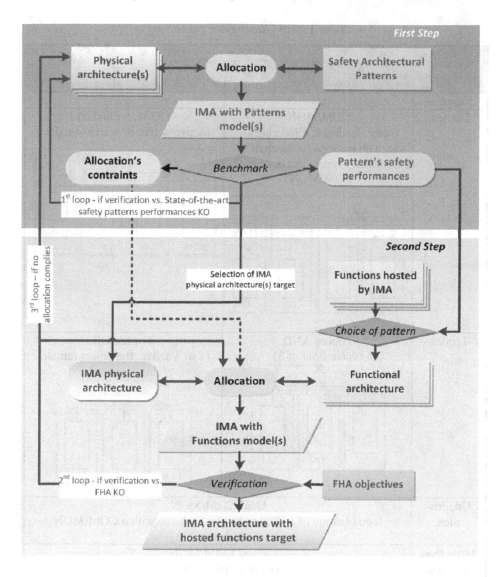

Fig. 2. Detail of modelling process

Table 1 presents a list of generic patterns identified in the designed avionics architectures, depending on the number of channels considered in the pattern (a "channel" is here related to one or several functional modules in series). Safety Architecture Patterns may be a combination of other Safety Patterns, for example the Triplex-AND pattern is made of three instances of a Simplex Pattern, combined in a two-out-of-three voter scheme.

Table 1. Safety Architecture Patterns

Safety Pattern type		
Number of channels	Design for high Integrity	Design for Availability
Simplex	n/a	n/a
Duplex	COM/MON (voter, feedback, CRC checks, etc. with passivation mechanism located in user system or in COM/MON)	DUAL redundant (active-active or active-standby)
Triplex	Triplex-AND (voter 1 out of 3)	Triplex-OR (1 to 3 active, the others remaining standby)
Quadru-plex	Dual COM/MON (combination of a Dual redundant scheme with a COM/MON scheme)	
More than 4 channels	Quad COM/MON Triple Triplex-AND ...	

Safety objectives are affected to Safety Patterns, depending on the safety objectives and performances generally associated to these kinds of architectures, as shown in **Fig. 3** (for example, a COM-MON architecture aims to respond to integrity objectives at the highest level – i.e. generally for Failure Conditions classified CAT, but without any availability criteria). The classification proposed in **Fig. 3** is based on the following reliability assumptions : hardware platforms with a MTBF (Mean Time Between Failures) between 100 000 and 10 000 Flight Hours, and with a coverage rate of internal Built-In Tests around 95%. Latent failures not detected at equipment level by its internal monitoring are assumed to be covered and detected at function or system level with an adequate test time interval.

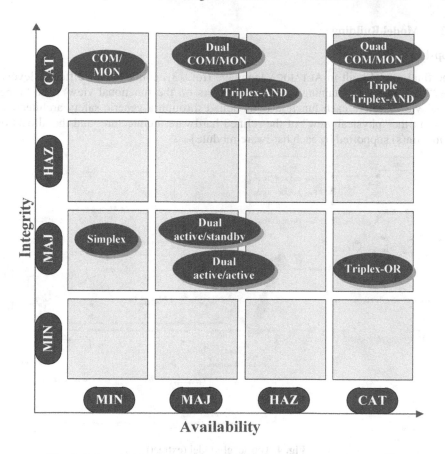

Fig. 3. Safety Architecture Patterns and their targeted safety objectives[2]

The use of Safety Architectural patterns allows then to compare the several IMA hardware architectures with "standardized" safety objectives, even in early validation when the functional allocation to hardware modules is not yet defined. Validation of the whole avionics system regarding safety objectives is also reduced, as each embedded function is associated to an Architectural pattern, according to the safety performances the function shall reach. Therefore, only Failure Conditions related to combination of functions in the Functional Hazard Analysis have to be analysed in the second validation loop described in **Fig. 2**. Incidentally, in the further steps of design, providing Architectural Patterns, associated to their "safety usage domain", helps to homogenize and rationalize the design of the whole set of functions embedded on the Integrated Modular Avionics.

---

[2] This illustration is not meant to be exhaustive, nor valid in any cases. Especially, Development Assurance Levels and Independence aspects are not considered here.

2.2   Model Building

Top-Level Model

The final model built in ALTARICA language (ref. [3]) contains four different levels : the "FHA view" (containing model's observers on the functional view) ; the "functional view" where each function is modelled through a generic safety architectural pattern ; the "physical view" of the refined hardware architecture; and the allocation {function(s) supported by each hardware module}.

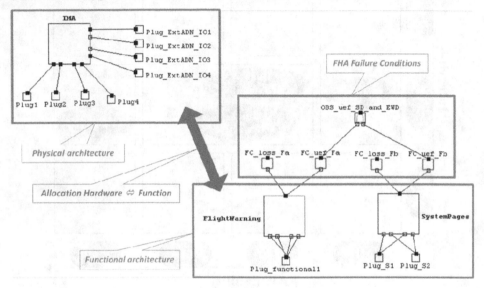

Fig. 4. Top-level model (extract)

"Functional" View

The functional view is composed of the Safety Architectural Patterns or of the functions embedded on the Integrated Modular Avionics, each of them being figured by its Safety Pattern.

A Safety Architectural Pattern is typically break-down into one or several modular channels, that contain, in our model, the following modules to cope with the modular avionics intended functions :

- Input / Output module(s),
- Processing module(s),
- A basic safety logic function (e.g. master-salve redundancy, voter m/n, etc.), related to the type of modeled pattern, arranging its several channels,
- Communication nodes between IO and processing modules representing Virtual Link paths through Avionics Data Network,
- External interfaces : input(s) that are either connected to other patterns' outputs or plugged if not used ; and output(s) that are linked to model observers of data (loss of data or corrupted data) for safety assessment purpose.

Patterns may be connected to each other's, to modelize dependencies in the functional architecture (e.g. Patterns in serial or COM/MON arrangements).

A node in ALTARICA language is characterized by :

- A name : unique identifier in the system model,
- Flows : inputs and outputs characterized by their range domain (boolean, enumerated values, etc.),
- One or several states characterized by their range domain (same as for flows),
- Events (failure modes or functional events),
- A behaviour : relationships between states and events (State Automata) and between states and flows (assertions).
- And may be linked to a library provided by the tool, to allow its re-use in other parts of the model.

Fig. 5 gives standard State Automata and its translation into ALTARICA code for a low-level generic node of any pattern. This node has one nominal state (SAFE) and two degraded faulty states (LOST and ERRoneous behavior), and two failure events (loss and error) ; the node has one input and one output, which have three possible values : ok (i.e. data is valid and correct), invalid (i.e. data is not computed, not available or provided but out of expected range and detected invalid), or corrupted (i.e. data is considered valid by the receiver but is erroneous in a misleading way).

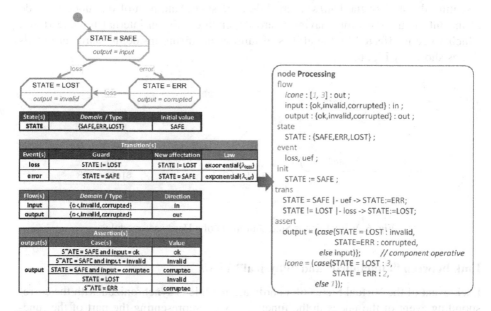

Fig. 5. standard Node's State Automata and tabular description, with its translation into ALTARICA code

This generic basic node may be used in the functional view for basic nodes of safety patterns (e.g. for "IOx" or "Processing" nodes) as well as in the physical view of system architecture, except that nodes used in the "physical" architecture view have probability laws attached to their failure events. Of course, specific hardware or functional items (e.g. Avionics Data network, voters, redundant sources selection, etc.) have specific behaviours and thus specific ALTARICA code.

"Physical" View

The Integrated Modular Avionics systems that we want to assess are composed of several Inputs/Outputs modules, several Processing modules, interfaced themselves and with several Display Units through an Avionics Data Network.

The physical architecture is refined at a logical level, and includes hardware dependencies such as redundancies and monitoring between items of different modules (e.g. Continuous Built-In-Test of one hardware item performed by another item, internal Power Supply redundancies, etc.) and also potential common modes of resources (Aircraft Power Supply busses, End-Systems to communicate through the avionics network, ...).

Failures are then propagated inside the "physical view", taking into account internal logical safety mechanisms through flows interfacing the different hardware modules (see left part of **Fig. 7**). For each hardware module of the IMA system, a virtual node named "virtual status" is added in the model at the module logical outputs, representing the state of the hardware module : the state Automata of this node is made of instantaneous transitions having guard depending only on internal module flows, which value is affected by the effects of failures occurring inside the hardware module, as shown by **Fig. 6**.

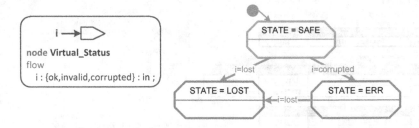

Fig. 6. Virtual Status State Automata of a Hardware module

Link between "Functional" and "Physical" Views

Each event of the Virtual Status of a hardware module is synchronized with the corresponding event of the nodes in the functional view representing the part of the function hosted by the hardware module, as shown in **Fig. 7**.

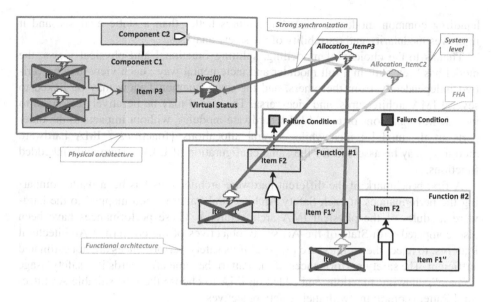

Fig. 7. Failures propagation inside physical architecture and effects to Functional Architecture failure propagation

These synchronizations are automatically generated from an allocation {function(s)/hardware module} table determined with the system designer. For the Avionics Data network modelling, the synchronizations of hardware switch failures with Communication nodes representing Virtual Link paths in the functional view are automatically generated according to the network routing configuration table based on network topology specific to each analyzed IMA architecture.

The choice of events synchronization to interface the different views offers the possibility of separately exploiting the functional or the physical model view (e.g. computing in a first stage minimal cutsets of the functional architecture to validate it, independently from the physical architecture). Synchronizations are "strong" synchronizations, meaning that synchronized events cannot be individually triggered, so when the allocation {function(s)/hardware module} is completed, only hardware failures are observed in the model results, dividing the number of events involved in minimal cutsets by five for the more complex functional views.

Thanks to the synchronization of hardware failure events with functional failure events, failures occurring inside the physical view are instantaneously propagated to the functional view. Then, minimal cutsets of refined hardware failures leading to each Failure Condition, linked to observers on data outputs in the functional view, may be automatically computed from the model and quantified based on the quantitative failure rates associated to hardware items failures modes.

3   Conclusion

The Model-based approach is well adapted to perform early validation of several system architectures, as it supports complex and dynamic systems modelling, handling common modes or cascading failures better than a static analysis, and it improves modularity and reusability of the safety analyses.

Thanks to the choices of modelling, splitting functional and physical views, the model has been built in a full modular and incremental way : each view may be verified independently from the others, and the same functional view may be linked to several IMA architectures, and vice-versa. The model may be iteratively extended to include new functions or to add IMA hardware modules, without impacts to the older parts of the model ; meanwhile, several allocations {functions / IMA hardware modules} may be assessed for the same configuration of IMA system and embedded functions.

A first benchmark of the different hardware architectures has been made comparing the performances of each Safety Architectural Pattern when mapped to the hardware modules of the physical IMA architecture(s). These performances have been also compared with State-of-the-Art safety objectives of the concerned Architectural Patterns, to reject the architecture proposal if its safety performances are not estimated sufficient. The safety performances of the Pattern become afterwards its "safety usage domain", allowing functions embedded on IMA to choose the best suitable Architectural Pattern complying with their safety objectives.

This step may also result in allocation's {function(s) supported by each hardware} constraints (e.g. to achieve segregation constraints at Aircraft level) ; in that case, Pattern's safety performances will be guaranteed only if allocation's constraints are fulfilled. Of course, in the benchmark results, IMA architectures generated no allocation's constraints for a particular Architectural Pattern are privileged, as they provide a better modularity for the integration of hosted functions.

Our Case study deals with about : 14 hardware modules in the physical view (resulting in 190 events), 15 avionics functions and 35 Failure Conditions in the functional view (resulting in 1300 events). For each system architecture, several variants (10 to 20) of allocation of pattern's items have been assessed. The resulting computation times are very satisfactory (less than 15 seconds per FC for cutsets at the order 3, which allow to identify all architecture design issues at this stage of the safety assessment).

Assessment of IMA architectures with Safety Architectural Patterns and with full targeted Aircraft functions configuration has then allowed to highlight the architectures offering the best safety performances, taking into account also dispatch constraints. Yet, Development Assurance Level (DAL) criteria and Independence Requirements face to common modes have not been considered in our case study, as they were deemed to be less stringent than quantitative objectives for our problematic : that is the benchmark and the sizing of several avionics systems composed of hardware items expected to be developed at the highest DAL level (DAL A) but similar. However, the verification of allocation independence face to common failures of shared resources is still performed by checking the order of Minimal Cutsets ("no single failure" criteria for the Catastrophic Failure Conditions) ; and the verification of DAL allocation to software items may also be performed by checking the Functional Failure Sets resulting from the Minimal Cutsets for each Failure Condition computed on the functional view model, independently from the allocation to hardware items.

This Model-based Approach rises however some issues concerning the validation and the completeness of allocation problem resolution (some of them may be solved by SAT-solvers as described in ref. [5]) we would like to address in further works related to our case study :

1. How to validate the allocation {functions / hardware module} performed in a separate table taking into account the model of the physical architecture : for example, by verifying that functions connected in the functional view are allocated to modules really connected in the physical view,
2. If an architecture is assessed Not OK vs. safety objectives, how to be sure that any other allocation {functions / hardware module} with extended allocation constraints will not be compliant with these safety objectives ?
3. If an architecture is assessed OK vs. safety objectives of Safety Architectural Patterns, how to be sure that this analysis cover all possible allocation {pattern's modules / hardware modules} ?
4. And is it possible to determine the optimal allocation {functions / IMA hardware module}, which reduces the number of IMA channels and network connections, and still compliant with safety objectives, taking into account additional allocation constraints (independence or co-location between functions, etc.)

References

1. SAE AEROSPACE, Aerospace recommended practice – Guidelines and Methods for conducting the safety assessment – SAE ARP4761
2. EUROCAE / SAE AEROSPACE, Aerospace recommended practice – Guidelines for Development of Civil Aircraft and Systems –EUROCAE ED-79A / SAE ARP 4754A
3. Arnold, A., Point, G., Griffault, A., Rauzy, A.: LaBRI, Université Bordeaux I and CNRS (UMR5800). The Altarica Formalism for Describing Concurrent Systems. Fundamenta Informaticae 34 (2000)
4. Rauzy, A.: Mode automata and their compilation into fault. Reliability Engineering and System Safety 78, 1–12 (2002)
5. Armoush, A.: Design Patterns for Safety critical Embedded Systems, Ph.D. Thesis Report (2010)
6. Sagaspe, L.: Allocation sûre dans les systèmes aéronautiques: Modélisation, Vérification et Génération,, Ph.D. Thesis Report, Université Bordeaux 1 (2008)
7. Seguin, C., Papadopoulos, C., et al.: Model-based safety assessment for the three stages of refinement ofthe system development process in ARP4754A, SAE 2011 AeroTech (2011)

Exploring the Impact of Different Cost Heuristics in the Allocation of Safety Integrity Levels

Luís Silva Azevedo[1], David Parker[1], Yiannis Papadopoulos[1], Martin Walker[1], Ioannis Sorokos[1], and Rui Esteves Araújo[2]

[1] Department of Computer Science, University of Hull, Hull, UK
{l.p.azevedo,i.sorokos}@2012.hull.ac.uk,
{d.j.parker,y.i.papadopoulos,martin.walker}@hull.ac.uk
[2] INESC TEC, Faculdade de Engenharia, Universidade do Porto, Portugal
raraujo@fe.up.pt

Abstract. Contemporary safety standards prescribe processes in which system safety requirements, captured early and expressed in the form of Safety Integrity Levels (SILs), are iteratively allocated to architectural elements. Different SILs reflect different requirements stringencies and consequently different development costs. Therefore, the allocation of safety requirements is not a simple problem of applying an allocation "algebra" as treated by most standards; it is a complex optimisation problem, one of finding a strategy that minimises cost whilst meeting safety requirements. One difficulty is the lack of a commonly agreed heuristic for how costs increase between SILs. In this paper, we define this important problem; then we take the example of an automotive system and using an automated approach show that different cost heuristics lead to different optimal SIL allocations. Without automation it would have been impossible to explore the vast space of allocations and to discuss the subtleties involved in this problem.

Keywords: Dependability Analysis, Requirements Analysis, Functional Safety, SIL Allocation and Decomposition, Cost Optimisation.

1 Introduction

Safety Standards, such as IEC 61508, ISO 26262, and ARP4754-A, introduce a system of classification for different levels of safety: IEC 61508 popularised the Safety Integrity Level (SIL), while ISO 26262 and ARP4754-A introduced domain-specific versions of this concept — the Automotive Safety Integrity Level (ASIL) for the automotive domain and the Development Assurance Level (DAL) for the aerospace domain. All of these serve as qualitative indicators of the required level of safety of a function or component, and generally they are broken down into 5 levels, ranging from strict requirements (e.g. SIL4, ASIL D, DAL A) to no special requirements (e.g. SIL0, QM, DAL E). These safety levels are employed as part of a top-down requirements distribution process. We focus on ISO 26262 guidelines as we will be analysing an automotive system; however, other standards prescribe analogous rules for requirements definition, allocation and decomposition. In ISO 26262 the process of

F. Ortmeier and A. Rauzy (Eds.): IMBSA 2014, LNCS 8822, pp. 70–81, 2014.
© Springer International Publishing Switzerland 2014

elicitation starts with a hazard and risk analysis which identifies the various malfunctions that may take place and what hazards may arise as a result. The severity, likelihood, and controllability of these hazards are then considered, and on the basis of this risk analysis, an ASIL is assigned to them; this ASIL assignment is intended to generate the necessary requirements throughout the system architecture that ensure that any risks will be decreased to an acceptable level. At this point, system level safety requirements, termed Safety Goals (SGs), are formulated, linked to system functions and inherit the ASILs of the hazard they are meant to prevent.

During subsequent development of the system, traceability to the original ASILs is maintained at all times. As the system design is refined into more detailed architectures, the original ASILs are allocated and can be decomposed throughout new sub-components and sub-functions of the design. ISO 26262 prescribes an "ASIL algebra" to guide this process, where the various integrity levels are translated into integers (ASIL QM = 0; A = 1; B = 2; C = 3 and D = 4). The algebra is essentially an abstraction and simplification of techniques for combining probabilities under assumptions of statistical independence of failures. In this approach, components that can directly cause the corruption of a SG are assigned with the ASIL of that hazard; if, on the other hand, multiple independent components must fail together to cause a SG violation, they are allowed to share the burden of complying with the ASIL of that SG; the rationale here is that the components' total ASIL must add up to the safety level of the SG. For example, a safety level like ASIL B can be met by two independent components which each individually only meeting ASIL A (and thus effectively A + A = B).

In following the decomposition rules, there are various concerns. The first concern is raised by the complexity of modern safety-critical systems. The trend is for these architectures to become systems of systems, where multiple functions are delivered by complex networked architectural topologies and where functions can share components. The ISO standard is lacking in providing examples and detailed guidelines to support ASIL allocation in these systems. Possibly due to this lack of clarity, practitioners often make mistakes [1]. Furthermore, the safety engineer's tasks include understanding architectural failure behaviour, ensuring that component failure independence constraints are met, working efficiently through the many possible combinations for allocations, and confirming that the decomposed low-level requirements still add up to the original high-level requirements. Performing all of these manually in such complex architectures is practically impossible, and here again the standard fails to give guidance on automated support.

The second concern relates to the way SIL decomposition is being formulated in the standards as a problem solely focused on safety, where the single goal is to arrive at an allocation of integrity requirements to components of the system architecture that fulfils a set of properly elicited system level safety requirements. Naturally, standards are focused on safety, so cost implications are not really considered. On the other hand, there is no doubt that the cost implications of SIL allocation are very relevant to developers of systems. We believe there are benefits to be found if the problem of safety requirement allocation is defined in a broader way which includes costs. Indeed, developing a component according to a given SIL, means that a set of development and validation activities needs to be undertaken. They are translated into time, efforts and in the end costs, and vary with the specific SIL prescribed to a component. Potentially, many allocation possibilities may be available, and in order to find the most advantageous, the problem needs to consider their different cost implications. To illustrate the issue, we need to turn to the very fundamentals of the techniques described in the standards. ISO 26262 gives a range of options for ASIL decomposition. For example a function with an SG that requires ASIL B can be implemented with an architecture of two components which, assuming that they fail independently, may inherit ASILs B and QM *or* A and A respectively. When such options exist, cost typically provides the deciding criterion. This is precisely where the development cost differences implied by different ASILs can reveal decomposition strategies that are more cost-effective than others. During the design phase, when requirement allocation and decomposition take place, exact development costs are naturally hard to obtain. However, cost analyses can still be made on the basis of some heuristic that expresses the relative cost differences of complying with the different ASILs. For example, taking the above example, if considering a logarithmic cost increase between ASILs (ASIL QM = 0; A = 10; B = 100; C = 1000; D = 10000), when decomposing a SIL B amongst two components, C_1 and C_2, one single optimal solution is revealed.

- C_1 (ASIL QM) + C_2 (ASIL B): 0 + 100 = 100;
- **C_1 (ASIL A) + C_2 (ASIL A): 10 + 10 = 20;**
- C_1 (ASIL B) + C_2 (ASIL QM) = 100.

The example must be read carefully, not to suggest that the above is a trivial problem where decomposition opportunities can be examined independently. Components are often participating in multiple functions and numerous chains of conflicting constraints must be examined to find cost-optimal SIL allocations. This is a complex combinatorial problem where *the satisfaction of safety requirements is simply a constraint that must be met, while the real objective is the optimisation of cost.*

It is important to stress that this is not a hypothetical, but a real, important and pertinent problem. The concern about cost implications of ASILs is already evident in the automotive domain. Indeed, there has been continuous discussion within the automotive Functional Safety community to determine an appropriate ASIL cost heuristic (see for example ISO 26262 LinkedIn Forum [2]). One proposal, for instance, suggests that the cost increase between ASIL B and C is bigger than the ones from A to B and C to D. We believe that the community is aware of the importance of a plausible cost heuristic for estimating the costs of meeting safety requirements. In this paper we want to advance this discussion further by showing, with the aid of automation, that what can be seen as "optimal satisfaction" of safety requirement is in fact defined by the nature of this cost heuristic.

In section 2 we briefly outline a recently developed method for a largely automated, cost-aware, model-based allocation of safety requirements in the form of SILs. In section 3 we apply this method to a case study performed on an automotive hybrid braking system. We assume two different cost heuristics and discuss the implications for SIL allocation. Finally in section 4 we summarise, conclude and point to future work.

2   Automatic and Optimal Decomposition of SILs

To address some of the concerns discussed above, we have recently been developing techniques [3, 4] to help automate SIL allocation and decomposition processes by extending the framework of the model-based dependability analysis tool HiP-HOPS (Hierarchically Performed Hazard Origin and Propagation Studies) [5]. HiP-HOPS is built around the concept of annotating the components of a system model with local failure logic. From these local descriptions, HiP-HOPS can synthesise fault trees for the whole system, describing how the individual component failures can propagate throughout the rest of the system and lead to hazardous conditions in the system output functionality. HiP-HOPS is aware of which components are independent by means of the assumption made in the fault propagation model and the fault tree analysis and it can automatically determine the opportunities for requirements decomposition. On the basis of this information, the tool next establishes a set of constraints based on the ASIL 'algebra' described by ISO 26262, but it can also use any analogous rules from standards affecting other industry sectors, such as the aerospace industry. Finally, HiP-HOPS initiates a search for the ASIL allocations that, while fulfilling such requirements constraints, minimize the total system's ASIL dependent costs according to some cost heuristic defined by the system designer. In related work, Mader *et al* [6] built a linear programming problem to minimize the sum of ASILs assigned to an architecture. In the aerospace sector, Bieber, Delmas and Seguin [7] used pseudo-Boolean logic to formulate the DAL decomposition problem; similarly to the work presented by Mader *et al*, the sum of DALs across the components of a system is minimized. In both cases, this can be understood as utilizing a linear fitness function to evaluate the different SIL allocation alternatives; the costs implications of each integrity level increase proportionally to the integer assigned to them by the SIL algebras. Assuming a linear cost growth is fairly simplistic and the use of other cost heuristics can be validly applied.

Our early research has shown that the number of potential combinations of allocations typically produces a vast search space. Therefore, recent work has focused on the use of metaheuristics that are known to be efficient in exploring large search spaces. Furthermore, meta-heuristics include the versatility, not present in many deterministic algorithms, to solve problems with different characteristics; this is important as we allow the system designer to input any ASIL cost function, and these have implications in the nature of the optimisation problem. Initial investigation on this has included implementations of genetic algorithms [8], a metaheuristic based on the concept of natural evolution, where a set of *candidate* solutions evolve, through *crossover* and *mutation* operations, during a fixed number of *generations* into (near) optimal solutions. More recently we have found significant improvements in solution quality and processing efficiency using a Tabu search technique [9] which is based on the work of Hansen and Lih [10]. In Tabu Search a single solution exists at any given iteration. Specialized local search algorithms are used for that solution to travel throughout the search space together with memory mechanisms that increase diversity and grant global exploration capabilities to the algorithm. Our technique makes use of a steepest descent approach for neighbourhood exploration: the cost reductions of decrementing each of the ASILs in the current solution are analysed and the failure mode's ASIL for which this cost variation is the highest is decremented. When decrementing an ASIL means violating any decomposition constraint, a mildest ascent direction is followed by incrementing the ASIL of the failure mode which results in the lowest system cost growth. At this moment a memory mechanism forbids reverse moves for a dynamic number of iterations p. This is important in avoiding returning to local optima. While descending, a similar mechanism exists, prohibiting reverse moves for p' iterations; this allows introducing further diversity in the search by reducing the possibility of switching behaviours between solutions.

It should be noted that HiP-HOPS assigns ASILs to component failure modes instead of the components themselves. This means that there is a greater level of refinement in this method, so for example an omission of an output can be assigned a different ASIL from a commission of the output if they lead to different effects at system level. In turn, higher integrity will be required by the subcomponents that can directly or indirectly cause the omission. This feature is clearly useful for the case where a component presents more than one type of failure and therefore requirements can be more appropriately tailored in dealing with each one of them. Strictly speaking, this approach does not agree with the ISO 26262 standard, which requires that a single ASIL is allocated to a component. HiP-HOPS can easily revert to this simpler model of allocation for compatibility with the standard, assigning an ASIL to a component on the basis of its most severe failure mode. However, we believe that when requirements are allocated to subsystems which are further developed as complex networks of components, and when allocation of subsystem safety requirements to these components must be achieved, then a more refined and recursive approach where the "subsystem" can be treated as a "system" that has multiple SGs and ASIL requirements is preferable. This, we believe, could be a point worth considering in the future evolution of the ISO 26262 standard.

Finally, HiP-HOPS SIL allocation extension should be regarded as a tool to inform decision making. Ultimately, it is up to the system designer to deliberate on the list of SIL allocation possibilities supplied by the tool and make decisions on how the system architecture should evolve and how refined requirements derived from the Safety Goals are being distributed throughout the components.

In the next section we apply our automated approach to a brake-by-wire system, and in the process demonstrate the impacts of ASIL-imposed cost consideration in deriving efficient allocation strategies.

3   ASIL Allocation Cost Impacts on a Hybrid Braking System

3.1   Hybrid Brake System Description

In our work towards automating and optimising ASIL allocation we have been utilizing the model of a Hybrid Braking System (HBS) for electrical vehicles as a case study to demonstrate our advances. The model is analysed in detail in [11] and is based on a system introduced by Castro *et al* [12] where braking is achieved using the combined efforts of two actuators: In-Wheel Motors (IWMs) and Electromechanical

Brakes (EMBs). IWMs decrease the kinetic energy of a vehicle transforming it into electrical energy. The latter is fed to car's powertrain batteries thus increasing driving range. However, the IWMs have limitations in regards to the amount of braking they can produce, namely at some speed regimes, or when the powertrain's batteries are close to or at a full state of charge. In that way, EMBs are used dynamically with IWMs to provide the total braking required. The HBS is a brake-by-wire system where there is no mechanical or hydraulic link between the braking pedal and the actuators. We have developed a model for the system that for illustrative purposes only considers the braking of one wheel. The model is depicted in Figure 1.

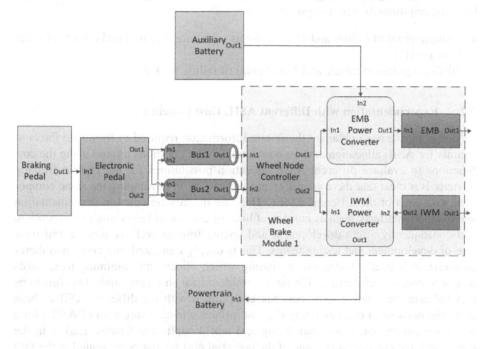

Fig. 1. Hybrid Braking System Model

For the architecture of the HBS, it is considered when the driver presses the braking pedal, his actions are sensed and processed on a redundant Electronic Pedal Unit. Braking requests are generated for each of the vehicles wheels and are sent via a duplex communications bus; these demands are received at a local Wheel Node Controller (WNC) that performs calculations for the division between electromechanical and electrical braking and sends commands accordingly to the power converters that control the two types of actuators. While braking, electrical power flows from the low voltage Auxiliary Battery to the EMB; the IWM, on the other hand, acts as a generator and provides energy for the Powertrain Battery. It needs to be noted that the elements of the power architecture should be regarded as subsystems composed of multiple components. The Powertrain Battery subsystem includes, for example, a Battery Management System, and the Power Converters integrate electronic driver circuits.

For this illustrative case study we have considered two hazards: "Omission of braking" (H1) and "Braking with the wrong value" (H2). For the purpose of demonstration, H1 and H2 have been assigned with ASILs D and C, respectively. The two hazards were linked to model output deviations in the following manner:

- H1: Omission of IWM.out1 AND Omission of EMB.out1
- H2: Wrong Value of IWM.out1 OR Wrong Value of EMB.out1

We have derived failure expressions for each of the components of the HBS architecture [11]. HiP-HOPS then automatically synthesized fault trees for each of the hazards, and through their analysis unveiled:

- 1 single point of failure and 18 dual points of failure (i.e. minimal cutsets of order two) for H1;
- 10 single points of failure and 1 dual point of failure for H2.

3.2   Experimentation with Different ASIL Cost Functions

At this point we have obtained the failure information required to formulate the constraints for ASIL allocation and we now focus on the questions around using the cost functions to evaluate different ASIL allocation possibilities for the Hybrid Braking System. It is clear that there are different implications in developing the same component with each of the different ASILs. They are directly reflected in implementation and evaluation efforts, such as number of lines of code or of safety analysis execution, and consequently affect development and testing time as well as average and peak size of development and testing teams. This is deeply translated into costs, and therefore one is logically interested in finding which allocations minimize these costs across a system architecture. We have considered for this case study two functions that indicate the relative costs between compliance with the different ASILs; these serve the purpose of demonstrating the cost influence in choosing a set of ASILs for a given system design, rather than being real world applicable figures. Earlier in the paper we have mentioned that one of the potential cost heuristics presented in the ISO 26262 LinkedIn forum indicated a larger cost jump between ASILs B and C than the ones from A to B and C to D. In meeting this consideration we have formulated the *Experiential-I* cost function shown in Table 1, where the cost between B and C (20) is twice the variation between any of the other ASILs (10). We have also established a second one, *Experiential-II*, which maintains that the cost difference between ASILs B and C (15) is greater than from A to B and C to D (10). However, this function instead assumes that the cost jump between no safety considerations – ASIL QM – and ASIL A is the biggest (20).

Table 1. ASIL Cost Heuristics

Cost Heuristics / ASILs	QM	A	B	C	D
Experiential-I	0	10	20	40	50
Experiential-II	0	20	30	45	55

3.3 Cost Optimal ASIL Allocations for the Hybrid Braking System

There are 24 failure modes in the HBS and 5 different ASILs that can be allocated to each one of them. This gives a total search space size of 5^{24} ($\approx 5.96 \times 10^{16}$), which is still small enough to be finished with the exhaustive search techniques described in [3]; all optimal solutions are therefore unambiguously known. It is worth noting however, that our Tabu Search and Genetic Algorithms are able to find these allocations very efficiently. To allow discussion, we display the optimal solutions in Table 2.

Table 2. HBS Optimal ASIL Allocations for Experiential-I and Experiential-II Cost Functions

	Optimal Solutions				
	Exp-I Cost: 390	Exp-II Cost: 585			
Components' Failure Modes	#1	#1	#2	#3	#4
Braking Pedal Omission	4	4	4	4	4
Braking Pedal Value	1	1	1	1	1
Electronic Pedal Omission 1	2	4	4	4	4
Electronic Pedal Omission 2	2	0	0	0	0
Electronic Pedal Value 1	1	1	1	1	1
Electronic Pedal Value 2	0	0	0	0	0
Bus1 Omission	2	0	4	0	4
Bus2 Omission	2	4	0	4	0
WNC Omission 1	2	0	0	4	4
WNC Omission 2	2	4	4	0	0
WNC Value 1	1	1	1	1	1
WNC Value 2	1	1	1	1	1
Auxiliary Battery Omission	2	0	0	4	4
Auxiliary Battery Value	1	1	1	1	1
Powertrain Battery Omission	2	4	4	0	0
Powertrain Battery Value	1	1	1	1	1
EMB Power Converter Omission	2	0	0	4	4
EMB Power Converter Value	1	1	1	1	1
IWM Power Converter Omission	2	4	4	0	0
IWM Power Converter Value	1	1	1	1	1
EMB Omission	2	0	0	4	4
EMB Value	1	1	1	1	1
IWM Omission	2	4	4	0	0
IWM Value	1	1	1	1	1

There are obvious differences between the results of using each of the cost heuristics. The most immediate is that *Experiential-I* yields only one optimal allocation whereas *Experiential-II* yields four solutions with the same minimal cost. A closer look tells us that none of the optimal solutions of *Experiential-II* matches the one from *Experiential-I*. In this way, the choice of cost heuristic would have a definite impact on the integrity of specific components, for example, in deciding that an Omission Failure would impose development and validation measures of ASIL B (*Experiential-I*) or ASIL D/QM (*Experiential-II*) within component EMB. It is of course possible that for the HBS or another system, two different cost heuristics may work in a way that yields exactly the same optimal solution(s). However, what is important to remember is that the latter does not represent the general case, as we have demonstrated, and that the cost heuristic defines which allocation is cost-optimal. We believe this is an important realisation and should kickstart some work towards defining a plausible and widely accepted cost heuristic that could both inform automated analyses, such as the one presented in this paper, and more generally inform decisions about how to optimise allocation of safety requirements during design refinement.

3.4   Costs Refinement for More Accurate Optimal ASIL Allocations

While the results above do demonstrate the need for a unified ASIL fitness function, one can argue that it is unrealistic to consider that the efforts associated with developing a processing unit of ASIL D are even close to those required for developing a High Voltage Battery subsystem with an equal integrity level. In meeting such concerns, we have refined our approach to allow a greater granularity in costs estimation, providing the user with the ability to establish categories of components and assign relative cost weights to them. This feature is demonstrated below.

Reutilising the HBS case study, we have divided the components of its architecture in to 3 categories, as shown in Table 3. Again this was done for the sole purpose of demonstration and more accurate and meaningful divisions may be found. In the same way, we have simplified the costs of individual failure modes for illustrative purposes, and have considered that the efforts in dealing with Value and Omission failures are equal within the same component.

Table 3. HBS Components Divided in 3 Categories

Programmable Electronics	Electronic Low Voltage	Electronic High Voltage
Electronic Pedal	Auxiliary Battery	IWM
WNC	EMB Power Converter	IWM Power Converter
Communication Buses	EMB	Powertrain Battery
-	Braking Pedal	-

We have assumed the *Programmable Electronics* category is the least expensive, and have used it as the base category for relative costs definition. We have estimated that the *Electronic Low Voltage* components are 3 times more expensive than *Programmable Electronics*. It is a given that when one adds features and/or redundancy to a system, the development costs increase. That is to say, growing complexity is usually tied to an increase in risk of defect and consequently the investment in safety measures escalates. In this way, taking into account the much larger complexity usually involved in both the software and hardware elements of a high voltage architecture, *Electronic High Voltage* was assigned with the highest cost jump: 5 times the price of *Programmable Electronics*. Note that in this class we can find the main components of the traction drive system with critical expensive parts and multiple control units with embedded software. We have reapplied the two cost functions of Table 1 and have used them in conjunction with the cost weights of the 3 component categories we have devised. Our technique yielded the optimal solutions presented in Table 4.

Table 4. HBS Optimal ASIL Allocations for Experiential-I and Experiential-II Cost Functions With Cost Weights for Components Categories

	Optimal Solutions		
	Exp-I Cost: 1030	Exp-II Cost: 1425	
Components FM	#1	#1	#2
Braking Pedal Omission	4	4	4
Braking Pedal Value	1	1	1
Electronic Pedal Omission 1	2	4	4
Electronic Pedal Omission 2	2	0	0
Electronic Pedal Value 1	1	1	1
Electronic Pedal Value 2	0	0	0
Bus1 Omission	2	0	4
Bus2 Omission	2	4	0
WNC Omission 1	4	4	4
WNC Omission 2	0	0	0
WNC Value 1	1	1	1
WNC Value 2	1	1	1
Auxiliary Battery Omission	4	4	4
Auxiliary Battery Value	1	1	1
Powertrain Battery Omission	0	0	0
Powertrain Battery Value	1	1	1
EMB Power Converter Omission	4	4	4
EMB Power Converter Value	1	1	1
IWM Power Converter Omission	0	0	0
IWM Power Converter Value	1	1	1
EMB Omission	4	4	4
EMB Value	1	1	1
IWM Omission	0	0	0
IWM Value	1	1	1

It is interesting to observe that using the cost weights between components categories reveals a new optimal solution for the *Experiential-I* function, whereas for *Experiential-II* the optimal solutions are a subset of the ones encountered earlier (#3 and #4 of Table 3). Even so, the minimal cost solution of *Experiential-I* is still different to the ones yielded by *Experiential-II*. Moreover, the higher cost assigned to the *Electronic High Power* category clearly biased the optimal solutions towards utilizing low ASILs for the failure modes of its components.

From the results above it was possible to demonstrate further that the use of different cost heuristics impacts the optimal allocation of ASILs, this time in the presence of relative cost differences between categories of components. Furthermore, the use of more specific cost information allowed us to reveal optimal solutions which are likely to be more accurate. For the case of the *Experiential-II* cost function, two of the solutions already identified as optimal in the previous section remained optimal following the refinement of costs. Finally, the introduction of categories and relative cost weights changes the nature of the optimisation problem; nonetheless, as in the previous step, our metaheuristics techniques were able to find the optimal solutions for this experiment, further validating their capabilities in dealing effectively with various formulations of the SIL allocation problem.

4   Conclusions

We have argued that the application of SIL allocation and decomposition is a complex combinatorial optimisation problem which must consider the optimisation of costs and not just the satisfaction of safety requirements constraints imposed by standardised SILs decomposition algebras. Through the use of a Hybrid Braking System case study we have demonstrated that such cost consideration allowed us to identify which are the most promising solutions, an effort that clearly contributes to a more efficient and cost-effective refinement of designs for safety-critical systems. Our example was equally important in revealing that different cost heuristics imply different optimality considerations; in this regard, work needs to be undertaken within each industry sector to identify plausible cost heuristics so that SIL allocation choices can be made with more confidence.

All of the deliberations above were only possible due to the use of an automated framework that enabled the exploration of the vast number of ASIL allocation solutions in our case study in the presence of different ASIL cost functions. While a definitive cost heuristic is presently not available, our method is flexible in using any that a system designer finds more suitable. Furthermore, some industries, like the automotive industry where ISO 26262 was introduced in late 2011, are still undergoing a shift from developing entire systems via application of ISO26262 towards processes in which there is reuse of Off the Shelf ASIL compliant parts. It is therefore likely that ASIL costs and their relationships might change, and it is important that our method maintains its versatility. Finally, our approach allows for designers to input costs in different levels of granularity; for example establishing categories of components with relative cost weights or even specific ASIL-dependant costs for each component. This further contributes to a more accurate determination of the best ASIL allocation strategies.

References

1. Ward, D.D., Crozier, S.E.: The uses and abuses of ASIL decomposition in ISO 26262. In: 7th IET International Conference on System Safety, incorporating the Cyber Security Conference (2012)
2. Allen, M.: Cost Versus ASIL. ISO 26262 Functional Safety [LinkedIn] (February 2, 2012), http://www.linkedin.com/groups/Cost-versus-ASIL-2308567.S.92692199?view=&srchtype=discussedNews&gid=2308567&item=92692199&type=member&trk=eml-anet_dig-b_pd-ttl-cn&ut=1evtvoEm1QcBw1 (accessed May 1, 2014)

3. Papadopoulos, Y., Walker, M., Reiser, M.-O., Weber, M., Chen, D., Törngren, S.D., Abele, A., Stappert, F., Lönn, H., Berntsson, L., Johansson, R., Tagliabo, F., Torchiaro, S., Sandberg, A.: Automatic Allocation of Safety Integrity Levels. In: Proceedings of the 1st Workshop on Critical Automotive applications: Robustness and Safety (CARS 2010), Valencia, Spain, April 27, pp. 7–10. ACM, New York (2010), doi:10.1145/1772643.1772646, ISBN: 978-1-60558-915-2

4. Azevedo, L.S., Parker, D., Walker, M., Papadopoulos, Y., Araujo, R.E.: Assisted Assignment of Automotive Safety Requirements. IEEE Software 31, 62–68 (2014)

5. Papadopoulos, Y., Walker, M., Parker, D., Rüde, E., Hamann, R., Uhlig, A., Grätz, U., Lien, R.: Engineering Failure Analysis & Design Optimisation with HiP-HOPS. Journal of Engineering Failure Analysis 18(2), 590–608 (2011) doi:10.1016/j.engfailanal.2010.09.025, ISSN: 1350 6307

6. Mader, R., Armengaud, E., Leitner, A., Steger, C.: Automatic and Optimal Allocation of Safety Integrity Levels. In: Proceedings of the Reliability and Maintainability Symposium (RAMS 2012), Reno, NV, USA, January 23-26, pp. 1–6 (2012), doi:10.1109/RAMS.2012.6175431, ISBN: 978-1-4577-1849-6

7. Bieber, P., Delmas, R., Seguin, C.: DALculus – theory and tool for development assurance level allocation. In: Flammini, F., Bologna, S., Vittorini, V. (eds.) SAFECOMP 2011. LNCS, vol. 6894, pp. 43–56. Springer, Heidelberg (2011)

8. Parker, D., Walker, M., Azevedo, L.S., Papadopoulos, Y., Araújo, R.E.: Automatic decomposition and allocation of safety integrity levels using a penalty-based genetic algorithm. In: Ali, M., Bosse, T., Hindriks, K.V., Hoogendoorn, M., Jonker, C.M., Treur, J. (eds.) IEA/AIE 2013. LNCS, vol. 7906, pp. 449–459. Springer, Heidelberg (2013)

9. Azevedo L.S., Parker D., Walker M., Papadopoulos Y., and Araujo R. E.: Automatic Decomposition of Safety Integrity Levels: Optimisation by Tabu Search. 2nd Workshop on Critical Automotive applications: Robustness & Safety (CARS), at the 32nd International Conference on Computer Safety, Reliability, and Security (SAFECOMP 2013), Toulouse, France (2013)

10. Hansen, P., Lih, K.-W.: Heuristic reliability optimization by tabu search. Annals of Operations Research (63), 321–336 (1996)

11. Azevedo, L.P.: Hybrid Braking System for Electrical Vehicles: Functional Safety, M.Sc. thesis, Dept. Elect. Eng., Porto Univ., Porto, Portugal (2012)

12. de Castro, R., Araújo, R.E., Freitas, D.: Hybrid ABS with Electric motor and friction Brakes. Presented at the IAVSD2011 - 22nd International Symposium on Dynamics of Vehicles on Roads and Tracks, Manchester, UK (2011)

An Integrated Process for FDIR Design in Aerospace

Benjamin Bittner[1], Marco Bozzano[1], Alessandro Cimatti[1], Regis De Ferluc[2], Marco Gario[1], Andrea Guiotto[3], and Yuri Yushtein[4]

[1] Fondazione Bruno Kessler, Trento, Italy
[2] Thales Alenia Space, France
[3] Thales Alenia Space, Italy
[4] European Space Agency (ESA), ESTEC, Noordwijk, The Netherlands

Abstract. The correct operation of complex critical systems increasingly relies on the ability to detect and recover from faults. The design of Fault Detection, Isolation and Recovery (FDIR) sub-systems is highly challenging, due to the complexity of the underlying system, the number of faults to be considered and their dynamics. Existing industrial practices for FDIR are often based on ad-hoc solutions, that are conceived and developed late in the design process, and do not consider the software- and system-level RAMS analyses data (e.g., FTA and FMEA).

In this paper we propose the FAME process: a novel, model-based, integrated process for FDIR design, that addresses the shortcomings of existing practices. This process aims at enabling a consistent and timely FDIR conception, development, verification and validation. The process is supported by the FAME environment, a model-based toolset that encompasses a wide range of formal analyses, and supports the FDIR design by providing functionality to define mission and FDIR requirements, fault propagation modeling, and automated synthesis of FDIR models. The FAME process and environment have been developed within an ESA-funded study, and have been thoroughly evaluated by the industrial partners on a case study derived from the ExoMars project.

1 Introduction

The design of critical systems in aerospace is a very complex and highly challenging task, as it requires assembling heterogeneous components, implemented either in hardware or in software, and taking into account their interactions. Moreover, safety- and mission-critical systems have to obey several sorts of functional and non-functional requirements, including (real-)time constraints, safety and dependability requirements. The correct operation of such systems increasingly relies on the ability to detect and recover from faults. The design of Fault Detection, Isolation and Recovery (FDIR) sub-systems is highly challenging, due to the complexity of the systems to be controlled, the number of faults and failure combinations to be considered, their effects and interactions.

Currently, there is no defined FDIR development process for aerospace coherently addressing the full FDIR lifecycle, and including the corresponding

F. Ortmeier and A. Rauzy (Eds.): IMBSA 2014, LNCS 8822, pp. 82–95, 2014.
© Springer International Publishing Switzerland 2014

verification and validation perspective. Current approaches are poorly phased: no dedicated approach to FDIR development exists, which can be employed starting from the early system development phases, and is able to take into account the design and RAMS data from both software and system perspective. Existing practices are often based on ad-hoc solutions, that are conceived and developed late in the design process. In particular, results of Software and System (Hardware) RAMS activities (e.g., FTA and FMEA), become available late in the process, leading to late initiation of the FDIR development, which has a detrimental effect on the eventual FDIR maturity.

Furthermore, no underlying, unifying model for various fault identification methods is available, making it difficult to ensure that the FDIR design is complete. There is a conflict between the bottom-up and top-down approaches: FMEA (bottom-up) can not be completed until system design has sufficient levels of details, whereas FTA (top-down) does not guarantee that every possible component failure mode which contributes to system failure has been considered. Finally, FDIR complexity limits the possibility to effectively determine the propagation of failures in terms of time.

To address these shortcomings, we propose a novel and comprehensive process for FDIR design, called the FAME process. This process aims at enabling a consistent and timely FDIR conception, development, verification and validation. It enables the specification and analysis of failure propagation using fault propagation models, the possibility to specify a set of relevant and decomposable requirements for FDIR, and to model, or synthesize, FDIR components that comply with the requirements. Finally, it enables verification of the effectiveness of FDIR. The FAME process is supported by a model-based toolset for FDIR development and verification: the FAME environment. The process and environment have been thoroughly evaluated by the industrial partners on a case study derived from the ExoMars project.

This work has been carried out as a response to an invitation to tender of the European Space Agency on the topic of FDIR development and verification. This study builds upon the previous COMPASS study [8,14], whose goal was to develop a comprehensive methodology and toolset for model-based development and verification of aerospace systems, supporting verification capabilities ranging from requirements analysis to functional verification, safety assessment, performability evaluation, diagnosis and diagnosability.

The paper is structured as follows. In Sect. 2 we present the FAME process, and in Sect. 3 we discuss tool support. In Sect. 4 we present the evaluation on the case study. In Sect. 5 and Sect. 6 we discuss related work and conclude.

2   The FAME Process

The proposed FDIR design process is schematically illustrated in Fig. 1. This picture shows the input and outputs of the activities, and illustrates how the "classical" design process can be improved, and supported, using formal technologies. The main novelties provided by the formal environment are:

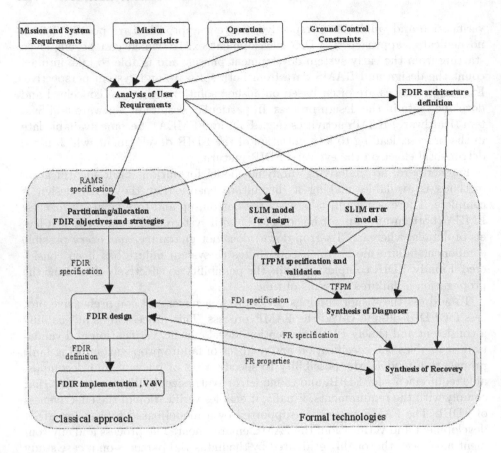

Fig. 1. Process Overview

- Formal modeling of both nominal and error models (i.e., taking into account faulty behaviors) in SLIM [9] (System-Level Integrated Modeling Language – a variant of AADL).
- Formal verification and validation capabilities, including RAMS analysis (e.g., Fault Tree Analysis, FMEA) carried out on the formal model.
- Modeling of fault propagation using so-called TFPM (Timed Failure Propagation Models).
- Formal definition of requirements for FDIR.
- Automatic synthesis of fault detection and fault recovery components (encoded in SLIM), starting from the TFPM and the FDIR requirements.

In this view, formal modeling and synthesis of FDIR is carried out in parallel with the classical process. The FAME process is technology independent, therefore, SLIM models could be replaced with other formal models, if available. Fig. 2 describes the process.

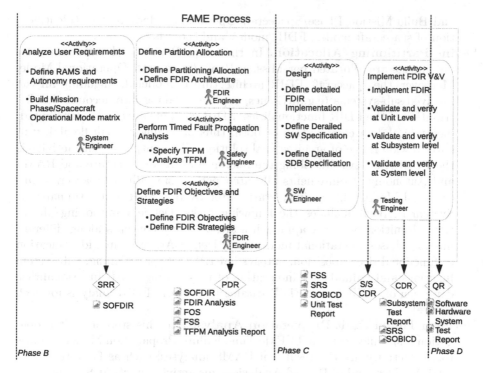

Fig. 2. FAME Process

The process is instantiated onto the ECSS standards [15]. In particular, it makes reference to lifecycle phases B, C, D, milestones such as SRR (System Requirements Review), PDR (Preliminary Design Review), CDR (Critical Design Review) and QR (Qualification Review), and to artifacts such as SOFDIR (System Operations and FDIR Requirements), FOS (FDIR Objectives Specification), FSS (FDIR Strategies Specification) and so on. The process is composed of the following steps:

Analyze User Requirements. The purpose of this activity is the collection and the analysis of all the user requirements that impact the design of FDIR. The requirements are analyzed to derive the FDIR objectives, and define their impact on the spacecraft design from system level down to unit level. The output of this activity is a document, containing the specification of the spacecraft FDIR operational concept. It starts at the beginning of System Phase B and terminates before System SRR. This activity includes the following tasks: Define RAMS and Autonomy requirements (identification of critical functions and redundancy schemes, classification of failures into failure levels, identification of FDIR levels, identification of pre-existing components to be re-used, definition of fail-safe and fail-operational strategies), and Build Mission Phase/Spacecraft Operational Mode matrix (identification of spacecraft modes, FDIR modes, and their association).

Define Partitioning/Allocation. In this step, RAMS and Autonomy Requirements are allocated per Mission Phase/Spacecraft Operational Mode. Moreover, the spacecraft FDIR architecture is modeled, including all the involved sub-systems (e.g., avionics, payload), taking into account the distribution of the FDIR functionalities. FDIR components can be distributed, hierarchical or a combination of both, thus providing enough flexibility to cover a wide range of architectural solutions. The output of this activity is the FDIR Analysis, describing the reference FDIR architecture and RAMS and Autonomy Requirements allocated per Mission Phase/Spacecraft Operational Mode. This activity starts after System SRR and terminates at System PDR. It includes the following tasks: Define Partitioning/allocation (definition of FDIR approach and autonomy concepts along different mission phases/operational modes) and Define Architecture (identification of functional decomposition, sub-system HW/SW partitioning, sub-system functions and redundancy, integration of pre-existing FDIR functionalities, definition of FDIR levels, FDIR catalogue, perform FDIR analysis for each failure).

Perform Timed Fault Propagation Analysis. In this step, a fault propagation is specified using a TFPM (Time Failure Propagation Model). Inputs to this activity are the results of RAMS analyses, such as fault trees and FMEA tables, and of Hazard Analysis. This activity starts at SRR and terminates at PDR. It includes the following tasks: Specify TFPM (taking into account the definition of the fault propagation model, starting from mission and system requirements, RAMS and hazard analysis, and specification of the observability information) and Analyze TFPM (whose goal is to check the correctness/completeness of the TFPM with respect to the system model, and analyze the suitability of the TFPM as a model for diagnosability, taking into account its observability characteristics).

Define FDIR Objectives and Strategies. The goal of this step is to specify FDIR Objectives (at system-level) and FDIR Strategies (at sub-system level), starting from RAMS and Autonomy Requirements, and exploiting the previous results on FDIR and fault propagation analysis. This activity starts after System SRR and terminates at System PDR (it can be done in parallel with the previous activity). It includes: Define FDIR Objectives (including the definition of objectives, such as required behavior in presence of failures) and Define FDIR Strategies (representing the FDIR functional steps to be performed, given the fault observation and the objective).

Design. This step is concerned with the design of the various FDIR sub-systems, and the corresponding software and data base, on the basis of the FDIR Reference Architecture. This activity starts at System PDR and terminates at Sub-System CDR. It includes: Define detailed FDIR implementation (identification of parameters to be monitored, ranges, isolation and reconfiguration actions), Define Detailed SW Specification (analyze the suitability of the available PUS services, and extend them as needed with new functionalities)

Table 1. Tool support for FAME process

Phase	Tool Functionality	Rationale
Analyze User Requirements	System Modeling & Fault Extension	Formal system modeling – nominal and faulty behavior (in SLIM); automatic model extension
	Formal Analyses	Derive requirements on FDIR design (input for following phases)
	Mission Modeling	Definition of mission, phases, and spacecraft configurations
Define Partitioning/Allocation	System Modeling	Modeling of context, scope, and FDIR architecture
	Formal Analyses	Derive and collect FDIR requirements
Define FDIR Objectives and Strategies	FDIR Requirements Modeling	Modeling of FDIR objectives and strategies, definition of pre-existing components to be re-used, and FDIR hierarchy
Perform Time Fault Propagation Analysis	Formal Analyses	Derive information on causality and fault propagation (input for TFPG modeling)
	TFPG Modeling	TFPG modeling, editing, viewing
	TFPG Analyses	TFPG behavioral validation, TFPG effectiveness validation, TFPG synthesis
Design	FDIR Modeling/Synthesis	Formal modeling and automatic synthesis of FDIR
	Formal Analyses	FDIR effectiveness verification
Implement FDIR, V&V	*Contract-based testing*	*Support for automatic generation of test suites*

and Define Detailed Spacecraft Data Base (SDB) specification (insert monitoring information, define the recovery actions, and the link between monitoring and recovery actions).

Implement FDIR, V&V. The last step is concerned with the implementation of FDIR in hardware and/or software, and its verification and validation with respect to the specifications. This activity starts at Sub-System PDR and terminates at System QR. It includes the following tasks: Implement FDIR and Validate and verify (this is typically carried out using a testing campaign, and repeated for Unit level, sub-system level and system level).

3 Tool Support

The FAME process is supported by a tool – called the FAME environment. Table 1 schematically illustrates tool support for the different process phases. Each phase of the FAME process is mapped with one or more tool functionalities – for each functionality, an explanation of its purpose is provided (the *contract-based testing* functionality is listed in italics, as it is part of future work).

The FAME environment is built on top of COMPASS [8], a framework for model-based design and verification, that provides several verification capabilities, including simulation, property verification, RAMS analysis (FTA, FMEA), diagnosability and FDIR analysis. The tool is freely distributed within the ESA member states. In the rest of this section, we briefly describe the capabilities that are specific of the FAME process, and in particular we focus on the underlying technological solutions. We refer to [5,16] for more details.

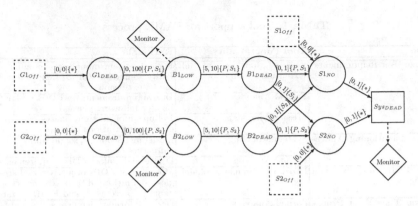

Fig. 3. An example of a TFPG

Mission and FDIR Specifications. FAME provides the possibility to specify the Mission Phase/Spacecraft Operational Mode matrix, including information on phases, operational modes, and spacecraft configurations. Phase/mode pairs can be tracked by FDIR to contextualize its strategies. FDIR requirements may be linked to specific phase/mode combinations, and they include the specification of spacecraft configurations as recovery targets, the specification of alarms that need to be fired, and the integration of existing FDIR components.

Fault Propagation Analysis. Timed Failure Propagation Graphs (TFPGs) are used to model temporal interactions of failures and their effects [1]. TFPGs model how failures propagate, affecting various monitored and unmonitored properties, and are thus an abstract view of the underlying system. An example is shown in Fig. 3. A TFPG consists of basic failure events, discrepancy nodes representing off-nominal system properties, and edges connecting these nodes, representing possible propagation paths. The edges are constrained by system modes (they are enabled only in those modes). Finally, edges contain lower and upper time bounds for the failure propagations. FAME supports loading, syntactic verification, displaying, editing of TFPGs, and definition of nodes using basic expressions over system variables (to interpret the behaviors of the system in terms of the TFPG). FAME allows checking whether the system exhibits failure propagations that are not captured by the TFPG (*behavioral validation*), namely that all links between discrepancies and timing information are correct. If wrong values are present, a counter-example is produced to guide the user in the refinement process. If no counter-example is found, the analysis guarantees that the timing values are correctly specified. The tool also allows checking the TFPG adequacy as a model for diagnosis, using diagnosability analysis [12]. This is called *(diagnosability) effectiveness validation*. This analysis enables the identification of the failure modes that are not diagnosable. Finally, a (prototype) function based on FTA is available which enables the automatic derivation from the system model of a basic TFPG without precise timing and mode information.

FDIR Synthesis. The FAME environment supports fully automated synthesis of diagnosis (FD) and recovery (FR) components, starting from an extended

SLIM model, a TFPG, an FDIR specification, and an optional sampling rate. FD synthesis [7] creates a diagnoser that generates a set of alarms for each specified failure, by monitoring the available sensors. The FR model can be synthesized using conformant planning [13]; it provides for each specified alarm and phase/-mode pair a recovery plan, i.e., a sequence of actions that guarantee to achieve the target under any circumstance. After synthesis, the FD and FR components are connected (in such a way that a generated alarm triggers the corresponding recovery plan) and combined with the original SLIM nominal model.

4   Case Study

The evaluation of the FAME process and environment was performed by Thales Alenia Space on a sub-set of the Trace Gas Orbiter (TGO) of the ExoMars project. The ESA ExoMars system will be launched in 2016 and will arrive at Mars approximately 9 months later in 2016. It is composed of a spacecraft that will carry an Entry and Descent Module (EDM) demonstrator. During the transit from Earth to Mars, the TGO will carry and provide power and other services to the EDM. The release of the EDM will take place prior to the critical Mars Orbit Insertion (MOI) manoeuvre by the TGO. After capture by Mars gravitation field, the TGO will orbit around Mars and provide support to the EDM. Once the EDM surface operations are completed, the TGO will start a science data acquisition phase. Near the end of this phase, the 2018 mission should arrive at Mars so that the emphasis may shift to the Rover support.

The case study was chosen since it provides an opportunity for evaluating all the aspects of the approach. In particular, it presents a complexity level that is representative of the classical complexity level in this domain. An FDIR design for the ExoMars TGO has already been developed, although the design has not yet been completely frozen. This provides the opportunity of comparing the results obtained with the FAME process with the existing results and, at the same time, provide feedback to the ExoMars team on the FDIR design.

The ExoMars mission can be divided into several mission phases, but in our case study we only consider the Mars Orbit Insertion (MOI). In this phase, several operational modes are used, including nominal modes (Routine - ROUT), safe modes (SAFE_1, SAFE_2) or degraded modes (Manouver in critical conditions - MAN_C) used by the FDIR when reconfiguration is required. The main functional chain considered during the case study is the Guidance, Navigation and Control (GNC) function which encompasses sensors, control software, and actuators. The goal of this sub-system is to maintain the correct spacecraft attitude. The faults that were considered are those related to the units that can lead to the main feared event considered in this study: the loss of spacecraft attitude.

4.1   Evaluation Criteria

In order to evaluate the FAME process and environment, we defined a set of questions, that are intended to evaluate the process, the technological choices and the prototype environment independently.

Item	Fault	Failure Detect Method	Local Effect	System Effect
IMU_001	Sensor signal is too low	EXT	Continuous self-reset of IMU	No measure is sent
IMU_002	Sensor output is biased	EXT	None	Biased output from sensor channel
IMU_003	Sensor output is erroneous	INT	Loss of RLG dither control	Erroneous output from sensor channel

Fig. 4. FMECA Table

Process. Is the process suitable for an industrial project, and coherent with the applicable standards, and the project lifecycle? What are its benefits with respect to the current industrial process? Are there any blocking points, issues, or concerns which could limit its application? Was any insight gained from modeling and specifying the requirements in a more formal way? How do the results obtained with FAME compare with the results obtained by the ExoMars team?

Technology. Is TFPG formalism suitable for handling space domain FDIR issues? Can all relevant constraints be expressed in the modeling language?

Environment. Is the FAME environment suitable for industrial needs ? Is the GUI efficient? Does the prototype help in modeling the FDIR-related aspects of the system? Did the synthesized TFPG resemble the manually designed one?

4.2   FAME Process Applied to the Case Study

We used the system architectural and behavioral information, and information concerning the mission phases and operational modes, as inputs to model the nominal system. Modeling was done in the SLIM [9] language.

Feared Event Analysis and FMECA. The first activity for safety analysis is the Feared Event Analysis. We are interested in the feared events coming from the units realizing the acquisition of the spacecraft attitude: the Inertial Management Units (IMU). We consider three possible failure modes: *No measure*, *Biased measure* and *Erroneous measures*. The only failure mode that is not diagnosable is biased measure, while absence of measure and erroneous measures are detectable either by rate control, or by cross-checking with other readings. Using documentation and FMECA from IMU equipment supplier, the IMU FMECA Items are analyzed and those having impact on the system are selected. Others are discarded with justification. Fig. 4 gives a selection of three FMECA items of the IMU equipment. We can see that the local and system effects can be matched with the failure modes identified in the previous feared event analysis.

Error Model and Fault Injection. Using the FMECA information, the system can be enriched with faulty behaviors. Thus, an *error model* is defined for the IMU component; the FMECA items are translated to error events, the failure modes are translated to error states, and the local / system effects are used to define the fault injections [10,8].

Failure Propagation Modeling. Sub-sets of system failures have been considered in order to simplify the analysis, e.g., in cold redundancy the failures of nominal equipment are analyzed independently of the failures of the redundant equipment. We start by considering the IMU equipment: in any mission phase where this unit is used, the failures propagate into the system (at this stage no FDIR prevents the propagation), and impact the spacecraft attitude, leading to the feared event we are interested in: loss of the spacecraft attitude. This fault propagation is modeled in the SLIM model by implementing for each function the effect on its outputs given erroneous input values. Since fault propagation may not be immediate, it is important to consider timing information. Function implementations therefore introduce delays in this propagation. Given the nominal SLIM model, the error models and the fault injections, and based on the consolidated failure propagation analysis performed using the TFPG, we can perform fault tree analysis for the case study - the results are as expected.

Analysis and Specification of FDIR User Requirements. For our case study, a set of requirements coming from the ExoMars TGO project are analyzed to produce FDIR objectives, strategies, and specifications – that are in turn provided to the FAME environment. The complete FDIR specification for the case study defines one alarm for each of the selected faults (Fig. 4) and for each of the IMUs, thus providing a total of 6 alarms in the specification. Each alarm is associated with a recovery requirement for each possible phase and mode combination. In total, this provides us with 24 recovery requirements, 12 for each IMU unit – the nominal one (IMU1) and the redundant one (IMU2).

Timed Fault Propagation Graph Modeling. Instead of building a global TFPG that would cover all failures of the system for all modes, the approach we adopted is to build several TFPGs covering the failures of respectively the nominal and the redundant IMU. With the current FAME environment only one TFPG is taken into account for the FDIR specification and the FD and FR synthesis. Therefore, independent FD and FR blocks are obtained for the two equipment units, leading to a decentralized FDIR. From the SLIM model enhanced with timing aspects and the error model, the TFPG model for IMU_1 failures is defined manually or synthesized using the toolset. The modeled TFPG is shown in Fig. 5. On this TFPG we can see the three failure modes of the nominal IMU equipment propagating in the system. On the propagation path, discrepancies are induced; some of them are observable, whereas some are not. Associations between discrepancies modes and system model define the relation between nodes in the TFPG and the original system. The TFPG is validated using behavioral and effectiveness validation analysis provided by the tool, verifying that the diagnosability of the system is well captured in the TFPG.

Fault Detection and Recovery Synthesis. The fault detection synthesis is run based on the fault detection specification. The result is an FD SLIM module that encodes a finite state machine with 2413 states. The fault recovery synthesis is run based on the fault recovery specification, only considering IMU_1. The result is an FR SLIM module with recoveries (6 recoveries out of 9 are found). The missing recoveries identify situations in which there is no strategy that can guarantee the recovery (note that it might be possible to find strategies that would work under certain circumstances, however the tool focuses on finding solutions that always work).

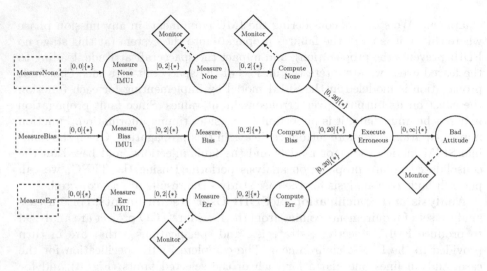

Fig. 5. Case study TFPG

FDIR Verification. In order to verify the resulting FDIR, both the SLIM system model extended with fault injections and the synthesized SLIM FDIR components have to be loaded into the COMPASS toolset for performing FDIR analysis (Fault Detection verification and Fault reconfiguration verification). As the synthesized FD model has numerous states, a lot of memory is required to load it in the toolset, which may require a powerful machine. The FD component is hard to verify by looking at the synthesized SLIM file, whereas the FR components can be checked easily in order to understand the content of the reconfiguration sequences.

4.3   FAME Prototype Toolset Evaluation

The case study allowed us to evaluate the FAME prototype environment, and to provide some answers for our evaluation criteria, as discussed below.

Process. We believe that the FAME process is suitable for an industrial project, and coherent with the applicable standards and project lifecycle. This is particularly true when dealing with single failure tolerant systems, since the analysis of fault propagation is performed in isolation for each failure or group of failures. If multiple failure tolerance is required, this approach should be consolidated to find the best way to analyze the failure combinations. Projects can benefit from FAME in the initial phases where FDIR is not yet defined. Time spent for analysis of mission requirements can be reduced by using FAME tool. The FAME process can be inserted easily in the current industrial process, provided that the users receive training on TFPGs. The synthesized SLIM models can be used as a starting point to implement HW and SW. Moreover, compared with the current industrial process, FAME permits to rely on early analysis of the robustness of the system and early design of FDIR. Formal modeling also allows to clarify the design, and to consider the system as a whole. Formalization is desired in order to prevent (mis-)interpretation, and forces the definition of clear requirements. Traditionally, time in failure propagation is often a major concern; the FAME process takes a step towards simplifying this type of analysis. Compared to the ExoMars project, the FDIR specification was similar to the real one; moreover, fault propagation analysis was not addressed at the same level, and FAME produced richer results. Fault Detection and Reconfiguration cannot be compared with the real project results, since they represent a completely novel approach relying on synthesis and time aware diagnosers.

Technology. SLIM enables a good characterization of the system; however, adding external constraints might be required in order to perform efficient model analysis (e.g., FR synthesis). The TFPG formalism seems to be adequate to handle the description of failure propagation during the FDIR design. Although the timing information for transitions is well understood, the mode information is not yet well understood from the user perspective. This has to be investigated further, in order to understand how this piece of information be exploited to model TFPGs per each failure (or sub-set thereof). This "mode" information will certainly be useful when dealing with TFPG combination. Unfortunately, the application of the FAME process to the industrial world may be limited by the state-space explosion when introducing time on complex models. This might impact the possibility of performing certain analyses or the automated synthesis process. It would be important to explore existing techniques from the formal methods community (e.g., contract-based design [11]) to deal with this problem.

Environment. The prototype environment is able to support the FAME process. Moreover, the structure of the synthesized TFPG was exactly the same as the one designed manually. Some limitations should be addressed in order to simplify the application of the process. The TFPG editing capabilities of the prototype FAME environment could be improved. The environment provides both textual editing and graphical view. Unfortunately, both methods are not user-friendly when dealing with big graphs. The environment provides little support to the traceability of requirements; this however could help improve the design cycle. Finally, another possible limitation could come from the incompatibility of formalisms used by the eco-system of tooling already in-use in the space domain. For instance, TAS uses an in-house modeling tool (Melody Advance) to model the system from early stages of the development process to later stages. Modeling is a time- and cost-consuming activity, hence a project can not afford to develop several models of the same system in different languages. It is recommended that SLIM models used in the FAME process are not created from scratch, but derived from existing models of the system. This is partly achievable, and a connection with Melody Advance seems possible.

5 Related Work

There are several previous works on model-based formal verification and failure analysis. The TOPCASED project [4] provides a toolchain that translates AADL and its Behavior Annex into Fiacre, and from Fiacre into timed Petri nets, which can be then model checked using the TINA toolbox. In [19], the authors present an ontology-based transformation of AADL models into the Altarica formal language; they can detect lack of model elements and semantically inconsistent parts of the system, but timed or hybrid extensions remain out of scope. Another AADL-based tool is ADeS [2] for simulation of system architectures. In [18], the authors present a framework for model based safety analysis, that covers both probabilistic and qualitative analysis; transformations into state-of-the-art model checkers, including PRISM and NuSMV, are available. Finally the FAME tool is based on the SLIM variant of AADL, however similar technologies are also available for the NuSMV family of languages [20,21].

[17] contains an interesting account of different notations for evaluating component-based systems and failure propagation, namely FPTNs, HiP-HOPS, CFTs and SEFTs. While TFPGs contain explicit temporal information, such as non-deterministic propagation timings and dependency on system modes, other models (e.g., SEFTs) enable the definition of probabilistically distributed delays, they provide FTA-like notation using temporal gates, and they can be evaluated quantitatively. A more detailed comparison will be done as part of future work.

As regards the FDIR modeling and process, in [3] the authors explore a few alternatives for modeling and verification of FDIR sub-components, using languages such as Altarica, SCADE, SLIM and the COMPASS tool; the FAME process and tool address some of the questions the authors raise, and also provide fault propagation analysis. Finally, [6] analyzes some of the issues for the development and validation of FDIR; FDIR functions, mechanisms and are expressed in AADL models and verified using the Uppaal model checker.

6   Conclusions and Future Work

In this paper we have presented a novel, model-based, dedicated process for FDIR development, verification and validation in aerospace. This process allows for a consistent and timely FDIR conception, development, verification and validation. The process is based on formal model-based approaches that enforce a high level of rigor and consistency; it can be integrated with the system and software development lifecycle, and it enables to effectively use the available mission and system requirements and the RAMS analysis data. The process has been successfully evaluated within an industrial setting.

As part of our future work, we will consider the extension of our framework in a few directions. In particular, we will investigate the specification of FDIR requirements, and synthesis of FDIR, in presence of decentralized or distributed architectures, where coordination is needed between different FDIR sub-components. In this context, FDIR decomposition can be driven by notions such as scope, context, and level of authority of FDIR. In the same area, we will explore the possibility to decompose, possibly hierarchically, the specification of fault propagation using multiple failure propagation models.

References

1. Abdelwahed, S., Karsai, G., Mahadevan, N., Ofsthun, S.C.: Practical implementation of diagnosis systems using timed failure propagation graph models. IEEE Transactions on Instrumentation and Measurement 58(2), 240–247 (2009)
2. ADeS, a simulator for AADL., http://www.axlog.fr/aadl/ades_en.html
3. Bensana, E., Pucel, X., Seguin, C.: Improving FDIR of Spacecraft Systems with Advanced Tools and Concepts. In: Proc. ERTS (2014)
4. Berthomieu, B., Bodeveix, J.P., Farail, P., Filali, M., Garavel, H., Gaufillet, P., Lang, F., Vernadat, F., et al.: Fiacre: An Intermediate Language for Model Verification in the TOPCASED Environment. In: Proc. ERTS (2008)
5. Bittner, B., Bozzano, M., Cimatti, A., De Ferluc, R., Gario, M., Guiotto, A., Yushtein, Y.: An Integrated Process for FDIR Design in Aerospace. In: Ortmeier, F., Rauzy, A. (eds.) IMBSA 2014. LNCS, vol. 8822, pp. 82–95. Springer, Heidelberg (2014)
6. Blanquart, J.-P., Valadeau, P.: Model-based FDIR development and validation. In: Proc. MBSAW (2011)
7. Bozzano, M., Cimatti, A., Gario, M., Tonetta, S.: A formal framework for the specification, verification and synthesis of diagnosers. In: Workshops at the Twenty-Seventh AAAI Conference on Artificial Intelligence (2013)
8. Bozzano, M., Cimatti, A., Katoen, J.-P., Nguyen, V.Y., Noll, T., Roveri, M.: Safety, dependability, and performance analysis of extended AADL models. The Computer Journal (March 2010) doi: 10.1093/com
9. Bozzano, M., Cimatti, A., Nguyen, V.Y., Noll, T., Katoen, J.-P., Roveri, M.: Codesign of Dependable Systems: A Component-Based Modeling Language. In: Proc. MEMOCODE 2009 (2009)
10. Bozzano, M., Villafiorita, A.: The FSAP/NuSMV-SA Safety Analysis Platform. Software Tools for Technology Transfer 9(1), 5–24 (2007)
11. Cimatti, A., Dorigatti, M., Tonetta, S.: OCRA: A tool for checking the refinement of temporal contracts. In: ASE, pp. 702–705 (2013)
12. Cimatti, A., Pecheur, C., Cavada, R.: Formal Verification of Diagnosability via Symbolic Model Checking. In: Proc. IJCAI, pp. 363–369. Morgan Kaufmann (2003)
13. Cimatti, A., Roveri, M., Bertoli, P.: Conformant planning via symbolic model checking and heuristic search. Artificial Intelligence 159(1), 127–206 (2004)
14. The COMPASS Project, http://compass.informatik.rwth-aachen.de
15. European Cooperation for Space Standardization. European cooperation for space standardization web site, http://www.ecss.nl/.
16. The FAME Project, http://es.fbk.eu/projects/fame
17. Grunske, L., Kaiser, B., Papadopoulos, Y.: Model-driven safety evaluation with state-event-based component failure annotations. In: Heineman, G.T., Crnković, I., Schmidt, H.W., Stafford, J.A., Ren, X.-M., Wallnau, K. (eds.) CBSE 2005. LNCS, vol. 3489, pp. 33–48. Springer, Heidelberg (2005)
18. Güdemann, M., Ortmeier, F.: A Framework for Qualitative and Quantitative Formal Model-Based Safety Analysis. In: Proc. HASE, pp. 132–141 (2010)
19. Mokos, K., Meditskos, G., Katsaros, P., Bassiliades, N., Vasiliades, V.: Ontology-Based Model Driven Engineering for Safety Verification. In: Proc. SEAA, pp. 47–54. IEEE (2010)
20. The nuXmv model checker, https://nuxmv.fbk.eu
21. The XSAP safety analysis platform, https://es.fbk.eu/tools/xsap

Reliability Analysis of Dynamic Systems by Translating Temporal Fault Trees into Bayesian Networks

Sohag Kabir, Martin Walker, and Yiannis Papadopoulos

Department of Computer Science, University of Hull, Hull, UK
{s.kabir@2012.,martin.walker@,y.i.papadopoulos@}hull.ac.uk

Abstract. Classical combinatorial fault trees can be used to assess combinations of failures but are unable to capture sequences of faults, which are important in complex dynamic systems. A number of proposed techniques extend fault tree analysis for dynamic systems. One of such technique, Pandora, introduces temporal gates to capture the sequencing of events and allows qualitative analysis of temporal fault trees. Pandora can be easily integrated in model-based design and analysis techniques. It is, therefore, useful to explore the possible avenues for quantitative analysis of Pandora temporal fault trees, and we identify Bayesian Networks as a possible framework for such analysis. We describe how Pandora fault trees can be translated to Bayesian Networks for dynamic dependability analysis and demonstrate the process on a simplified fuel system model. The conversion facilitates predictive reliability analysis of Pandora fault trees, but also opens the way for post-hoc diagnostic analysis of failures.

1 Introduction

Fault Tree Analysis (FTA) is a well-established and widely used method for evaluating system reliability which utilizes graphical representation based on Boolean logic to show logical connections between different faults and their causes [16]. FTA is a deductive analysis method, which means analysis starts with a system failure known as the top event and works backwards to determine its root causes. From a fault tree, it is possible to understand how combinations of failures of different components or certain environmental circumstances can lead to system failure. Qualitative analysis of fault trees are performed by reducing them to minimal cut sets (MCSs) which are the smallest combinations of failure events that are necessary and sufficient to cause system failure.

Increasingly, systems are getting more complex and their behaviour is becoming more dynamic as the behaviour of the system changes, functions and their failure modes vary, as do the flows between components of the architecture and the potential deviations of those flows. Due to this complex behaviour and the many possible interactions between the components, assessing the effects of combinations of failure events is not enough by itself to capture the system failure behaviour; in addition, understanding the order in which they fail is also required for a more accurate failure model. However, classical combinatorial fault trees are unable to capture this sequence-dependent dynamic behaviour [3, 5].

F. Ortmeier and A. Rauzy (Eds.): IMBSA 2014, LNCS 8822, pp. 96–109, 2014.

To overcome this limitation, a number of dynamic analysis techniques have been introduced, such as Dynamic Fault Trees (DFTs) [6] and Pandora temporal fault trees (TFTs) [18]. DFTs are traditionally analysed by translating them into Markov chains (MCs), but the major shortcoming of a Markov model is that for large and complex systems, it becomes very large and complicated and therefore difficult to construct and analyse. Alternatives have also been proposed, such as an algebraic framework to model dynamic gates of DFTs; this allows qualitative [11] and quantitative [12] analysis of DFTs.

Pandora introduces temporal gates to capture sequence-dependent behaviour and provides temporal logic to allow qualitative analysis. This technique can be used to determine minimal cut sequences (MCSQs) of temporal fault trees, which are the smallest sequences of events that are necessary to cause the top events, analogous to minimal cut sets of conventional fault trees. As temporal expressions are usually complex when compared to Boolean expressions, temporal laws can be used to minimise the expressions and therefore reduce complexity [17]. Like DFTs, Pandora temporal fault trees can also be solved by mapping them into MCs, but again this can lead to issues with the state-space explosion problem.

Bayesian Networks (BNs) have previously been used in the analysis of combinatorial fault trees, e.g. in [1]. They offer a number of advantages, alleviating some of the typical constraints of FTs, e.g. the need for statistical independence of events and exponential distributions of failure rate of events. They also allow both predictive and diagnostic analysis [13]. BNs can also be used to help minimise the state-space explosion problem by allowing compact representation of temporal dependencies among the system components and sequence-dependent failure behaviours [10], which has led to their use for analysing DFTs [2, 14]. However, so far no attempts have been made to use BNs to solve Pandora temporal fault trees. One of the advantages of Pandora is that it can be integrated well in model based design and analysis techniques. It has been shown, for instance in [17], that Pandora expressions incorporating sequence operators can be used to describe the local failure logic of components and then synthesis into temporal fault trees from systems models, e.g. expressed in popular notations such as SysML, EAST-ADL, AADL or Matlab Simulink, where models have been annotated with Pandora expressions. The principle has been shown within the HiP-HOPS model-based safety analysis tool, which has been connected experimentally to several commonly used modelling notations. Given the increasing importance of model-based design and analysis, and the potential use of Pandora in this context, we believe that it is both theoretically and practically useful to explore possible avenues for improved analysis of Pandora temporal fault trees. Therefore, in this paper, we show how the BNs can also be used to solve Pandora temporal fault trees, and thus enable us to perform quantitative analysis of Pandora TFTs focusing on prediction of reliability.

The rest of paper is organized as follows: Section 2 presents the fundamentals of Pandora temporal fault trees. The basic concepts of Bayesian Networks are presented in Section 3. Section 4 describes the method for converting Pandora temporal fault trees into Bayesian Networks. The method is then illustrated by applying it to a case study in Section 5. Finally, concluding remarks are presented in Section 6.

2 Introduction to Pandora Temporal Fault Trees

2.1 Pandora Temporal Gates

Pandora extends conventional FTs by defining three temporal gates: Priority-AND (PAND), Priority-OR (POR), and Simultaneous-AND (SAND). These gates allow analysts to represent sequences or simultaneous occurrence of events as part of a fault tree.

Priority-AND (PAND): The Priority-AND (PAND) gate is not a new gate and has been used in FTA as far back as the 1970s [8], and also features in the Dynamic Fault Tree methodology. However, it was never properly defined for use in qualitative analysis, resulting in ambiguous behaviour. In Pandora, therefore, the PAND gate is defined as being true only if the following conditions are true:

- All input events occur
- Input events occur from left to right
- No input events occur simultaneously

The symbol '$<$' is used to represent the PAND gate in logical expressions, i.e., $X < Y$ means (X PAND Y) where X and Y are both failure events. The fault tree symbol of the PAND gate is shown in Fig.1 (I).

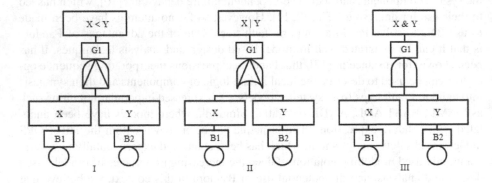

Fig. 1. Pandora temporal gates. (I) PAND. (II) POR. (III) SAND.

Priority-OR (POR): Like the PAND gate, the Priority-OR (POR) gate also defines a sequence, but it specifies an ordered disjunction rather than an ordered conjunction. It is used to indicate that one input event has priority and must occur first for the POR to be true, but does not require all other input events to occur as well. The POR can therefore be used to represent trigger conditions where the occurrence of the priority event means that subsequent events may have no effect. The POR is true only if:

- Its left-most (priority) input event occurs
- No other input event occurs before the priority input event
- No other input event occurs at the same time as the priority input event

The symbol '|' is used to represent the POR gate in logical expressions, thus $X|Y$ means (X POR Y) and the fault tree symbol of the POR gate is shown in Fig.1 (II).

Simultaneous-AND (SAND): The Simultaneous-AND or SAND gate is used to define situations where an outcome is only triggered if two or more events occur simultaneously. For example, this can happen because of a common cause, or because the events have a different effect if they occur approximately simultaneously as opposed to in a sequence. It is true only if:

- All input events occur
- All the events occur at the same time

The symbol '&' is used to represent the SAND gate in logical expressions and the fault tree symbol of the SAND gate is shown in Fig.1 (III).

We further use '+' to represent OR and '·' to represent AND. The SAND gate has the highest priority in a logical expression, then PAND, POR, AND, and OR. Therefore $P+Q\&R<S|T$ is equivalent to $P+(((Q\&R)<S)|T)$.

2.2 Pandora Temporal Logic

As well as the three temporal gates, Pandora also defines a set of temporal laws that describe the behaviour of the gates and how they relate to each other and to the standard Boolean AND and OR gates. These laws can all be proved, e.g. with temporal truth tables as in [18], and form the basis for qualitative analysis of Pandora's temporal fault trees, allowing reduction and minimisation of the expressions to obtain the minimal cut sequences, or MCSQs.

Most important of these laws are the Completion Laws [18], which relate the temporal gates to the Boolean gates:

- Conjunctive Completion Law: $X \cdot Y$ $\Leftrightarrow$ $X<Y + X\&Y + Y<X$
- Disjunctive Completion Law: $X+Y$ $\Leftrightarrow$ $X|Y + X\&Y + Y|X$
- Reductive Completion Law: X $\Leftrightarrow$ $Y<X + X\&Y + X|Y$

2.3 Time Representation in Pandora Temporal Fault Trees

Pandora makes few assumptions about the model of time used in any particular system; time can be interval or point-based, discrete or continuous, or some hybrid thereof. The result is a flexible approach that can be adapted to both design-time exploration of possible failures and run-time diagnosis of faults that have already occurred. Pandora does impose three key restrictions, however:

- The model of time used must be linear, not branching;

- Events are persistent (i.e., once occurred, they remain in a 'true' state indefinitely)
- Events occur instantly (i.e., go from 'false' to 'true' with no delay).

As long as these restrictions are followed, there are only three possible temporal relations between two events: before, simultaneous, and after. These are all covered by the temporal gates PAND, SAND, and POR introduced above. In Pandora, therefore, the exact time at which an event occurs is not as important as the order in which the events occur; all that matters is whether an event occurs before, after, or at the same time as another event, as this is what defines the sequence.

3   Bayesian Networks

Bayesian Networks are based on a well-defined theory of probabilistic reasoning and provide a graphical framework to represent uncertain knowledge in artificial intelligence [15]. BNs consist of a qualitative part and a quantitative part. The qualitative part is a directed acyclic graph of nodes and arcs, like the one shown in Fig.2. The nodes of the graph represent the random variables (events) and arcs represent dependencies or cause-effect relation among nodes.

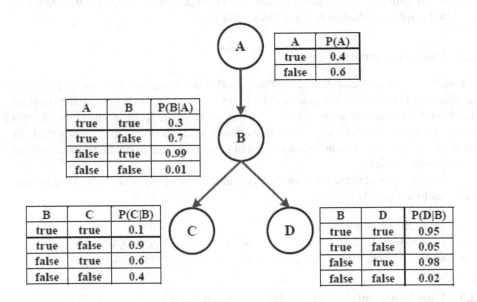

Fig. 2. A Simple Bayesian Network

In Bayesian Network, a node X is said to be the parent of another node Y if there is an arrow from node X to node Y, e.g. node A is a parent of node B in Fig.2. A node without parent is known as a root node and node without a child is called a leaf node e.g. node A is a root node and node C and D are leaf nodes in Fig.2.

The quantitative part of BNs consists of a prior probability table for each of the root nodes and a conditional probability table (CPT) for each of the other nodes given the status of their parents. For example, in Fig.2, the root node A has a prior probability table which shows the probability of A being in any of the permissible states, e.g. P (A = true) = 0.4. At the same time all other nodes have their own CPT. The CPT of a node shows the probability of that node being in any of its permissible states given the states of its parent nodes. For example, from the CPT of node D, we can see that the probability of the node D be true given that its parent B is false is 0.98, i.e., P (D=true| B=false) = 0.98. A set of conditional independence statements are the main consideration while making BN models and conditional independence information can be obtained from the BN model by employing the rules of d-separation [15]. The joint probability distribution of a set of random variables $\{X_1, X_2, X_3, \cdots, X_n\}$ can be determined from conditional independence assumptions and using a chain rule as explained in [15]:

$$P(X_1, X_2, \cdots, X_{n-1}, X_n) = \prod_{i=1}^{n} P(X_i | Parent(X_i)) \qquad (1)$$

If A and B are two random events and evidence is found that event B has occurred, then using the Bayes theorem, the posterior probability of event A on condition that B has happened can be defined as:

$$P(A|B) = \frac{P(B|A)\,P(A)}{P(B)} \qquad (2)$$

where $P(A)$ and $P(B)$ are the prior probabilities of event A and B respectively.

BNs provide a robust probabilistic method of reasoning under uncertainty and they are capable of combining different sources of information to provide a global assessment of dependability attributes such as reliability and safety, therefore they have received much attention in last decade in the area of dependability analysis [1, 9].

4   Conversion of Temporal Fault Trees into Bayesian Networks

In order to convert temporal fault trees into BNs, it is required to understand how Pandora represents the sequencing of events. As mentioned earlier, in Pandora "the exact time at which an event occurs is not important—the only thing that matters is when it occurs relative to the other events, i.e. which comes first, which comes second, which comes last etc." [18]. Therefore, sequence values, an abstraction of the relative time at which an event occurs are used in Pandora instead of a quantitative, absolute metric of time. If an event has not occurred then that event is given a sequence value 0. If an event has occurred then it is given a sequence value greater than 0 to indicate when it occurred relative to other events, i.e., all sequence value greater than 0 represents logical true, but the higher the value the later the events occurred, e.g. sequence value 1 means the event occurred first, 2 means it occurred second and so on. If two or more events occur simultaneously, then they will have the same sequence value. These same sequence values also make up the basis of temporal truth tables used in Pandora, as they combine the truth state (true/false) with the relative time of occurrence for each event.

Table 1. Temporal Truth Table for all gates in Pandora

X	Y	X OR Y	X AND Y	X POR Y	X PAND Y	X SAND Y
0	0	0	0	0	0	0
0	1	1	0	0	0	0
1	0	1	0	1	0	0
1	1	1	1	0	0	1
1	2	1	2	1	2	0
2	1	1	2	0	0	0
2	2	2	2	0	0	2

A temporal truth table showing the sequence values for each gate in Pandora given the sequence values of each input event are provided above:

The first step in the conversion process is to translate the Pandora TFT into an equivalent discrete-time Bayesian Network, where each root node of the BN represents a basic event of the TFT and each gate (including both Boolean and temporal gates) of the TFT is represented as intermediate node. The root nodes must then each have a prior probability table defined, while the intermediate nodes must each have a conditional probability table (CPT) defined. The conversion of the TFT to BN is a simple one-to-one mapping from basic events and gates to root and intermediate nodes in which the original fault tree connections are maintained as parent/child relationships, but the prior probability table and CPT are populated based on the failure probability distributions of the basic events and the behaviour of the gates used in the temporal fault trees.

As the outcome of each temporal gate is dependent on the relative sequence values of the events involved in those gates, we divide the mission time T into n intervals from $t=0$ to $t=T$, where n must be at least equal to the number of events, following the similar concept used in [2]. Each time interval represents a possible non-zero sequence value used in Pandora, during which the state of an event may change from not occurred (false) to occurred (true). At the beginning of the system operation, a component is considered as not failed therefore given a sequence value 0 (i.e., the component is in State 0) and this value remains the same until the component fails. If a component fails in interval 1, then it will have the sequence value 1, and so on.

The value of the events in each interval can be treated as a specific state. If an event is in State 0, then it means it has sequence value 0 (i.e., it did not occur). If an event is in State 1, then it means it occurred in interval 1, and if it is in State 2, then it occurred in interval 2, and so forth. This allows us to construct a CPT for all possible states of the input events to a gate, showing the probability that the gate will be in a particular state (i.e., has a given sequence value) depending on the states (sequence values) of the input events.

Note that in Pandora the outcome of any gate can be either true or false but every true value is associated with sequence information, i.e., the relative time at which the gate becomes true. Therefore, the probability of a node representing a gate being in a certain state given the state information of its parent nodes can either be 0 or 1. As an example, let us consider a 2 input POR gate. For simplicity, we choose n=2 and thus divide the mission time T into 2 intervals. This yields three possible states for each event: state 0, in which an event does not occur at all during the mission time T; state 1, in which the event occurs in the interval [0, T/2], and state 2, in which the event occurs in the interval [T/2, T]. Each state is then associated with a probability, namely the probability of the event being in that state.

Fig.3 illustrates this example and shows the POR gate with two input events and its equivalent BN, where the events are independent. In the BN, nodes X and Y represent the independent events X and Y and their prior probability tables are populated from the failure rate information of the component failure modes X and Y respectively.

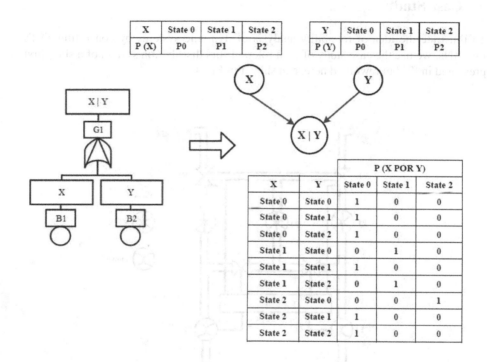

Fig. 3. Two input POR gate and its equivalent BN

The arcs from node X and Y to node (X|Y) shows the dependency of the POR gate outcome on its input events X and Y. The CPT shows the behaviour of the POR gate, i.e., it is true if its left-most (priority) input event occurs and no other events occur before or at the same as the priority event. A 1 in the State 0 column of the CPT means the outcome of POR gate is false — i.e., that it has a 100% probability of not occurring at all during the mission time T given those particular input states. Similarly, a 1 in the State 1 column means that it has a 100% probability of occurring during interval 1 given those particular inputs, and the same for State 2 and interval 2.

For example, we can say that the probability that the POR gate will be in State 0 given that event X is in State 1 and event Y is State 0 is 0, i.e., P(X POR Y= State 0 |

X= State1, Y= State 0) = 0. This is as we would expect, since the POR gate will have the same sequence value as its priority event if the left-most (priority) event X occurs and the other event Y does not occur. Instead, the POR outcome should be in State 1, i.e. P(X POR Y= State 1 | X= State1, Y= State 0) = 1. This can also be seen in the temporal truth table in Table 1: if X is 1 and Y is 0, then X POR Y should also be 1. This procedure can be repeated for all the gates used in Pandora such that their CPTs will resemble their equivalent temporal truth tables. It is possible to represent a TFT in different logically equivalent forms. In our experiments, translation of equivalent TFTs appear to produce equivalent BNs, although we have yet to prove this formally.

5   Case Study

To illustrate the idea of reliability analysis of dynamic systems by converting TFTs into BNs, we use the case study of fault tolerant fuel distribution system of a ship, first presented in [7] but reworked here, and shown in Fig.4.

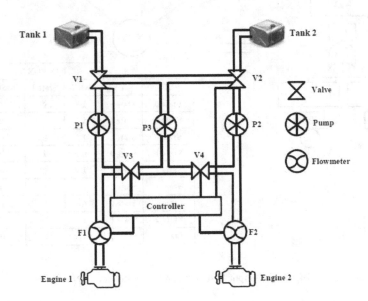

Fig. 4. Fault tolerant fuel distribution system

Under ordinary operation, there are two primary fuel flows: Engine 1 gets fuel from Tank 1 through Pump 1 (P1), and Engine 2 gets fuel from Tank 2 through Pump 2 (P2). Flowmeter 1 (F1) and Flowmeter 2 (F2) monitor the rate of fuel flow to Engine 1 and Engine 2 respectively and report it back to the Controller. On detecting insufficient fuel flow to either of the engine, the Controller introduces dynamic behaviour to this system by activating standby Pump 3 (P3) and redirecting fuel flow accordingly using the valves V1-V4. For example, if insufficient fuel flow to Engine 1 is detected, then the Controller can activate Pump 3 and open Valves 1 and 3 (V1 and V3), and thus fuel flows to Engine 1 through Pump 3 instead of Pump 1. On the other hand if a problem with fuel flow to Engine 2 is detected then Pump 3 will be activated and Valves 2 and 4 (V2 and V4) will be opened instead. Therefore, Pump 3 can take over the task of either Pump 1 or Pump 2, but not both. A failure of both Pump 1 and Pump 2 will cause at least one engine to be starved of fuel; for example, if Pump 1 fails and Pump 3 replaces it, then Pump 3 will no longer be available to replace Pump 2 if Pump 2 subsequently fails. This results in degraded propulsion functionality for the vessel, as speed and manoeuvrability will be reduced.

Pandora temporal gates can be used to model the dynamic behaviour in this scenario and helps to correctly capture the sequences of events that lead to failure. For simplicity, internal failure of the engines themselves is left out of the scope of this analysis. The Pandora temporal fault tree for the failure behaviour of Engine 1 of the fault tolerant fuel distribution system was constructed via model-based synthesis from Pandora descriptions of local failure logic of components and it is shown in Fig.5. As the failure of Engine 1 and Engine2 are caused by the similar events in the opposite sequences, the TFT of failure behaviour of Engine 2 looks almost identical except that P1 and P2 are reversed, and so is omitted for brevity. The basic events in the following TFT are:

- P1/P2/P3   = Failure of Pump 1/2/3 (e.g. blockage or mechanical failure)
- V1/V3   = Failure of Valve 1/3 (e.g. blockage or stuck closed)
- S1   = Failure of Flowmeter 1 (e.g. sensor readings stuck high)
- CF   = Failure of Controller

The TFT of Fig.5 is converted into a discrete-time BN following the procedure described in Section 4, shown in Fig.6. Failure rates of all components are assumed to be exponentially distributed and the values of the failure rates of each component are shown in Table 2. The prior probability table of each root node is populated based on the failure rate of corresponding component and the conditional probability tables of each intermediate node are populated following the same procedure described in Section 4.

Table 2. Failure rates of components of fuel distribution system

Component	Failure rate/hour (λ)
Tanks	1.5E-5
Valve1 & Valve2	1E-5
Valve3 & Valve4	6E-6
Pump1 & Pump2 & Pump3	3.2E-5
Flowmeter Sensor	2.5E-6
Controller	5E-7

The computation for the system failure probability or unreliability using the BN is performed using the modified version of the JavaBayes tool [4] considering mission time T= 10000 hours. The probability of top event occurrence for different values of n is shown Table 3. For comparison, an analytical technique [7] for solving the TFT

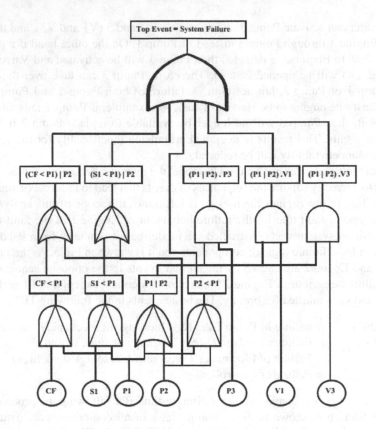

Fig. 5. TFT of failure behaviour of Engine 1

yields a value of 0.1353. We can see that as the value of n increases, the accuracy of the approximation increases and the value of top event probability converges towards a ceiling value.

Execution time is taken as an average over 5 runs for each value of n and increases by a factor of approximately 1.6 for every additional interval, but it also results in greater accuracy. Therefore, the value of n represents the tradeoff one can make between the execution time and the accuracy. In this case, an acceptable tradeoff can be found at value of $n = 12$ which could provide reasonable accuracy.

6   Conclusion

In this paper, we have discussed how a recent extension of fault tree analysis, Pandora, allows capturing sequence dependent failure behaviour in dependability analysis. An advantage of Pandora is that it is easily integrated in increasingly popular model-based design and analysis techniques. In this paper we identified BNs as a potential framework for improved solving of Pandora temporal fault trees. BNs provide a robust probabilistic method of reasoning under uncertainty and they are capable of combining different

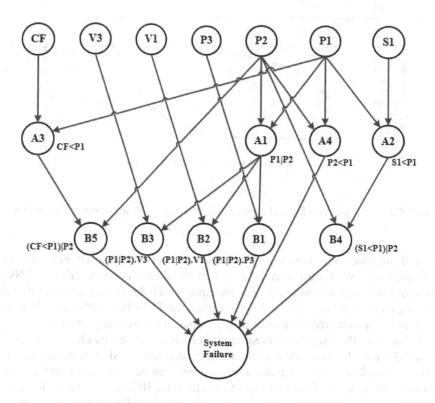

Fig. 6. Bayesian Network of failure behaviour of Engine 1

Table 3. Top event probability of redundant fuel distribution system

n	Top Event Probability	Average Execution Time (ms)
3	0.1114	15.6
4	0.1159	25.2
5	0.1187	40.6
6	0.1205	74.8
7	0.1218	149.6
8	0.1227	306.0
9	0.1235	493.0
10	0.1242	1011.2
12	0.1250	3070.0
15	0.1260	12879.4
17	0.1264	29162.8
20	0.1268	84889.0

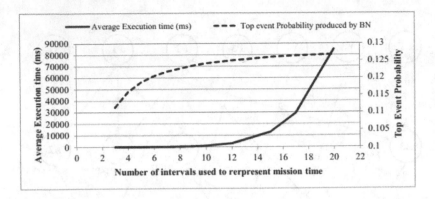

Fig. 7. Changes in unreliability and average execution time with the change of value of n

sources of information to provide a global assessment of dependability in terms of its various attributes. We have presented a way of translating Pandora TFTs to BNs to perform dynamic dependability analysis focusing on reliability and demonstrated the process on an example case study. After mapping the TFTs into a BN, the BN model was solved to perform predictive analysis to compute the top event probability, i.e. system unreliability. The execution speed and precision of the results obtained from the proposed BN model is dependent on the number time slots used to represent the mission time. Therefore, users can make a tradeoff between execution time and accuracy by choosing the number of time intervals to model in the BN. At present, we have considered the system components as non-repairable, but in the future, we hope to extend this work by considering reparability of components. At the same time we have a plan to perform a numerical comparison between the performance of the BN-based solution to Pandora TFTs and other existing solution techniques, e.g. Markov chains. The conversion presented in this paper also opens the road for demonstrating the ability for post-hoc diagnostic analysis of failures in the context of Pandora-enabled model-based dependability analysis, a process which involves calculating and updating the posterior probability of nodes given observed evidence in other nodes.

References

1. Bobbio, A., Portinale, L., Minichino, M., Ciancamerla, E.: Improving the analysis of dependable systems by mapping fault trees into Bayesian networks. Reliability Engineering & System Safety 71(3), 249–260 (2001)
2. Boudali, H., Dugan, J.: A new bayesian network approach to solve dynamic fault trees. In: Proceedings of Annual Reliability and Maintainability Symposium, pp. 451–456 (January 2005)
3. Bruns, G., Anderson, S.: Validating Safety Models with Fault Trees. In: Górski, J. (ed.) SAFECOMP 1993, pp. 21–30. Springer, London (1993)
4. Cozman, F.: JavaBayes (2001), http://www.cs.cmu.edu/~javabayes/
5. Dugan, J.B., Bavuso, S.J., Boyd, M.A.: Fault Trees and Sequence Dependencies. In: Proceedings of Annual Reliability and Maintainability Symposium, pp. 286–293 (January 1990)

6. Dugan, J.B., Bavuso, S.J., Boyd, M.A.: Dynamic fault-tree models for fault-tolerant computer systems. IEEE Transactions on Reliability 41(3), 363–377 (1992)
7. Edifor, E., Walker, M., Gordon, N.: Quantification of Priority-OR Gates in Temporal Fault Trees. In: Ortmeier, F., Lipaczewski, M. (eds.) SAFECOMP 2012. LNCS, vol. 7612, pp. 99–110. Springer, Heidelberg (2012)
8. Fussell, J., Aber, E., Rahl, R.: On the Quantitative Analysis of Priority-AND Failure Logic. IEEE Transactions on Reliability R-25(5), 324–326 (1976)
9. Langseth, H., Portinale, L.: Bayesian networks in reliability. Reliability Engineering & System Safety 92(1), 92–108 (2007)
10. Marquez, D., Neil, M., Fenton, N.: Solving Dynamic Fault Trees using a New Hybrid Bayesian Network Inference Algorithm. In: 16th Mediterranean Conference on Control and Automation, pp. 609–614. IEEE (2008)
11. Merle, G., Roussel, J.M., Lesage, J.J.: Algebraic determination of the structure function of Dynamic Fault Trees. Reliability Engineering & System Safety 96(2), 267–277 (2011)
12. Merle, G., Roussel, J.M., Lesage, J.J.: Quantitative Analysis of Dynamic Fault Trees Based on the Structure Function. Quality and Reliability Engineering International 30(1), 143–156 (2014)
13. Montani, S., Portinale, L., Bobbio, A., Codetta-Raiteri, D.: Radyban: A tool for reliability analysis of dynamic fault trees through conversion into dynamic Bayesian networks. Reliability Engineering & System Safety 93(7), 922–932 (2008)
14. Montani, S., Portinale, L., Bobbio, A., Varesio, M., Codetta-Raiteri, D.: A tool for automatically translating Dynamic Fault Trees into Dynamic Bayesian Networks. In: Annual Reliability and Maintainability Symposium (RAMS 2006), pp. 434–441. IEEE (2006)
15. Pearl, J.: Probabilistic reasoning in intelligent systems: Networks of Plausible Inference. Morgan Kaufmann (1988)
16. Vesely, W., Dugan, J., Fragola, J., Minarick, R.J.: Fault Tree Handbook with Aerospace Applications. Tech. rep., NASA office of safety and mission assurance, Washington, DC (2002)
17. Walker, M., Papadopoulos, Y.: Qualitative temporal analysis: Towards a full implementation of the Fault Tree Handbook. Control Engineering Practice 17(10), 1115–1125 (2009)
18. Walker, M.D.: Pandora: A Logic for the Qualitative Analysis of Temporal Fault Trees. Ph.D. thesis, University of Hull (2009)

metaFMEA-A Framework for Reusable FMEAs

Kai Höfig[1], Marc Zeller[1], and Lars Grunske[2]

[1] Siemens AG, Corporate Technology,
Otto-Hahn-Ring 6, 81739 München, Germany
{kai.hoefig,marc.zeller}@siemens.com
http://www.siemens.com/
[2] University of Stuttgart, Institute of Software Technology,
Universitätsstraße 38, 70569 Stuttgart, Germany
{lars.grunske}@informatik.uni-stuttgart.de
http://www.iste.uni-stuttgart.de/

Abstract. Failure mode and effects analysis (FMEA), is a widely used deductive failure analysis for safety critical systems. Since modern safety critical systems tend to increased complexity, automation and tool support have a long history in research and industry. Whereas compact embedded systems can be analyzed using FMEA in a manually maintained table using for example a spreadsheet application, complex systems easily result in an unmanageable long table especially when larger development teams are involved. During the application of the methodology in industry, two central problems were observed. First, textually described effects are interpreted differently and lead to inconsistencies. Second, one component often is used multiple times in a system, e.g. in electronic circuits where huge circuits are build using a small number of electronic devices. Each implementation of a component results in the same failure modes in a FMEA. Manually inserting them is error prone and adding a new failure mode to an existing component can be very time consuming. Therefore, we describe here a meta model that is capable to solve the aforementioned problems of different inconsistencies and analyze the benefits of this meta model in a tool implementation along with a case study.

Keywords: FMEA, FMEDA, model-based safety engineering.

1 Introduction

Safety critical systems are ubiquitous in our daily lives and can be found in various domains such as automotive, railway, aerospace, healthcare and industrial automation. Responsible design and analysis provides the required quality and safety of such systems. Since modern safety critical systems tend to increased complexity, automation and tool support have a long history in research and industry.

Failure mode and effects analysis (FMEA), is an inductive reasoning (forward logic) single point of failure analysis for safety critical systems. It examines the consequences of potential failures on the functionality of a system.

F. Ortmeier and A. Rauzy (Eds.): IMBSA 2014, LNCS 8822, pp. 110–122, 2014.

Different variations of FMEAs are currently used in many domains to analyze safety critical systems, e.g. for software or processes, and can either be qualitative or quantitative. All variations have in common, that they analyze failure modes of elements and their effects on the analyzed system. In [25] a generic quantified FMEA is described for a domain independent application of electrical/electronic/programmable electronic systems. Without the quantifications, the described FMEA is also generic for the qualitative variation of the analysis. The variation of a FMEA as described in [25] is called a Failure Mode Effects and Diagnostic Analysis or sometimes also called Failure Mode Effects and Diagnostic Coverage Analysis (FMEDA).

Whereas compact embedded systems can be analyzed using FMEA in a manually maintained table using for example a spreadsheet application, complex systems easily result in an unmanageable long table especially when larger development teams are involved. During the application of the methodology in industry, two central problems were observed. First, textually described effects are interpreted differently and lead to inconsistencies. This makes it complicated to analyze the table for failure modes that result in the same effect with a different textual description. This information is for example required for diagnostic reasons when an effect is observed and its source shall be found. Second, One component often is used multiple times in a system, e.g. in electronic circuits where huge circuits are build using a small number of electronic devices. Each implementation of a component results in the same failure modes in a FMEA. Manually inserting them is error prone and adding a new failure mode to an existing component can be very time consuming.

To tackle these challenges, we present *metaFMEA*, a meta model that allows reuse of parts, their failure modes, effects and measures. The model is implemented in a tool and was evaluated in a industrial case study from the healthcare sector. In the following section 2 the existing approaches are summarized. In section 3, an example for a FMEDA is drawn to further describe the challenges introduced in this section. After that, the meta model for automated FMEDA analyzes *metaFMEA* is presented in section 4. This model is implemented in a tool and the applicability in industrial projects is analyzed in section 5. Section 6 summarizes this paper and gives an perspective for future work.

The presented work shows that reuse in FMEA can be manged using *metaFMEA*. This reuse also supports consistency and overcomes time consuming and error prone manual tasks. The presented case study provides an overview about the strong impact *metaFMEA* can have.

2   Related Work

The research presented in this paper is related to the general research area on model-based safety evaluation of software system and reuse of safety artefact as a sub-area of model-based safety evaluation.

Model-Based Safety Evaluation. The use of models in safety engineering processes has gained increasing attention in the last decade [27,33,35]. Specifically the idea is to support automatic generation of safety artifacts such as fault trees [1,4,5,8,17,18,20,28,36,38,37,40,42,34,44] or FMEA tables [10,11,12,39,43] from a system models. To construct the safety artefact the system models are often annotated with failure propagation models [14,15,18,31,29,38]. These failure propagation models are commonly combinatorial in nature thus producing static fault trees. This is also driven by the industrial need to certify [9,25,26] their system with static fault trees. Only rarely more advanced safety evaluation models such as Dynamic Fault Trees (DFTs) [2,3,13,16], Generalized Stochastic Petri Nets (GSPNs)[41], State-Event Fault Trees (SEFTs) [21,29,30] or Markov models [7,6]. Beside annotating an architecture specification there is also their are also approaches to construct a safety artefact via model checking techniques [19,22,23,24,32].

The *metaFMEA* approach developed in this paper complements these techniques, especially the once that generate FMEA tables from a system or architecture specification. For these model-based safety evaluation approaches the frame work presented reusable FMEAs could add significant productivity gains. **Reusable Model-Based Safety Analysis.** In the development of a safety-critical system similar components may result in similar safety evaluation models. However, significant use of safety evaluation models is still rare and should be handled with great care. In fault trees a common way of reusing is to copy an entire subtree. However, Kaiser et al. [21,31,29,30] realized that fault trees should be reused as subgraphs, and created Component Fault Trees and State-Event Fault Trees (SEFTs). The line of research results the ability to reuse an entire subgraph, via typing them and so called in- and out-failure ports that serve as interfaces to the rest of the fault tree. In another line of research Wolforth et al. [45,46,47] created a language extension for HiP-HOPS [38] that allow for pattern-based specification of reusable failure propagation models. As a result, reuse of safety models between similar components and from common patterns is possible. From the reused failure propagation models via the HiP-HOPS [38] methodology complete fault trees can be automatically constructed.

Our approach *metaFMEA* significantly differs from the presented approaches because we are focusing on Failure Mode Effects and Diagnostic Coverage Analysis (FMEDA) tables as the underlying safety artifact. Furthermore, we report our practical experience when reusing FMEDA table entries in the *metaFMEA* methodology.

3   Example for a Typical FMEDA

A FMEDA as described in [25], is typically developed using a manually maintained table with the support of a spreadsheet application. Table 1 shows an example of such an analysis for the failure modes and effects of two different parts of an electronic circuit. C101 is a capacitor with 100nF for 120V and its purpose is to smooth the output of an electronic circuit. R305 is a resistor with 10kOhm and its purpose is to regulate the amplification factor of an electronic circuit. The failure modes of these parts are open and short circuit and their failure rate is given in *Failure In Time*, whereas $1FIT = 1*10^{-9}$ per hour. The failure mode *short circuit* of C101 and *open circuit* of R305 result in the dangerous effect that the amplification factor of the circuit exceeds its limitations. Vice versa, the failure mode *open circuit* of C101 and *short circuit* of R305 have no effect. The dangerous effects are both detected by a pulsed runtime test with a diagnostic coverage of 90%. This results in a failure rate of dangerous undetected failures of 1FIT and 2FIT for both parts. Vice versa, the residual rate for detected dangerous failures is 9FIT and 18FIT.

Table 1. FMEDA example for two parts of a circuit

Circuit ID	C101		R305	
Type	Capacitor		Resistor	
Part	100nF/120V		10kOhm	
Function	smooth output		regulates amplification factor	
Failure Mode	short circuit	open circuit	short circuit	open circuit
λ	10	10	20	20
Effect	amplification factor exceeds limitations	no effect	no effect	amplification factor exceeds limitations
Classification	Dangerous	Safe	Safe	Dangerous
Diagnosis	pulsed test	n/a	n/a	pulsed test
Coverage	90	n/a	n/a	90
λ_{du}	1	n/a	n/a	2
λ_{dd}	9	n/a	n/a	18

A manually maintained table, especially if implemented in a spreadsheet application, contains some automation, e.g., the calculation of the values for the different failure rates. Nevertheless the aforementioned problems as described in section 1 cannot be solved using such a system or such an implementation.

3.1 Inconsistency of Failure Effects

Typically FMEA tables are long and can contain thousands of lines for complex systems. In addition, the tables are not filled by a single person but by a team of engineers and designers. That one and the same failure effect is described textually in multiple ways thus is highly probable. To analyze the table for a specific failure mode, e.g. how often the failure effect *amplification factor exceeds limitations* is contained within the table cannot be analyzed since it might be described textually different for every occurrence of that effect. Without a consistent description, no quantification for this effect is possible since it would require clustering all different descriptions of that effect within one class. Vice versa, for a given failure mode during runtime of the system the FMEDA table can be used for diagnosis. This can be a time consuming and error prone task if the effect is described differently. The same applies to diagnostic measures.

3.2 Inconsistency of Failure Modes

In large systems, especially in electronic circuits, components or devices are used over and over again, e.g. the capacitor or resistor of the example. For every implementation of a part within the system, the same failure modes have to be analyzed in the FMEDA table. For large tables, the consistency cannot be guaranteed. Furthermore, if during the design of the system a new failure mode is discovered that was not analyzed before, this new failure mode has to be added to every occurrence of the corresponding part. For a large list or for an already large amount of existing failure modes for a component it can be very time consuming and error prone to manually add the new failure mode to every occurrence of the component or to check whether the failure mode is among the already analyzed failure modes for every occurrence of the part. For diagnosis, possible sources of failures remain undetected.

In the next section, a meta model is described that is able to overcome this problems with inconsistencies by utilizing the different relations between failure modes, components and effects.

4   Meta Model Enabling Reuse in FMEA Analyses

In this section, the meta model is described that is used to document the relevant elements and their relations of the here described methodology of an reusable FMEA. This *metaFMEA* model is capable to reflect the classic elements of the FMEA as described in section 3 but extends the methodology by utilizing the relations. In this way, the reuse-functionality is enabled solving the problems as described in section 1.

Figure 1 shows the meta model for a FMEA analysis using generic parts and failure modes. To break down a larger system into manageable parts, a FMEA consists of multiple assemblies. Each assembly is a set of analyzable elements of the system that build somehow a logic unit, e.g. a certain area of an electronic circuit diagram. Each element of an assembly is an instance of a specific part, e.g, an electronic device. Each part instance is related to a part from a part list. The part list stores all parts that can be used to build a system. Each part from the part list or from the set of parts has an associated set of failure modes. A failure mode describes a specific kind of failure that a part can have. Since a part has a quantified behavior to fail, here referred to as a FIT, a failure mode has a percentage to assign a percentage part of the quantified failure behavior of the part to the specific failure mode. Parts and failure modes are data that come from a global data source and are therefore associated to the area marked as collaborative.

Since in the analyzed system, the failure mode instances that stem from the failure modes from the collaborative data can have different effects in different assemblies or systems, they are instantiated. This is done in the meta model by adding an instance of a failure mode from the collaborative data, the failure mode instance element. This element has an associated effect element holding the information (description) about the effect of the failure mode instance on the system. The effect is classified and quantified in a category, E.g. into the categories safe, dangerous and dontcare to mark an effect as not harmful (safe), with no effects on the outcome of the analysis (dontcare), or as harmful (dangerous). Furthermore a failure mode instance has an associated so-called measure. A measure protects from the effect to occur, e.g., if a failure mode instance is detected during the runtime of the analyzed system and the system is set into a shut down state (safe state) to prevent the effect. Since mechanisms detecting failure mode instances during the runtime of a system are mostly not 100% effective, the effect have an associated effectiveness, e.g., a quantified percentage value (diagnostic coverage). Since effects and measures occur multiple times in the analysis of a system, they are here associated to the reuse area of thee diagram.

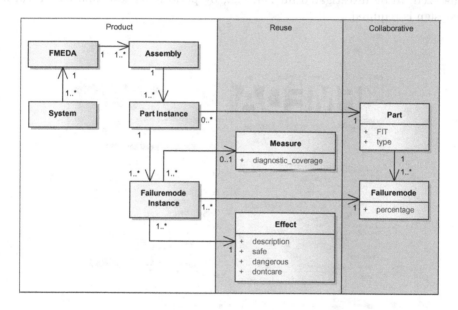

Fig. 1. Meta model for reusable FMEDA *metaFMEA*

5   Evaluation

In this section, we present briefly a tool implementation of the model as described in section 4 and draw conclusions from a case study we did in the healthcare sector.

5.1   Tool Implementation

Figure 2 shows a screenshot of a tool implementing the methodology as presented in section 4. This tool allows to split up the analyzed system into assemblies.

Each assembly holds a certain set of parts to be analyzed. Each part has a list of associated failure modes, effects and measures. The failure modes come from a part list which contains parts and their failure modes. Every time the part is used in an assembly, a new instance of that part is generated. If the failure modes of a part are altered, the changes are automatically distributed to all references where the part is implemented. The effects of a failure mode can also be reused. Once initiated, an existing failure mode can selected via a drop-down menu and associated to another failure mode. The same mechanism is available for the measures. Furthermore, we added local effects as a textual field to add a reason for the reuse of an effect. Another feature that is not available in classic FMEDA analyzes is to color code a failure mode. Here we used the classifications *done, in progress* and *critical* to mark failure modes as already analyzed, to be investigated further, e.g., by performing test, and as critical if redesign is required.

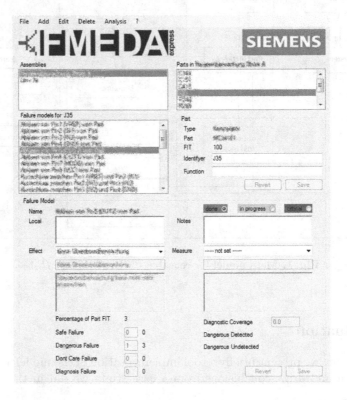

Fig. 2. Screenshot of FMEDAexpress, a tool implementing the meta model and automations as presented in this paper

5.2   Case Study

The case study was a FMEDA of an electronic circuit measuring a safety-critical multidimensional sensor value. If the sensor value exceeds limitations, the possible actions of the systems are limited (safety function). The electronic circuit consists of 723 parts as shown in table 2. Among them are 388 resistors and 194 capacitors. Each capacitor and resistor has only two failure modes. Furthermore complex parts have a more complex safety relevant behavior. This is mainly a result of the higher number of pins and their combinations of short circuit and open circuit. The system was divided into 94 assemblies to reduce the complexity of the analysis.

Table 2. Electronic parts involved in the case study circuit, their number of implementations in the circuit and the number of failure modes for each implementation

Part	Occurrence	Failure modes
Resistors	388	2
Capacitors	194	2
Comparator A	38	19
Comparator B	37	19
Transistor	28	6
Operational Amplifier A	11	31
Diode	8	4
Digital Potentiometer	6	63
Voltage Monitor	4	21
Current Limiter	3	24
DC/DC Converter	2	8
Operational Amplifier B	1	31
Demultiplexer	1	45
Multiplexer	1	45
Low Drop Out Modulator	1	15

During the analysis of the system, we figured out that the number of analyzed failure modes for the operational amplifiers and the comparators were not enough (finding 1). At about half-time of the analysis activities, we had to extend the failure modes of these parts to also analyze short circuit between pins that were next to each other on a chip. Furthermore, operational amplifiers and comparators are implemented here with four devices on a chip and packaged in a single IC package. So, one implementation of such parts can easily interfere with another implementation.

As a result, the existing analysis had to be extended by 6 failure modes for each operational amplifier and comparator. There are 723 parts in total and 87 parts that are affected by the previously described finding. The number of failure modes that had to be inserted in the analysis sums up to 522. So, about 12% of the parts and 13% of the failure modes are affected by this finding. The methodology as described in section 4 is beneficial to implement the new circumstances in an existing analysis. First, the new failure modes that have to be inserted in the FMEA using the tool is reduced to 24, since 6 failure modes are added to each comparator (2 types) and operational amplifier (also 2 types) using the part list. Versus adding 522 failure modes in a manual table, this is a reduction by circa 95 percent. Furthermore, adding such a huge number of failure modes manually is error prone and hard to maintain. In the tool implementation, the part list is used to add the missing failure modes to the parts and they appear automatically at every implementation of such a part marked as *in progress* (see section 5.1). Analyzing them is still a manual task, but they can easily be spotted using the category.

Our second finding was that we used a very limited number of measures. In the entire analysis, we had seven measures to mitigate or detect the effect of failure modes. In total, these seven measures are used in approximately 1500 lines of the analysis. Table 3 shows how often a measure is used to mitigate an effect. The data is an extrapolation that stem from 13 assemblies since more data about the entire 94 assemblies is currently missing.

The methodology as described in section 4 allows to reference and reuse measures. This is beneficial, since once described, the measure can be applied over and over again. In a manually maintained table, often measures are reused by making a reference to the cell where the measure is described the first time. This is hard to maintain if this cell has to be changed. In our case study, changing either the diagnostic coverage or the description of a measure would affect an average of about 214 lines which is about 5.5% of the entire analysis. Looking up all forward references is error prone and the accuracy of the manually maintained FMEA cannot be guaranteed. Using the methodology as described in section 4, measures can be easily maintained and their description can be extended or changed using only a single element for one measure. Changes that affect the diagnostic coverage of a measure can be changed in the same way. This is beneficial if during the analysis more precise values are available or if the impact of a more accurate measure needs to be tested (impact analysis).

Table 3. Measures investigated during the analysis and number of occurrences marking how often a measure is used to mitigate a specific effect of a failure mode of an electronic part (extrapolation for 94 assemblies from data for 13 assemblies)

Measure	Occurrence in 13 assemblies	Extrapolation for 94 assemblies
Missing runtime test response	104	752
Value limits exceeded A	6	43
Current limits exceeded	19	137
Value Limits exceeded B	17	123
Redundant electrical part	1	7
Total loss of function	3	22
Value Limits exceeded C	54	390

Our third finding during the analysis was that we reused effects, especially within one assembly. The benefits for reusing effects is the same as for the second finding we described before for reusing measures. Only one effect exists and is referenced if it is reused. We observed here that a local effect often results in the same global effect. For example, the effect of an open circuit capacitor has a local effect within the assembly. This effect is described, but finally the effect is directly mitigated by the surrounding capacitors. On the one hand, this could also be modeled as a measure, on the other hand, this is a direct electronic effect and not a measure that was implemented as a safety function. This partition of an effect into a local and a global part was not used during this case study and will be implemented in the meta model and further investigated in our future work as described in the next section.

6 Conclusion and Future Work

In this paper, typical challenges during FMEA are described briefly in section 3. In section 4, the *metaFMEA* model is presented that aims at solving these challenges. Section 5 shows a tool implementation and evaluates the methodology in an industrial application. The aforementioned challenges of having inconsistencies as a result of mistakes when reusing parts, failure modes, effects and measures in a manually maintained table, were observed during the case study. They have an appreciable impact on the analysis and manually solving them is error prone and time consuming. Using the tool implementation and the *metaFMEA* model, the effort is significantly reduced and the tool provides support for a sound analysis. In our future work, we will further investigate the model and the tool implementation. In section 5.2 we described the phenomena that an effect is often partitioned into a local and a global part. This finding will be implemented in our meta model and further investigated in upcoming analyzes.

References

1. Adler, R., Förster, M., Trapp, M.: Determining Configuration Probabilities of Safety-Critical Adaptive Systems. In: 21st International Conference on Advanced Information Networking and Applications (AINA 2007), pp. 548–555. IEEE Computer Society (2007)
2. Amari, S., Dill, G., Howald, E.: A new approach to solve dynamic fault trees. In: Annual Reliability and Maintainability Symposium, pp. 374–379 (2003)
3. Bechta-Dugan, J., Bavuso, S., Boyd, M.: Dynamic fault-tree models for fault-tolerant computer systems. IEEE Transactions on Reliability 41(3), 363–377 (1992)
4. Bondavalli, A., Majzik, I., Mura, I.: Automated Dependability Analysis of UML Designs. IEEE International Symposium on Object-oriented Real-time distributed Computing 2 (1999)
5. Boulanger, J.L., Dao, V.Q.: Experiences from a model-based methodology for embedded electronic software in automobile. pp. 1–6 (April 2008)

6. Bozzano, M., Cimatti, A., Katoen, J.-P., Nguyen, V.Y., Noll, T., Roveri, M.: The COMPASS approach: Correctness, modelling and performability of aerospace systems. In: Buth, B., Rabe, G., Seyfarth, T. (eds.) SAFECOMP 2009. LNCS, vol. 5775, pp. 173–186. Springer, Heidelberg (2009)

7. Bozzano, M., Cimatti, A., Katoen, J.P., Nguyen, V.Y., Noll, T., Roveri, M.: Safety, dependability and performance analysis of extended aadl models. Comput. J. 54(5), 754–775 (2011)

8. Bretschneider, M., Holberg, H.J., Bode, E., Bruckner, I.: Model-based safety analysis of a flap control system. In: Proc. 14th Annual INCOSE Symposium (2004)

9. CENELEC EN 50126,128,129: CENELEC (European Committee for Electrotechnical Standardisation): Railway Applications – the specification and demonstration of Reliability, Availability, Maintainability and Safety, Railway Applications – Software for Railway Control and Protection Systems, Brussels (2000)

10. Cichocki, T., Górski, J.: Failure mode and effect analysis for safety-critical systems with software components. In: Koornneef, F., van der Meulen, M.J.P. (eds.) SAFECOMP 2000. LNCS, vol. 1943, pp. 382–394. Springer, Heidelberg (2000)

11. Cichocki, T., Górski, J.: Formal support for fault modelling and analysis. In: Voges, U. (ed.) SAFECOMP 2001. LNCS, vol. 2187, pp. 190–199. Springer, Heidelberg (2001)

12. David, P., Idasiak, V., Kratz, F.: Towards a Better Interaction Between Design and Dependability Analysis: FMEA Derived From UML/SysML Models. In: Safety, Reliability and Risk Analysis: Theory, Methods and Applications, pp. 2259–2266 (January 2008)

13. Dehlinger, J., Dugan, J.B.: Analyzing dynamic fault trees derived from model-based system architectures. Nuclear Engineering and Technology: An International Journal of the Korean Nuclear Society 40(5), 365–374 (2008)

14. Domis, D., Trapp, M.: Integrating Safety Analyses and Component-Based Design. In: Harrison, M.D., Sujan, M.-A. (eds.) SAFECOMP 2008. LNCS, vol. 5219, pp. 58–71. Springer, Heidelberg (2008)

15. Elmqvist, J., Nadjm-Tehrani, S.: Safety-Oriented Design of Component Assemblies using Safety Interfaces. Formal Aspects of Component Software (2006)

16. Ganesh, P., Dugan, J.: Automatic Synthesis of Dynamic Fault Trees from UML SystemModels. In: 13th International Symposium on Software Reliability Engineering, ISSRE (2002)

17. Giese, H., Tichy, M., Schilling, D.: Compositional hazard analysis of uml component and deployment models. In: Heisel, M., Liggesmeyer, P., Wittmann, S. (eds.) SAFECOMP 2004. LNCS, vol. 3219, pp. 166–179. Springer, Heidelberg (2004)

18. Grunske, L.: Towards an Integration of Standard Component-Based Safety Evaluation Techniques with SaveCCM. In: Hofmeister, C., Crnković, I., Reussner, R. (eds.) QoSA 2006. LNCS, vol. 4214, pp. 199–213. Springer, Heidelberg (2006)

19. Grunske, L., Colvin, R., Winter, K.: Probabilistic model-checking support for FMEA. In: Fourth International Conference on the Quantitative Evaluaiton of Systems (QEST 2007), pp. 119–128. IEEE Computer Society (2007)

20. Grunske, L., Kaiser, B.: Automatic generation of analyzable failure propagation models from component-level failure annotations. In: Fifth International Conference on Quality Software (QSIC 2005), Melbourne, September 19-20, pp. 117–123. IEEE Computer Society (2005)

21. Grunske, L., Kaiser, B., Papadopoulos, Y.: Model-driven safety evaluation with state-event-based component failure annotations. In: Heineman, G.T., Crnković, I., Schmidt, H.W., Stafford, J.A., Ren, X.-M., Wallnau, K. (eds.) CBSE 2005. LNCS, vol. 3489, pp. 33–48. Springer, Heidelberg (2005)

22. Güdemann, M., Ortmeier, F.: A framework for qualitative and quantitative formal model-based safety analysis. In: 12th IEEE High Assurance Systems Engineering Symposium, HASE 2010, San Jose, CA, USA, November 3-4, pp. 132–141. IEEE Computer Society Press (2010)
23. Güdemann, M., Ortmeier, F., Reif, W.: Using Deductive Cause-Consequence Analysis (DCCA) with SCADE. In: Saglietti, F., Oster, N. (eds.) SAFECOMP 2007. LNCS, vol. 4680, pp. 465–478. Springer, Heidelberg (2007)
24. Heimdahl, M.P.E., Choi, Y., Whalen, M.W.: Deviation analysis: A new use of model checking. Automated Software Engineering 12(3), 321–347 (2005)
25. IEC61508: International Standard IEC 61508, International Electrotechnical Commission (IEC) (1998)
26. ISO 26262: ISO/DIS 26262- Road vehicles – Functional safety (2009)
27. Joshi, A., Miller, S.P., Whalen, M., Heimdahl, M.P.E.: A proposal for model-based safety analysis. In: 24th AIAA/IEEE Digital Avionics Systems Conference (2005)
28. Joshi, A., Vestal, S., Binns., P.: Automatic Generation of Static Fault Trees from AADL Models. In: DSN Workshop on Architecting Dependable Systems. LNCS. Springer (2007)
29. Kaiser, B.: State/Event Fault Trees: A Safety and Reliability Analysis Technique for Software-Controlled Systems. Ph.D. thesis, Technische Universität Kaiserslautern, Fachbereich Informatik (2005)
30. Kaiser, B., Gramlich, C.: State-event-fault-trees – A safety analysis model for software controlled systems. In: Heisel, M., Liggesmeyer, P., Wittmann, S. (eds.) SAFECOMP 2004. LNCS, vol. 3219, pp. 195–209. Springer, Heidelberg (2004), doi:10.1016/j.ress.2006.10.010
31. Kaiser, B., Liggesmeyer, P., Mäckel, O.: A new component concept for fault trees. In: SCS 2003: Proceedings of the 8th Australian workshop on Safety critical systems and software, pp. 37–46. Australian Computer Society, Inc., Darlinghurst (2003)
32. Lipaczewski, M., Struck, S., Ortmeier, F.: Using tool-supported model based safety analysis - progress and experiences in saml development. In: 14th International IEEE Symposium on High-Assurance Systems Engineering, HASE 2012, Omaha, NE, USA, October 25-27, pp. 159–166. IEEE Computer Society (2012)
33. Lisagor, O., McDermid, J.A., York, U.K., Pumfrey, D.J.: Towards a Practicable Process for Automated Safety Analysis. In: 24th International System Safety Conference (2006)
34. Mahmud, N., Walker, M., Papadopoulos, Y.: Compositional synthesis of temporal fault trees from state machines. In: 2011 Sixth International Conference on Availability, Reliability and Security (ARES), pp. 429–435 (August 2011)
35. McDermid, J., Kelly, T.: Software in Safety Critical Systems: Achievement and Prediction, University of York, UK (2006)
36. de Miguel, M.A., Briones, J.F., Silva, J.P., Alonso, A.: Integration of safety analysis in model-driven software development. IET Software 2(3), 260–280 (2008)
37. Papadopoulos, Y., Maruhn, M.: Model-Based Automated Synthesis of Fault Trees from Matlab.Simulink Models. In: International Conference on Dependable Systems and Networks (2001)
38. Papadopoulos, Y., McDermid, J.A., Sasse, R., Heiner, G.: Analysis and synthesis of the behaviour of complex programmable electronic systems in conditions of failure. Int. Journal of Reliability Engineering and System Safety 71(3), 229–247 (2001)
39. Papadopoulos, Y., Parker, D., Grante, C.: Automating the failure modes and effects analysis of safety critical systems. In: Int. Symp. on High-Assurance Systems Engineering (HASE 2004), pp. 310–311. IEEE Comp. Society (2004)

40. Rae, A., Lindsay, P.: A behaviour-based method for fault tree generation. In: Proceedings of the 22nd International System Safety Conference, pp. 289–298 (2004)
41. Rugina, A.-E., Kanoun, K., Kaâniche, M.: A System Dependability Modeling Framework Using AADL and GSPNs. In: de Lemos, R., Gacek, C., Romanovsky, A. (eds.) Architecting Dependable Systems IV. LNCS, vol. 4615, pp. 14–38. Springer, Heidelberg (2007)
42. Szabo, G., Ternai, G.: Automatic Fault Tree Generation as a Support for Safety Studies of Railway Interlocking Systems. In: IFAC Symposium on Control in Transportation Systems (2009)
43. Walker, M., Papadopoulos, Y., Parker, D., et al.: Semi-automatic fmea supporting complex systems with combinations and sequences of failures. SAE Int. J. Passeng. Cars - Mech. Syst. 2(1), 791–802 (2009)
44. Walker, M., Papadopoulos, Y.: Qualitative temporal analysis: Towards a full implementation of the fault tree handbook. Control Engineering Practice 17(10), 1115–1125 (2009),
    http://www.sciencedirect.com/science/article/pii/S096706610800186X
45. Wolforth, I., Walker, M., Grunske, L., Papadopoulos, Y.: Generalizable safety annotations for specification of failure patterns. Softw., Pract. Exper. 40(5), 453–483 (2010)
46. Wolforth, I., Walker, M., Papadopoulos, Y.: A language for failure patterns and application in safety analysis. In: IEEE Conference on Dependable Computing Systems (DEPCOSA 2008). IEEE Computer Society (2008)
47. Wolforth, I., Walker, M., Papadopoulos, Y., Grunske, L.: Capture and reuse of composable failure patterns. IJCCBS 1(1/2/3), 128–147 (2010)

AltaRica 3 Based Models
for ISO 26262 Automotive Safety Mechanisms

Abraham Cherfi[1,2], Antoine Rauzy[3], and Michel Leeman[2]

[1] LIX - Ecole Polytechnique, route de Saclay, 91128 Palaiseau cedex, France
name@lix.polytechnique.fr
[2] GEEDS - Valeo, France
{firstname.lastname}@valeo.com
[3] Chaire Blériot-Fabre - Ecole Centrale de Paris, Grande Voie des Vignes,
92295 Châtenay-Malabry, France
{firstname.lastname}@ecp.fr

Abstract. Cars embed a steadily increasing number of Electric and Electronic Systems. The ISO 26262 defines a number of constraints, rules and requirements that the development of Automotive E/E Systems must obey in order to guaranty their Functional Safety. One of the means at hand to enhance the safety of these systems is to reinforce them with so-called Safety Mechanisms. The Standard discusses at length how to estimate the contribution of these mechanisms to Functional Safety. These calculations rely however on Fault Tree models or ad-hoc formulas that are hard to check for completeness and validity. In this article, we propose generic AltaRica 3 for Electric and Electronic Systems protected by first and second order safety mechanisms. These models are of a great help to clarify the behavior of these systems as well as to determine the domain of validity of simpler models such the above mentioned Fault Trees or ad-hoc formulas.

Keywords: Automotive Functional Safety, ISO 26262, Safety Mechanisms, AltaRica, Markov Models.

1   Introduction

Cars embed a steadily increasing number of Electric and Electronic Systems. In order to guaranty their Functional Safety, the ISO 26262 standard [1] was published in November 2011. This standard defines a number of constraints and rules that the development of automotive Electric and Electronic Systems must obey. One of the means at hand to enhance the safety of Electric and Electronic Systems is to reinforce them with so-called Safety Mechanisms. Safety Mechanisms are various types of devices that typically prevent spurious usages of the system, or warn the driver when something wrong happens.

The ISO 26262 standard discusses at length the use of these Safety Mechanisms and how to estimate their contribution to functional safety. To do so, it relies essentially on Fault Tree models or ad-hoc formula. Such models or formulas are indeed of

F. Ortmeier and A. Rauzy (Eds.): IMBSA 2014, LNCS 8822, pp. 123–136, 2014.

interest for practitioners, but they are only approximations. Without a more explicit representation of failure scenarios to serve as a reference, it is hard to check them for completeness, and understand their domain of validity and to ensure their accuracy. Explicit models have been proposed by several authors for Safety Instrumented System described in the mother IEC 61508 Standard [2] (see e.g. [3, 4]). In the case of the ISO 26262 standard, at least to our knowledge, this work has not been done yet.

The remainder of this article will be organized as follows:

First, in order to introduce the different types of safety mechanisms, we will present in Section 2 two typical examples of critical automotive systems. The first example will be based on the control of the Electric Motor Inverter with its detection based safety mechanisms, and the second example will be based on an Electric Seats Control Unit with its inhibition based safety mechanism. This will help us explains their behavior, and their influence on the systems implementing them.

Next to this, in Section 3, we will present our previously established Markov models [7] for the representation of the automotive safety mechanisms behaviors that will help us to explain the various parameter that must be taken into account.

After that, in Section 4, we will present the corresponding AltaRica 3 models for the previously defined examples. This will also help us to introduce more general models for the representation of these safety mechanisms. To finish, we discuss in the same section, the reachability graphs of the two models presented above, and compare them to the unfolded Markov models.

2   Two Typical Examples of Safety Mechanisms

In this section, we present two representative examples of automotive systems embedding safety mechanisms.

2.1   Vehicle Management Unit for Inversion

We shall first consider the case of a Vehicle Management Unit (VMU). In an electric vehicle, a VMU is responsible for commanding the electric motor inverter, among other functions. A VMU consists of a microcontroller which, given certain inputs (gas and brake pedal positions), sends a torque set-point to the inverter that in turn commands the electric motor (traction and regenerative braking), as illustrated in Figure 1. Such a VMU is a critical function: if the microcontroller gets stuck in a loop and continuously sends a command higher (or lower) than expected, it could lead to unintended vehicle acceleration or braking.

In order to prevent such hazards, a watchdog is added which is in charge of bringing the system to a safe state in case the microcontroller is detected to be stuck. The watchdog is an electronic component that is used to detect and recover from microcontroller malfunctions. The microcontroller refreshes regularly the watchdog in order to prevent him from timing out. If it gets stuck in a loop, the watchdog cannot be reset, so the watchdog times out and sends a reboot order to the microcontroller. Such a watchdog is a first order safety mechanism based on error detection.

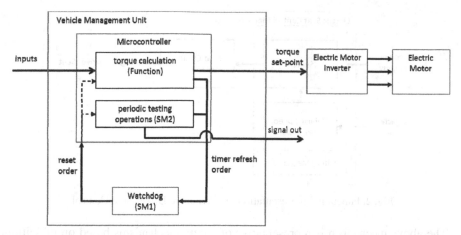

Fig. 1. Simplified functional representation of the Vehicle Management Unit for Inversion

As a physical component, the watchdog may fail (although the reliability of the watchdog is much higher than the one of the microcontroller). Also, the watchdog is able to detect only certain kind of errors of the microcontroller: typically, it is not able to detect memory corruption problems.

In order to ensure that the watchdog is working, the microcontroller tests the watchdog at each vehicle start (when the ignition is set on). The role of this second order mechanism is to warn the driver in a case of a problem with the watchdog. It may itself fail and is itself not able to catch all of the problems of the watchdog.

As the torque calculation function and the second order safety mechanism function are never executed in parallel, their failures are considered as independent (and are independent from watchdog failures).

The above example is representative of safety mechanisms based on error detection as embedded for instance in electric steering column controller, electric braking, several types of microcontrollers protected with watchdogs and more generally command-control systems.

2.2   Electric Driver Seats Control

Another type of safety mechanism is used in Electric Driver Seat Controls (EDSC). An EDSC allows the driver to tune his seat position. A spurious tuning action while the vehicle is running (over a certain speed, e.g. 10km/h) can indeed cause an accident, for instance because the driver is no longer able to reach the brake pedal or because he gets suddenly pushed onto the steering wheel.

In order to prevent this from happening, the system embeds a mechanism in charge of turning off the power supply of the EDSC when the vehicle is running. This first order mechanism is therefore based on inhibition. As previously, it is in general completed with a second order one in charge of testing it at each vehicle start (obviously, it cannot be tested while the vehicle is running).

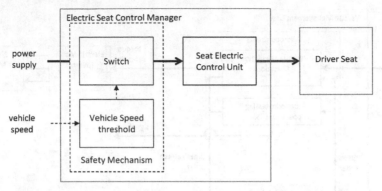

Fig. 2. Functional representation of an Electric Driver Seat Control

The above mechanism is representative of safety mechanisms based on inhibition, as embedded for instance in Electric Steering Column Lock, Automatic Doors opening systems and more generally all systems that must be inhibited when the speed of the vehicle gets above a given threshold.

2.3   Discussion

The implementation of the safety mechanisms presented in this section is a practical way to enhance the automotive systems safety without expensive physical redundancy. The majority of automotive first order safety mechanisms can be actually categorized in either of the two categories presented above:

- Most of them are based on error detection. The idea is to switch the system into a safe state when an error is detected. These safety mechanisms are usually made of two elements: the detection device and the actuation device.
- Some of them inhibit the system they protect when the vehicle is in a state where the failure of the system is potentially dangerous.

As a failure of the first order safety mechanism has in general no direct influence on the system it controls, it can hardly be perceived by the driver. A second order safety mechanism is thus often added in order to check periodically the availability of the first one, typically when the engine is turned on or the vehicle starts to move. The role of such a second order mechanism is to warn the driver.

3   Generic Markov Models

To have a clear understanding of the behavior of Electric and Electronic Systems in presence of failures (including those of safety mechanisms), the best method is probably to design state/transition models for these systems. As Markovian hypotheses can be verified or are at least approximated for calculation purposes, these models can be turned into Markov chains in a straightforward way.

In this section, we shall propose Markov chains for systems of each of the two above categories. These Markov chains are generic in the sense that one has just to adjust values of parameters (such as failure rates, coverage rates...) to assess the safety of a particular system. Markov chains presented hereafter can be subsequently embedded into larger Markov models or approximated either by means of Fault Tree constructs or by ad-hoc formulas. They serve as a reference.

3.1 Case of a Hardware Block Protected by a First Order Safety Mechanism Based on Detection

Let us consider first the case of a Hardware block HB protected by a first order safety mechanism SM1 based on error detection. The generic Markov chain for this system is given in Figure 3.

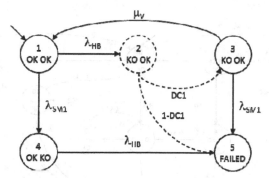

Fig. 3. Generic Markov Chain for a Hardware Block protected by a first order Safety Mechanism based on error detection

Such a system fails in a dangerous state if both the hardware block and the safety mechanism fail, no matter in which order. Therefore, the Markov chain encodes basically three failure scenarios.

In the initial state (1), both the hardware block and the safety mechanism are working properly. The failure rates λ_{HB} for the hardware block and λ_{SM1} are assumed to be constant over the time (no ageing effect). If the hardware block fails first, the system goes to state 2, where the safety mechanism detects or not this failure instantaneously. As a graphical convention, we denote instantaneous states and their outgoing probabilities by dashed lines, as on the figure. The probability not to detect the failure is 1-DC1, where DC1 stands for the diagnostic coverage of the safety mechanism. In the state (2), if the failure of the hard block is not detected the system goes to the failure state (5) (first failure scenario). Otherwise, it goes to the safe state (3). In this state, the mean time before the vehicle is taken to the garage is T_M, i.e. the repair rate of the hardware block is $\mu_V = 1/T_M$. Now, if the safety mechanism fails before the vehicle is repaired, then the system goes to the failure state (5) (second failure scenario). Otherwise it goes back to the initial state (1).

Finally, if, in the initial state, the safety mechanism fails before the hardware block fails, then the system goes to state (4). In this state, we have nothing to do but to wait until the hardware block fails to go into the failure state (5) (third failure scenario).

Note that since there is no mean to detect a failure of the safety mechanism, there is no mean to repair it neither. Moreover, we assume that neither the hardware block nor the safety mechanism are inspected during periodic maintenances of the vehicle. This hypothesis is realistic, although pessimistic.

3.2   Case of a Hardware Block Protected by a First Order Safety Mechanism Based on Detection and a Second Order Safety Mechanism

We shall consider now the case of a hardware block HB protected with a first order safety mechanism SM1 based on error detection which is itself tested by a second order safety mechanism each time the vehicle starts. The generic Markov chain for such a system is given Figure 4.

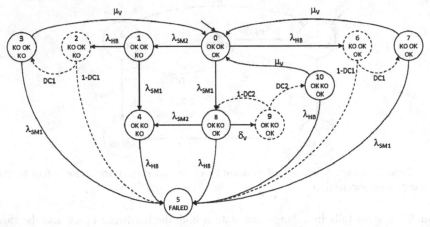

Fig. 4. Generic Markov Chain for a Hardware Block protected by a first order Safety Mechanism based on error detection and a second order Safety Mechanism

This model extends the previous one. The second order mechanism has its own failure rate λ_{SM2} as well as its own diagnostic coverage DC2. Note that it is assumed that when the vehicle is taken to the garage, it is fully repaired and is as good as new after this repair.

In the initial state (0), the hardware block HB and the two safety mechanisms SM1 and SM2 are assumed to work correctly. Now there are three possibilities:

- The second order mechanism fails first. In that case, according to our hypotheses, we are exactly in the same situation as if there was no second order mechanism. So the model obeys the same pattern as previously. We kept actually the same numbering of states 1 to 5 to emphasize this point.
- The hardware block fails first. This situation is also very similar to the previous one, for the second order mechanism plays no specific role in the subsequent scenarios. State 0, 6 and 7 are therefore symmetric to states 1, 2 and 3. The only difference stands in the availability of the second order mechanism.

- The interesting scenarios are therefore those where the first safety mechanism fails first, i.e. the system goes to state 8. We shall now develop these scenarios.

In state 8, we are in the situation where the first order safety mechanism failure is unnoticed. Here again there is a race condition amongst three possibilities:

- The hardware block fails first, before the current journey ends. In that case, the whole system fails (state 5).
- The second order safety mechanism fails first. In that case, we can make the pessimistic assumption that the driver did not notice the warning before this failure. So, we are back to the situation where there is no second order safety mechanism (and the first order one is failed), i.e. to state 4.
- The current journey ends before both the hardware block and the second order mechanism fail (state 9). We can assume that the mean time before the journey ends is Tj so that the transition rate between states 8 and 9 is $\delta_V = 1/T_J$. Now at the next start of the vehicle, the second order mechanism tests the first order one with a probability DC2 of successful detection. If the detection is successful (state 10) then either the driver takes the vehicle to the garage before the hardware block fails (in which case the system goes back to the initial state 0) or the hardware block fails first (in which case the whole system fails, i.e. goes to state 5). If the second order mechanism does not detect the failure of the first order one, then we have to wait for another start of the vehicle to make the test again (so the system goes back to state 8)

It is worth to note that the model described here is quite different from those proposed for Safety Instrumented Systems in references [3, 4]. The difference stands mainly in assumptions about the maintenance policy. As already pointed out, the designer of an automotive Electric and Electronic system has no control on maintenance. So, he has to make pessimistic hypotheses about what the driver will (reasonably) do.

3.3   Case of a Hardware Block Protected by a First Order Safety Mechanism Based on Inhibition and a Second Order Safety Mechanism

We shall now consider the case of a hardware block HB protected with a first order safety mechanism SM1 that inhibits the hardware block functionality, itself periodically tested by a second order safety mechanism SM2. The generic Markov chain for such a system is given in Figure 5. As the reader has immediately noticed, this model is embedded in the previous one. The reason is that if the hardware block fails before the first order safety mechanism, then there is nothing to inhibit and the system is safe (but of course not available).

Note also that there is no detection device and therefore no diagnostic coverage for the first order safety mechanism.

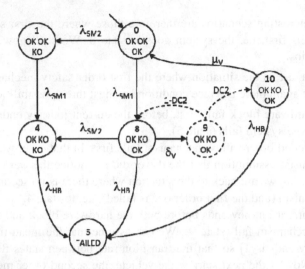

Fig. 5. Generic Markov chain for a Hardware Block protected by a first order Safety Mechanism based on inhibition and a second order Safety Mechanism

4   AltaRica 3.0 Models

In this section we present AltaRica 3 models for the representation of automotive safety mechanisms. One of the main objectives behind this is to be able to define generic classes for the different objects that are handled during the safety analyses and which allow the representation of their dysfunctional behavior.

AltaRica 3 is the latest evolution of event based modeling language "AltaRica" [8]. In this Language, the state of the system is described by means of variables, so, the modification of the system state can only happen when its variables values change. Also, the value of these variables can only change when an event is triggered.

Events can be associated with deterministic or stochastic delays. Models consist of hierarchical components interfaced in a discrete event system: their inputs and outputs can be connected and their transitions can be synchronized.

In the following sub sections, we will use the previously presented examples (Section 2), to explain our implementation of the automotive safety related components.

4.1   AltaRica 3 Models for the Vehicle Management Unit for Inversion

In this subsection, we will describe, element by element how to represent dysfunctional behavior of the VMU for inversion.

So, to begin, each of the considered objects (functional blocks and safety mechanisms) can have two states: working and failed. So, we create the corresponding variable type:

```
domain HardwareStatus{WORKING, FAILED}
```

We also know that each object can be subject to failure when it is working, and is considered as repaired after maintenance. Both maintenance and failure are considered as events, and are represented in our models by transitions with the same name.

With this in mind, we can already obtain the AltaRica model for a generic Hardware Block :

```
class HardwareBlock
  HardwareStatus self (init = WORKING);
  Boolean failed (reset = false);
  Boolean failureDetected (reset = false);
  Boolean safeMode (reset = false);
  event failure (delay = exponential(lambda));
  event maintenance;
  transition
    failure : self == WORKING -> self := FAILED;
    maintenance : true -> self := WORKING;
  assertion
    failed := self == FAILED;
    safeMode := failed and failureDetected;
end
```

We also have three Boolean variables for external communication:
- "failed", that allows to read the state of the hardware block (for examples In Section 2.1, when the refresh orders are not sent to the watch dog, this variable is set to "true").
- "safeMode", that allows to see if the hardware block is in safe mode. As defined in Section 2, the safe mode is engaged when the hardware block has failed ("failed" set to true) and its failure is contained by the first order safety mechanisms ("failureDetected" set to true).
- "failureDetected", is an input variable that allows to indicate if a failure is currently detected by the first order safety mechanism (this correspond to the restart order sent in the example Section 2.1).

In addition to those, a detection based first order safety mechanism must be able to detect and contain the failure of its associated hardware block.

In order to take into account the diagnostic coverage and its associated probabilities of detection we create two concurrent instantaneous transitions (as only one can be triggered at a time): One for the good detection of the hardware block failure and another for its wrong detection.

```
domain FaultStatus{DETECTED, PROPAGATION, NONE}
class DetectionBasedSafetyMechanism
  FaultStatus faultStatus (init = NONE);
  HardwareStatus self (init = WORKING);
  Boolean failed(reset = false);
  Boolean inputSignal (reset = false);
  Boolean sendSafeModeOrder (reset = false);
  event failure (delay = exponential(lambda));
  event goodDiagnostic(delay = 0, expectation = DC);
  event wrongDiagnostic(delay = 0, expectation = 1 - DC);
  event maintenance;
  transition
```

```
failure : self == WORKING ->
        {faultStatus := PROPAGATION; self := FAILED;}
goodDiagnostic: self == WORKING and inputSignal and
        faultStatus == NONE -> faultStatus := DETECTED;
wrongDiagnostic: self == WORKING and inputSignal and
        faultStatus == NONE -> faultStatus := PROPAGATION;
maintenance: true -> {faultStatus := NONE;
        self := WORKING;}

assertion
    failed := self == FAILED;
    sendSafeModeOrder := faultStatus == DETECTED;
end
```

We consider that the first order safety mechanism allows fault propagation in two cases: either the hardware block failure has not been detected (wrong diagnostic), or, the safety mechanism has failed, so it is impossible to stop the hardware block failure propagation.

By following the same logic, we can design the second order mechanism behavior:

```
domain SignalisationStatus {SIGNALED, NONE}
class SecondOrderSafetyMechanism
  FaultStatus faultStatus (init = NONE);
  HardwareStatus self (init = WORKING);
  SignalisationStatus signalisationStatus (init = NONE);
  Boolean inputSignal(reset = false);
  event failure (delay = exponential(lambda));
  event goodDiagnostic(delay = Td, expectation = DC);
  event wrongDiagnostic(delay = Td, expectation = 1 - DC;
event maintenance;
  transition
    failure : self == WORKING -> self := FAILED;
    goodDiagnostic: self == WORKING and
            faultStatus == NONE and inputSignal ->
            signalisationStatus := SIGNALED;
    wrongDiagnostic: self == WORKING and
            faultStatus == NONE and inputSignal -> skip;
    maintenance: true -> {self := WORKING;
            signalisationStatus := NONE;}
end
```

The main difference between this second order safety mechanism and the previously defined first order safety mechanism are the following:

-   The second order safety mechanism does not contain faults, it only signals them, and so, we consider that as long as a fault is signaled, it stays in this status even if the second order safety mechanism fails.
-   The diagnostic coverage events are periodically timed and not instantaneous as presented in the detection based first order safety mechanism. This represents the fact that the tests that only occurs at the vehicle start.

Now that we have the classes that correspond to each element in our system, we can combine them in order to represent the dysfunctional behavior of our vehicle management unit (VMU).

```
class VMU
  Microcontroller uc;
  DetectionBasedSafetyMechanism watchDog;
  event repairRequestedBySM1 (delay = tTau);
  event repairRequestedBySM2 (delay = tTau);
  observer HardwareStatus status =
      if(uc.torqueCalculationFunction.failed
      and watchDog.faultStatus == PROPAGATION)
      then FAILED
      else  WORKING;
  transition
    repairRequestedBySM1:
            watchDog.faultStatus==DETECTED -> skip; &
            !uc.torqueCalculationFunction.maintenance &
            !watchDog.maintenance &
            !uc.periodicTestingUnit.maintenance;
    repairRequestedBySM2:
            uc.periodicTestingUnit.signalisationStatus ==
            SIGNALED and
            not uc.torqueCalculationFunction.failed -> skip; &
            !uc.torqueCalculationFunction.maintenance &
            !watchDog.maintenance &
            !uc.periodicTestingUnit.maintenance;
    hide    uc.periodicTestingUnit.maintenance,
            watchDog.maintenance,
            uc.torqueCalculationFunction.maintenance;
  assertion
    watchDog.inputSignal :=
        uc.torqueCalculationFunction.failed;
    uc.periodicTestingUnit.inputSignal :=
        watchDog.failed;
    uc.torqueCalculationFunction.failureDetected :=
        watchDog.sendSafeModeOrder;
end
```

As detailed in Section 2.1, the VMU is composed by the microcontroller and a watchdog. The Microcontroller is in charge of two functions: The torque calculation function "torqueCalculationFunction" and the second order safety mechanism "periodicTestingUnit" in charge of testing the watchdog. We consider that the VMU fails only when the torque calculation function fails and when the watchdog can't contain the propagation.

Also, there are two events that lead to maintenance: either the failure of the torque function is detected by the watchdog or the failure of the watchdog is detected by the second order safety mechanism. This is represented respectively by the transitions "repairRequestedBySM1" and "repairRequestedBySM2".

4.2   AltaRica 3 Models for Electric Driver Seat Control

In this subpart, we present the modifications that are necessary in our previous model in order to be able to represent systems and components with first order safety mechanisms based on inhibition.

The main difference between this model and the previous one is in the type of the first order safety mechanism that is used. Indeed, as described in the section 2.2. This system implements a safety mechanism based on inhibition.

First of all, to realize this implementation, we consider that as long as the first order safety mechanism is active then the associated hardware block is not powered. Thus we change the failure transition of our hardware block by adding this condition:

```
failure : self == WORKING and powered -> self := FAILED;
```

We also must define the safety mechanism based on inhibition:

```
class InhibitionBasedSafetyMechanism
  HardwareStatus self (init = WORKING);
  Boolean failed (reset = false);
  Boolean functionInhibition (init = true);
  event failure (delay = exponential(lambda));
  event maintenance;
  transition
    failure : self == WORKING ->
        functionInhibition := false; self := FAILED;
    maintenance : true ->
        functionInhibition := true; self := WORKING;
  assertion
    failed := self == FAILED;
end
```

As we can see, as long as this safety mechanism is working, it forces the function inhibition by setting its Boolean communication output "functionInhibition" to the value "true".

For the second order safety mechanism behavior implementation, we use the one that was presented in the previous section.

To finish this implementation, we created the class EDSC that is in charge of combining the previously presented components:

```
class EDSC
  HardwareBlock driverSeatsManager;
  InhibitionBasedSafetyMechanism powerInhibition;
  SecondOrderSafetyMechanism periodicTestingUnit;
  event repairRequestedBySM2 (delay = tTau);
  observer HardwareStatus status =
    if (driverSeatsManager.failed) then FAILED
    else  WORKING;
  transition
    repairRequestedBySM2:
      periodicTestingUnit.signalisationStatus == SIGNALED
      and not driverSeatsManager.failed -> skip; &
      !powerInhibition.maintenance &
      !driverSeatsManager.maintenance &
      !periodicTestingUnit.maintenance;

    hide  periodicTestingUnit.maintenance,
          driverSeatsManager.maintenance,
          powerInhibition.maintenance;
  assertion
```

```
periodicTestingUnit.inputSignal :=
            powerInhibition.failed;
driverSeatsManager.powered :=
            not powerInhibition.functionInhibition;
end
```

As we can see, the only condition for the system failure is that the driver seat manager fails. But as the different objects were designed, this event can happen only after the failure of the inhibition based first order safety mechanism.

4.3   Reachability Graphs

Using a stepper, we built the reachability graph for each of the presented AltaRica models.

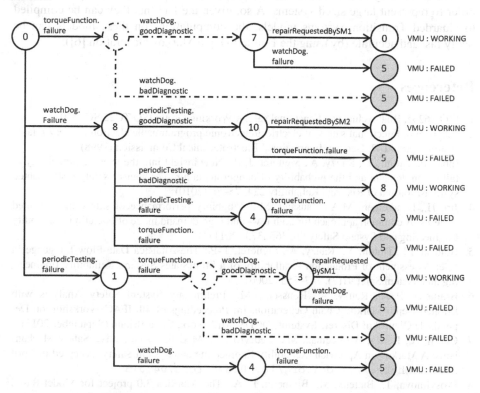

Fig. 6. Reachability graph of the VMU AltaRica 3 Model matched with the unfolded view of the corresponding Markov Model

As we can see in Figure 6, our VMU AltaRica model perfectly matches the Markov model presented in Figure 4. The states numbers in this graphic are the same as the ones presented in the corresponding Markov model. This allows us to say that AltaRica model presented in Section 4.1 provides good implementations of the automotive Safety Mechanisms.

The same work has been done to compare the model proposed in Section 4.2 with the one illustrated in Figure 5. In this case too, the two models perfectly match, allowing us to deduce that they provide good implementations of Automotive Safety Mechanisms.

5   Conclusion

In this article, we proposed AltaRica 3 models for the implementation of the behavior of large classes of automotive Electric and Electronic systems protected by first and possibly second order safety mechanisms. These models are generics in the sense that only few adjustments must be made in order to use them in most of the practical cases.

The modularity of the models that we proposed allows to easily combine them in order to represent large sized systems. Also, given the fact that they can be compiled to Guarded Transition Systems models, the computations on these models can be really fast and accurate (by using the Limited Depth Markov Generation [6]).

References

1. ISO 26262, Road vehicles – Functional safety, Working Group ISO TC22 SC3 (2011)
2. IEC 61508, Functional safety of electrical/electronic/programmable electronic safety-related systems, parts 1–7. Geneva: International Electrotechnical Commission (1998)
3. Innal, F., Dutuit, Y., Rauzy, A., Signoret, J.-P.: New insight into the average probability of failure on demand and the probability of dangerous failure per hour of safety instrumented systems. Journal of Risk and Reliability 224, 75–86 (2010)
4. Jin, H., Lundteigen, M.A., Rausand, M.: Reliability performance of safety instrumented systems: A common approach for both low- and high-demand mode of operation. Reliability Engineering and System Safety 96, 365–373 (2011)
5. Boiteau, M., Dutuit, Y., Rauzy, A., Signoret, J.-P.: The AltaRica Data-Flow Language in Use: Assessment of Production Availability of a MultiStates System. Reliability Engineering and System Safet 91(7), 747–755 (2006)
6. Brameret, P.-A., Rauzy, A., Roussel, J.M.: Preliminary System Safety Analysis with Limited Depth Markov Chain Generation. In: Proceedings of 4th IFAC Workshop on Dependable Control of Discrete Systems, DCDS 2013, York, Great Britain (September 2013)
7. Cherfi, A., Rauzy, A., Leeman, M., Meurville, F.: Modeling Automotive Safety Mechanisms: A Markovian Approach, Reliability Engineering and System Safety (accepted in April 2014), doi:http://dx.doi.org/10.1016/j.ress,04.013
8. Prosvirnova, T., Batteux, M., Brameret, P.-A.: The AltaRica 3.0 project for Model-Based Safety Assessment. In: DCDS 2013, York, Great Britain (September 2013)

A Pattern-Based Approach towards the Guided Reuse of Safety Mechanisms in the Automotive Domain

Maged Khalil, Alejandro Prieto, and Florian Hölzl

Fortiss GmbH, Software and Systems Engineering Dept., Guerickestr. 25, Munich, Germany
{khalil,hoelzl}@fortiss.org, alejandroprieto86@gmail.com

Abstract. The reuse of architectural measures or safety mechanisms is widely-spread in practice, especially in well-understood domains, as is reusing the corresponding safety-case to document the fulfillment of the target safety goal(s). This seems to harmonize well with the fact that safety standards recommend (if not dictate) performing many analyses during the concept phase of development as well as the early adoption of multiple measures at the architectural design level. Yet this front-loading is hindered by the fact that safety argumentation is not well-integrated into architectural models in the automotive domain and as such does not support comprehensible and reproducible argumentation nor any evidence for argument correctness. The reuse is neither systematic nor adequate.

Using a simplified description of safety mechanisms, we defined a pattern library capturing known solution algorithms and architectural measures/constraints in a seamless holistic model-based approach with corresponding tool support. Based on a meta-model encompassing both development artifacts and safety case elements, the pattern library encapsulates all the information necessary for reuse, which can then be integrated into existing development environments. This paper explores the model and the approach using an illustrative implementation example, along with the supporting workflow for the usage of the approach in both "designer" and "user" roles.

Keywords: Safety-critical systems, pattern-based design, architectures, safety cases, automotive, reuse.

1 Introduction

In practice, the reuse of architectural designs, development artifacts and entire code sequences is widely-spread, especially in well-understood domains. This also holds true for the development of safety-critical products, and extends to reusing the corresponding safety-cases aiming to document and prove the fulfillment of the underlying safety goals. This, however, is marred by several problems [18]:

- Most analyses (FMEA, FTA, etc.) have to be performed at system level, yet the components/ measures / safety mechanisms themselves need to be reused independently,
- and are not tied in any structured manner to other elements needed to provide the relevant context.

F. Ortmeier and A. Rauzy (Eds.): IMBSA 2014, LNCS 8822, pp. 137–151, 2014.
© Springer International Publishing Switzerland 2014

- Safety-cases in the automotive domain are not well integrated into architectural models and as such
- they do not provide comprehensible and reproducible argumentation
- nor any evidence for the correctness of the used arguments.

Reuse in a safety-critical context, and particularly the reuse of safety cases, is mostly ad-hoc, with loss of knowledge and traceability and lack of consistency or process maturity being the most widely spread and cited drawbacks [3], [18].

The use of patterns in the development of safety-critical products is already in wide spread use. Catalogues exist [14, 15] that discuss highly organized and well-known safety mechanisms, such as comparators or "1outof2" voters. Safety case templates can be generated, stored and reused for many categories of patterns. Some of these patterns are truly abstract and tackle higher system description levels, such as the "High Level Software Safety Argument Pattern Structure" presented in [12], while some can target a certain context, such as the use of Commercial-Off-The-Shelf (COTS) Components in a safety-critical context [13]. Patterns of safety cases for well-known problems have been suggested in academic literature [3, 4], [9, 11, 12, 13 and 14]. Further discussion is provided in [7], [18].

The reuse of safety mechanisms can be made both simpler and more robust through the encapsulation of all information into a consistent structured package, which can then be stored in a library element, along with the corresponding safety case to support it [18]. Dealing with non-functional requirements, especially safety, at later development stages is difficult and highly costly [2]. Front-loading these aspects into an integrated solution environment and properly leveraging the added value of a model-based approach to solving this problem requires automation using adequate tool support. This does not yet exist, despite these activities and analyses having mostly become part of the day-to-day business of safety-critical development [9]. The structure and usage of this reusable comprehensive library element concept in a seamless model-based development tool is the focus of this paper.

Chapter 2 details the problem. Chapter 3 explains our approach and gives an overview of the data model of the pattern library element as well as the usage process and most important attributes, supported by an example. In chapter 4 we discuss the impact of this contribution. In conclusion, we summarize our work and detail open research questions and future work in Chapter 5.

2   Problem

In our context, a typical reuse scenario would involve broadly reusing an architectural measure or design pattern, e.g., homogenous (hardware) duplex redundancy, in which a vulnerable single channel carrying a critical signal is duplicated to increase reliability, or more precisely one or more of the logical development artifacts employed, such as a comparator function. If the previous safety case is at all reused, it serves as a detached guide of what needs to be provided to close the case, i.e. serving a prescriptive role, which is arguably better than nothing [18]. Yet be it a design pattern or development artifact, a single item does not tell the entire story. For example, to correctly deploy homogenous redundancy, many other aspects have to be covered:

- one has to define the requirements the pattern fulfills,
- refine the requirements and draw up a specification,
- detail a (logical) component architecture,
- and optimize a deployment strategy that guarantees the duplicate components will not run on the same hardware resource.

These steps have to be preceded by feasibility checks or making explicit assumption about the system, e.g., that a second hardware channel is allowed, which is a contextual bit of information. This is not all; to justify reusing this pattern, one would also have to include any tests or information proving that this particular pattern is suitable for the goal it targets, as well as perhaps why this method and not another was chosen, e.g., why just use 2 channels and not a 2-out-of-3 pattern in our example.

Finally, all parts comprising this information, as well as their relations, which are more complex than simple traces, must be captured in a comprehensive and comprehensible manner which should also provide a suitable interface to the environment the reused element will be deployed in. Thus, the reuse of trusted design patterns or safety mechanisms cannot be confined to reusing the central artifact alone. Much of the information, in this case highly critical information, remains trapped in the heads of the developer and if mentioned at all most details remain implicit [18].

This gives rise to the need of some kind of encapsulation of the reusable safety mechanism (with requirements, specification, components, etc.), along with a minimum set of guarantees that can be achieved at that level and support via a solid argumentation. The encapsulation has to be structured, defining a minimum set of necessary information for correct reuse.

3   Approach

Using a simplified description of safety mechanisms according to the most common error management subtypes (avoidance/ detection/ handling) we define a pattern library covering known solution algorithms and architectural measures/constraints in a seamless holistic model-based approach with corresponding tool support. The pattern library comprises the minimum set of elements needed for correct reuse, i.e. the requirement the pattern covers, the specification of how one plans to implement it and the architecture elements/ measures / constraints required as well as the supporting safety case template and may include deployment or scheduling strategies, which would then be integrated into existing development environments. This enables an early analysis of hazards and risks, as well as the early adoption of multiple measures at the architectural design level during the concept phase, which is recommended (if not dictated) by many safety standards, e.g., [1].

Subsequently, fault types can be matched both to probable hazards but more importantly to the problem categories they fall into or are most similar to, from a system architecture design viewpoint. Combining this with known architectural constraints and patterns for solving them, we can thus reason about which types of architectural patterns are relevant for the system under analysis. The fault types, along with their requirements, are bundled with solution arguments, comprising components, their (sub-) architectures, deployment plans and schedules, into pattern libraries, which are rounded up by the corresponding safety-case templates or skeletons to provide argumentation for achieving the goals. Because our scope is safety mechanisms, the artifacts used here for safety argumentation all fall into the product information category of safety evidence [23].

Underlying the approach is the consistent use of patterns, as we previously described in [7], [9, 10], from the categorization of hazard types, over the abstract modeling of the respective safety concepts, and down to their implementation in the system architecture description, with a focus on providing argument chains in a seamless model-based environment. More details are given in [18]. Our proof-of-concept implementation leverages preexisting capabilities in our research CASE tool AUTOFOCUS3 (AF3) [8] (such as logical architecture description, model-based requirements engineering, model-checking, optimized deployments, safety case expression, among many others) [10], [16] to generate the artifacts for the safety mechanism libraries.

In this paper, we mainly focus on the structure and usage of elements from a library of reusable patterns, including the data models and workflow required to support seamless integration into a model-based development environment. Automation via tool-support is essential to achieve the intended advantages.

3.1   Structure Model of Library Element

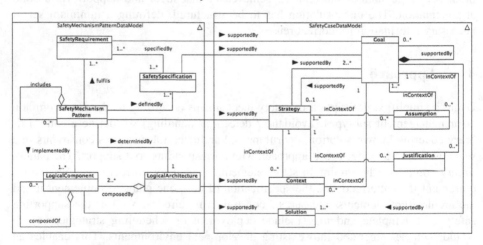

Fig. 1. Structure Model for Safety Mechanism Library Element

Figure (1) shows the basic structure model of a pattern library element. The right hand side is a safety case structure linked to the corresponding development artifacts on the left hand side, which in turn support each argumentation element. We use the Goal Structuring Notation (GSN) - in its Community Standard Version 1.0 [5] – for the graphical expression of safety cases as it was the most mature option suited to our needs. GSN is a structured (yet not formal) notation, which provides graphically differentiated basic safety case element types, such as goals, evidence, strategy, justification and so on, as well as a clear description of necessary and allowed connection types between these elements. Our decision to employ GSN is detailed in [7], [18].

While the left part of the model, which contains development artifacts, can entirely originate in one seamless tool (as will be shown in our implementation example in Section 3.3), this is not necessary. The development artifacts may reside in multiple repositories and be in varying formats; the binding element is the safety case shown on the right hand side, which gives the story and rationale behind the reusable pattern, organized by its relation to the *StructureModel* entities. This aspect is particularly important for a real world development context, which almost always entails a heterogeneous tool-chain.

Structure Model Elements
Figure (2) provides a closer look at the left hand side of figure (1), detailing the development artifacts library structure part. The definition and scope of these fundamental building blocks are in line with the system engineering view provided in the SPES2020 Project [20].

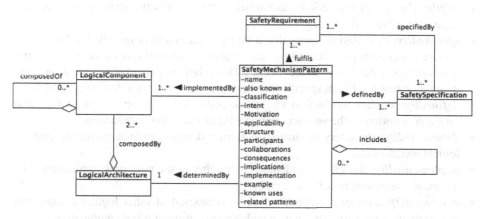

Fig. 2. Pattern Library Element: Structure Model for Development Artifacts

The entities of the safety mechanism pattern data model seen in figure (2) are:
- **SafetyMechanismPattern**: is a container object collecting information necessary for reuse, which is listed as a catalogue of attributes and adapted to the context of safety mechanism patterns. The majority of these attributes originated in the works of the Gang of Four [19] and were further consolidated for use in the safety field in Tim Kelly's works [14], [17]. Two clear exceptions are the attribute *Implications*, taken from [15], which describes how using a safety mechanism pattern affects other non-functional requirements such as reliability, modifiability, cost & execution times, and the attribute *Related Patterns*, which typically contains a purely nominal list of similar or affiliated patterns, but in our case is used to link related safety mechanism *classes*. This provides direct traceability and allows for a quick

propagation and adaptation of changes across related patterns, increasing confidence in reuse as well as the maintainability of the library.

- **SafetyRequirement**: details the requirement the pattern fulfils, as well as any safety related attributes, e.g., Safety Integrity Level.
- **SafetySpecification**: a concrete description of the safety mechanism's functional behavior and its interaction with the environment, and serves as a basis for the implementation in a logical component. It can be formal, e.g., in AF3 the behavior of safety mechanisms can be captured in state automata.
- **LogicalComponent**: is the implementation or concrete representation of a safety mechanism at software level, whose definition includes transfer behavior, e.g., code specification or a state automaton. It can be a composition of logical components which collectively determine the safety mechanism's behavior.
- **LogicalArchitecture**: defines the context of the safety mechanism pattern, by describing the boundaries / interface of the *LogicalComponent* implementing the mechanism as well as giving a description of any other components involved.

Structure Model Relations
The relationships between the model's entities are as follows:

- *fulfils*: The use of this safety mechanism pattern fulfils the stated safety requirement (or set thereof).
- *specifiedBy*: this relation shows that a safety requirement is *specified* or brought to a more concrete representation by one or more specifications of the implementation, providing the "how" to the "what". This relation is also bidirectional, because it could be that a solution specification *specifies* one or more safety requirements.
- *definedBy*: a safety mechanism's behavior is defined by its specification. Can also give a description of the architectural context of the safety mechanism.
- *determinedBy:* the safety mechanism pattern is determined by a unique structure or logical architecture.
- *implementedBy*: the safety mechanism belonging to the pattern is implemented by a logical component at software level.
- *composedOf*: a logical component *can be* composed of other logical components or simply direct descriptions, e.g., a code specification or a state automaton.
- *composedBy*: this relationship shows that a logical architecture or context of a safety mechanism is *composed by* at least two logical components, which interact with the safety mechanism's logical component. In its simplest form, one is an input and the other is an output component.
- *includes*: this relationship indicates that a safety mechanism pattern can include other patterns within its structure. This entails inheritance of the respective safety requirements, safety specification, logical component and the logical architecture of the related or reused safety mechanism patterns. The form and structure of inclusion has to be defined in a case-by-case manner.

Pattern Catalogue Attributes
Contrary to the typically purely verbose nature of capturing pattern attributes, our use of a model-based approach means that we are able to integrate this information and capture most of it into the elements of the structure model. This is a particularly

important feature, as verbose lists have a tendency to be overlooked, misused or misinterpreted and we consider them to constitute an obstacle to pattern reuse. The captured attributes are:

1. *Name*: captured in the name of the safety mechanism pattern itself.
2. *Classification*: states to which category of safety mechanisms (*Failure Avoidance, Failure Detection and Failure Containment/ Handling*) [14] the pattern belongs, and is captured in the structure of the library itself.
3. *Intent*: this attribute is captured in the *SafetyRequirement* entity.
4. *Motivation*: this attribute provides the rationale behind using the pattern and is captured in the safety requirement entity, with any additional, implementation-specific information being captured in the *SafetySpecification* entity.
5. *Applicability*: describes the architectural context of the safety mechanism as well as instantiation information and is captured by the *LogicalArchitecture* entity and augmented by the workflow described in section (3.2) of this paper.
6. *Structure*: this attribute is captured by the entities *LogicalComponent* and *LogicalArchitecture* and their relation.
7. *Participants*: are captured at an interaction level by the *LogicalArchitecture* entity and at a structural level by the structure of the safety mechanism library.
8. *Collaborations*: this attributed is captured by the structure of the safety mechanism library and the safety case supporting it.
9. *Consequences*: the parts of this attribute describing which components in the logical architecture or inside the safety mechanism's component have to be instantiated or further developed upon usage are captured in the structure model as well as in the workflow described in section (3.2).
10. *Implementation*: is partially captured in the *SafetySpecification* entity as well as the entities *LogicalComponent* and *LogicalArchitecture* and their relation.
11. *Related patterns*: this attribute is captured in the data model for inclusion relations by the recursive aggregation relation of the *SafetyMechanismPattern* entity.

Mapping to SafetyCaseModel
Having defined the development artefacts part of the structure model, a quick explanation of their mapping to the corresponding elements in the *SafetyCaseModel* seen on the right hand side of figure (1) is given next.

• **SafetyRequirement** – *supportedby* – **Goal**: the entry point to any reuse problem is a goal or requirement that has to be fulfilled.
• **SafetyMechanismPattern** – *supportedby* – **Strategy**: the information captured in the safety mechanism pattern and the information it contains lays out a plan for solving the problem, i.e. a strategy, and helps explains the relation between the elements of the pattern, most importantly their refinement and decomposition.
• **SafetySpecification** – *supportedby* – **Goal**: a safety specification is mapped to the (sub-)goal entity in the safety case data model, as it describes a refinement and decomposition of the higher level goals towards implementing a solution.
• **LogicalComponent** – *supportedby* – **Solution**: the logical component is the solution for the stated goal.

- **LogicalArchitecture** – *supportedby* – **Context**: the logical architecture provides context to the safety pattern and the logical component and its implementation, without which the pattern is either meaningless or cannot be described concisely.

3.2   Tool Implementation and Usage Workflow

Our approach and the implementation support in AF3 envision two roles: a safety mechanism *Developer* and a safety mechanism *User*. To support the *Developer* role a comprehensive analysis of many safety mechanisms was carried out, which identified three archetypes of structure models for capturing safety mechanisms in AF3. To save a new safety mechanism, the *Developer* has to decide which archetype best fits his need. The developer is aided in this task by a wizard, which also assures that library elements cannot be created without the mandatory information. These AF3 categories and the *Developer* role are not the focus of this paper.

For the *User* role, we must differentiate between using the library element in an already existing project or in a green field one, i.e. I need a redundant design for my function/application/system and wish to start with a comprehensive structure model that includes all the necessary artefacts and then fill in details later.

The analysis of the safety mechanisms and the usage roles, led to the identification of three categories for the usage of the artefacts captured in the library element. Taking the usage scenario into account, these categories define how each artefact in the library element will be added into the development environment. These are:

1. **Copy**: Artefacts are copied into the environment as is. *SafetyRequirements*, and *SafetySpecification* elements, along with all the *SafetyCaseModel* artefacts, are treated in this manner, as they are clearly defined static elements that do need to be changed upon usage.
2. **Instance**: artifacts are to be instantiated upon usage. This may include the input of some parameters by the users. *LogicalComponent* entities are always used in this manner. *LogicalArchitecture* elements are treated in this manner if and only if the usage mode is "green-field".
3. **Replace**: Artefacts are replaced by ones existing in the model. This mode applies to *LogicalArchitecture* elements and is obviously only usable when deploying the library element into a preexisting model. E.g., logical components stored in the library element to describe the interaction of the central safety mechanism component with its environment are replaced by existing components from the model, to which the library pattern / safety mechanism is to be applied.

The deployment of the library elements is guided by a wizard, whose function it is, among others, to ensure that library elements are deployed seamlessly. To that end, the wizard prompts the user at each step to link / map the components of the inserted library to their counterparts in the existing model. E.g., a comparator deployment prompts the user to select the two components whose outputs are to be compared, as well as the original requirement, which prompted the deployment of the comparator safety mechanism from the library in the first place. The development process still has to be monitored and approved at key decision points by a human expert.

The implementation carried out in AF3 currently covers four safety mechanisms, *1oo2Voting*, *Comparison*, *RangeCheck*, and *HomogeneousDuplexRedundancy* [14]. Continuing with the redundancy example introduced in Chapter 2, the following section illustrates the implementation using screenshots.

3.3   Implementation Example

Figure (3) shows an illustrative overview of the pattern library implementation. On the left are snapshots of screen grabs of functionalities for the generation of library artifacts in AF3 and on the right is an example for a simplified corresponding safety case, thus encapsulating all the information required to reuse the pattern.

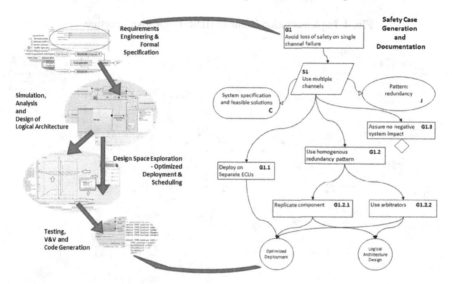

Fig. 3. Pattern Library Element: Simplified Illustration of Duplex Redundancy Pattern [18]

The interaction of the *HomogeneousDuplexRedundancy (HDR)* implementation example safety mechanism with its environment is captured in the *LogicalArchitecture* element shown in figure (4), with the corresponding safety case shown collapsed in figure (5). Using the relations described in the GSN standard [5] and implemented in AF3, it is possible to perform completeness and consistency checks on the safety case, such as "*solutions must stem from goals and no other elements*" or "*no open goals remain*". Not shown, due to space limitation but implemented with AF3, are the corresponding requirements or specification of any of the central *LogicalComponent* elements, e.g., the *Comparator*. Also possible but not shown, is a formal specification of mechanism behavior, allowing automatic test suite generation.

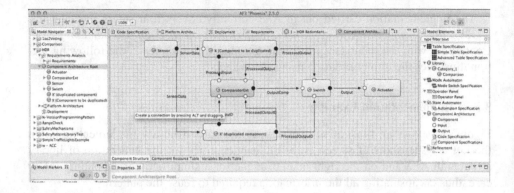

Fig. 4. Implementation Example HDR: LogicalArchitecture

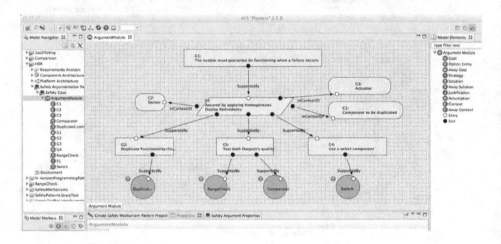

Fig. 5. Implementation Example HDR: SafetyCaseModel

3.4   Extended Structure Model

The library element is, however, incomplete for the HDR example without capturing
the deployment rules, which determine how the software components are assigned to
hardware units. This is a new piece of information and gives rise to the need to extend
the structure model with optional elements beyond the basic ones previously shown in
figure (1). To encapsulate more information, such as the deployment rule, or facilitate
a refinement of the specification, such as the categories provided by ISO26262 in its
functional and technical safety concepts, we extended the structure model as shown in
figure (6). Other elements could also be introduced to capture any other information
pertaining to the suitability of the safety mechanism, e.g., tests or analyses.

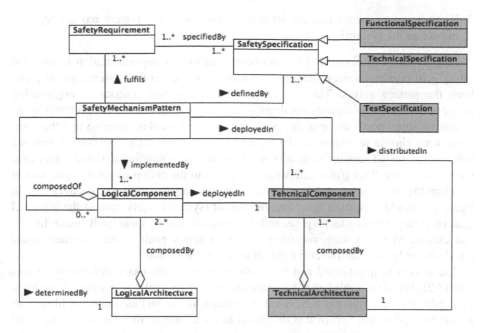

Fig. 6. Pattern Library Element: Extended Structure Model for Development Artifacts

3.5   Modular and Compositional Argumentation

The use of patterns as a way of documenting and reusing successful safety argument structures was pioneered by Kelly [17], who developed an example safety case pattern catalogue providing a number of generic solutions identified from existing safety cases. This was further developed by Weaver [11], who specifically developed a safety pattern catalogue for software. A software safety pattern catalogue was also developed by Ye [13], specifically to consider arguments about the safety of systems including COTS software products. Further discussion of these approaches' strengths and drawbacks is given in [12], [18].

These approaches all focused on generating safety case templates for known patterns, whereas the safety case templates themselves are the focus. Our approach encourages the encapsulation of the reusable development artifacts along with the supporting safety cases to enable correct and speedy reuse in a safety-critical context. The ARRL approach presented in the OPENCOSS project [22] offers a similar but more generalized workflow, yet our approach differs in that it catalogues existing information, targets a specific use case, and does not force a new framework or language on to the user.

Using our approach does give rise to at least three interesting questions:
1. What is an adequate boundary interface for modular compositional argumentation?
2. How do we guarantee that all goals (and sub-goals) have been identified?
    and more importantly,

3. How do we guarantee that the introduced pattern or component has no negative impact on the system?

As previously discussed in [18] and supported by our implementation results, the safety goal presents a very adequate boundary interface to the system, whose problems the pattern solves. This is alignment with common practice in engineering projects, where "requirements catalogues" are the standard mode of exchanging information about needs and evaluating results. To illustrate this, imagine that the comparator we choose to employ in the figure (3) example is a COTS HW/SW unit we buy from a trusted supplier who also provides the corresponding detailed safety case for the arbitrator. That (sub-) safety case snaps on to the collapsed safety case, shown in figure (5), at the safety sub-goal (Comparator) it satisfies. The entire safety case in figure (5) would then itself snap into the parent (system) safety case at the top-level goal boundary defining its purpose, and this process would repeat itself hierarchically and cumulatively. As such, satisfying all the system's goals at the interface would enable not only modular but also a cumulative argumentation.

The answer to questions 2 and 3 is partially given in the usage description in section (3.2). We do not think that a human expert can be totally taken out of the loop, especially if a deterministic behavioral description is not included into the library, as in our case. Thus key approval is delegated to the expert at all integration nodes and supported by automated tool checks, such as the one shown in figure (3), where the undeveloped safety goal $G1.3$, which leads to no solution and will as such be detected by the tool checks, serves as a reminder to carry out an impact analysis after integrating the safety mechanism (and its safety case) into the existing model. Similarly, we propose that assumptions made in library safety cases require the approval of the system integrator before acceptance. This check is easily implemented.

To achieve true compositionality, the underlying framework used to describe the behavior of each safety mechanism should support temporal logic, and the descriptions of both the components and the safety cases supporting them would have to be deterministic. Such descriptions lie outside the scope of this paper, which focuses on structural as opposed to behavioral models, and could be the subject of future work.

4   Impact and Contribution

The design of functional-safety systems is largely driven by best practices – like the use of fault monitors, safe states, or redundant paths. These best practices can often be presented in the form of patterns – both to describe a possible solution, but also to document an argumentation about their contribution to a safety case. The provision of a library of such patterns allows the identification and comprehensive (re-)use of suitable architectural measures and of corresponding components along with their safety cases, facilitating a cumulative if not compositional argumentation about the achieved safety goals.

The approach defines the structure of such a library, encapsulating all necessary information for a correct reuse of safety mechanisms. The approach not only adds new attributes to the ones known in pattern catalogue literature but also captures most of the information from these attributes into the model itself. This decreases reliance on the hitherto typically verbose attribute catalogue and we consider it to be a major bonus for the approach, as textual lists have a tendency to be overlooked, misused or misinterpreted and we consider them to constitute an obstacle to pattern reuse.

Furthermore, the approach features an explicit model-based representation of safety mechanisms within the context of their usage and the problems they solve. This has several advantages, including 1) a better characterization of the problem space addressed by the pattern – better than the textual description otherwise used in pattern templates, 2) a more natural representation of the transformations embodied in the application of the pattern, and 3) a better handle on the selection, rationale and application of the patterns [21].

Thus, the approach contributes to the optimization of development with respect to system safety in general, and specifically to safety-critical component reuse. We also believe the paradigm to be extensible to COTS (Commercial Of-The Shelf) components, as well as providing support for the "Safety Element out of Context" clause cited in safety standards, such as the ISO26262 [1].

5   Conclusion and Future Work

This paper presents the structure and workflow of an approach which facilitates the reuse of safety mechanisms by encapsulating relevant information in a pattern library with tool support. We furthermore explored the possibilities and showed the opportunities supported by this approach. A holistic pattern-based approach to the construction of safety-cases in a seamless model-based development of safety-critical systems requires several elements, the main constituents of which are:

1. A library of reusable argumentation patterns – both in form of problem patterns (e.g., faults like early, late, or wrong sensor information; temporal or spatial interference between functions) and solution patterns (e.g., error avoidance, detection, mitigation; sensor fault detection and correction mechanisms; partitioning mechanisms) – built from elements of a model-based description of the system under development (e.g., requirements, functions, SW-/HW-components, channels, busses, deployment strategies) as well as GSN safety cases (e.g., goals, solutions, justifications, contexts)
2. A mechanism for the instantiation (e.g., stuck at-/noise-like faults; different filter for fault detection) and application (e.g., linking to the corresponding HW- and SW-elements) of those patterns in a compositional fashion.
3. A mechanism to check the soundness of the constructed argumentation (e.g., no open sub-goals; all context are covered by corresponding system elements) w.r.t. to its structure.

Using the approach presented in this paper, we have shown the feasibility of handling all three of the above points to varying degrees. In the next step we are focusing on expanding our pattern library with more implementation examples to test for general applicability and scalability as well as examining adequate methods for cross-referencing and categorizing patterns. This will be followed by transporting the concepts into the significantly more detail-rich and ISO26262 automotive-safety specific SAFE Meta-model [6] and checking its feasibility and scalability in that context.

Acknowledgments. The AF3 project is a long-term ongoing tool development effort led by the fortiss department of "Software and Systems Engineering". The functionality provided currently is mainly the result of the joint work of: Florian Hölzl, Sabine Teufl, Mou Dongyue, Sebastian Voss, Daniel Ratiu. Many thanks also to the other members of the AF3 team.

Many thanks also go to the project partners from the SAFE/SAFE-E project [6], which served as a starting point for many of the concepts presented in this work. SAFE-E is part of the Eurostars program, which is powered by EUREKA and the European Community (ID 01|S1101) and funded by the German Ministry of Education and Research (BMBF) under the ID E!6095. Responsibility for the content rests with the authors.

References

1. ISO 26262 Standard, Road Vehicles Functional Safety (2011), http://www.iso.org
2. Lindstrom, D.R.: Five Ways to Destroy a Development Project. IEEE Software, 55–58 (September 1993)
3. Kelly, T., McDermid, J.: Safety case construction and reuse using patterns. In: 16th International Conference on Computer Safety, Reliability and Security, SAFECOMP (1997)
4. Wagner, S., Schätz, B., Puchner, S., Kock, P.: A Case Study on Safety Cases in the Automotive Domain: Modules, Patterns, and Models. In: Proc. International Symposium on Software Reliability Engineering (ISSRE 2010). IEEE Computer Society (2010)
5. Origin Consulting (York) Limited, on behalf of the Contributors."Goal Structuring Notation (GSN)". GSN COMMUNITY STANDARD VERSION 1 (November 2011)
6. The ITEA2 SAFE Project / The EUROSTARS SAFE-E Project, http://www.safe-project.eu
7. The SAFE / SAFE-E Consortium. Deliverable D3.1.3 / D3.4, Proposal for extension of Meta-model for safety-case modeling and documentation (2013), http://www.safe-project.eu
8. AutoFOCUS 3, research CASE tool, af3.fortiss.org, 2014 fortiss GmbH
9. Khalil, M.: Pattern-based methods for model-based safety-critical software architecture design. In: ZeMoSS 2013 Workshop at the SE 2013 in Aachen, Germany (2013)
10. Voss, S., Schätz, B., Khalil, M., Carlan, C.: A step towards Modular Certification using integrated model-based Safety Cases. In: VeriSure 2013 (2013)
11. Weaver, R.: The Safety of Software – Constructing and Assuring Arguments. PhD Thesis, Department of Computer Science, The University of York (2003)
12. Hawkins, R., Clegg, K., Alexander, R., Kelly, T.: Using a Software Safety Argument Pattern Catalogue: Two Case Studies. In: Flammini, F., Bologna, S., Vittorini, V. (eds.) SAFECOMP 2011. LNCS, vol. 6894, pp. 185–198. Springer, Heidelberg (2011)
13. Ye, F.: Justifying the Use of COTS Components within Safety Critical Applications. PhD Thesis, Department of Computer Science, The University of York (2005)
14. Wu, W., Kelly, T.: Safety Tactics for Software Architecture Design. In: Proceedings of the 28th Annual International Computer Software and Applications Conference (COMPSAC 2004), vol. 1, pp. 368–375. IEEE Computer Society, Washington, DC (2004)

15. Armoush, A.: Design Patterns for Safety-Critical Embedded Systems. Ph.D. Thesis, RWTH-Aachen (2010)
16. Voss, S., Schätz, B.: Deployment and Scheduling Synthesis for Mixed-Critical Shared-Memory Applications. In: Proceedings of the 20th Annual IEEE International Conference and Workshops on the Engineering of Computer Based Systems, ECBS (2013)
17. Kelly, T.: Arguing Safety – A Systematic Approach to Managing Safety Cases. PhD Thesis, Department of Computer Science, The University of York (1998)
18. Khalil, M., Schätz, B., Voss, S.: A Pattern-based Approach towards Modular Safety Analysis and Argumentation. In: Embedded Real Time Software and Systems Conference (ERTS 2014), Toulouse, France (2014)
19. Gamma, E., Helm, R., Johnson, R., Vlissides, J.: Design Patterns: Elements of Reusable Object-Oriented Software. Addison Wesley (1995)
20. SPES2020 Consortium. Pohl, K., Hönninger, H., Achatz, R., Broy, M.: Model-Based Engineering of Embedded Systems – The SPES 2020 Methodology. Springer (2012)
21. Mili, H., El-Boussaidi, G.: Representing and applying design patterns: what is the problem? In: Briand, L.C., Williams, C. (eds.) MoDELS 2005. LNCS, vol. 3713, pp. 186–200. Springer, Heidelberg (2005)
22. Verhulst, E.: OPENCOSS Project Presentation. "Cross-domain systems and safety engineering: Is it feasible?". Flanders Drive Seminar, Brussels (2013)
23. Nair, S., de la Vara, J.L., Sabetzadeh, M., Briand, L.: Classification, Structuring, and Assessment of Evidence for Safety: A Systematic Literature Review. In: 6th IEEE International Conference on Software Testing, Verification and Validation, ICST 2013 (2013)

Towards the Derivation of Guidelines
for the Deployment of Real-Time Tasks
on a Multicore Processor

Stefan Schmidhuber[1], Michael Deubzer[2], Ralph Mader[3], Michael Niemetz[1],
and Jürgen Mottok[1]

[1] Ostbayerische Technische Hochschule (OTH) Regensburg
Seybothstraße 2, 93053 Regensburg, Germany
{stefan.schmidhuber,michael.niemetz,juergen.mottok}@oth-regensburg.de
[2] Timing-Architects Embedded Systems GmbH
Bruderwöhrdstraße 15b, 93055 Regensburg, Germany
michael.deubzer@timing-architects.com
[3] Continental AG
Siemensstraße 12, 93055 Regensburg, Germany
Ralph.Mader@continental-corporation.com

Abstract. The deployment of automotive software on a multicore processor includes the task of mapping executables to cores. Given the number of possible solutions, integrators have to solve a complex problem. Considering multiple, often conflicting goals like minimizing task response times and memory consumption, complexity further increased with the advent of multicore processors. We present a model-based approach for deriving design rules supporting integrators with statically mapping tasks to a multicore ECU. First, an evolutionary algorithm is used to sample the design space. For each sample, a model-based analysis is performed, resulting in the required fitness values according to the system metric objectives. Finally, subsets of the sample population are used to derive deployment guidelines by evaluating similarities between highly ranked solutions. This reduces the number of solutions to be considered by the integrators by orders of magnitude. In a case-study, we demonstrate the developed approach on an artificial automotive engine management system.

Keywords: Real-time systems, embedded multicore systems, runnable partitioning, task-to-core mapping, software integration, design space exploration, evolutionary algorithms.

1 Motivation

Engine management systems in the automotive domain evolved during the past 20 years from simple map based control for the ignition timing towards more and more complex algorithms closely controlling the combustion process of an engine. The need for close control comes along with an increased demand for

F. Ortmeier and A. Rauzy (Eds.): IMBSA 2014, LNCS 8822, pp. 152–165, 2014.

calculation power. In the last decades the standard way to increase the performance of a processor was to increase the clock-frequency. However, such an increase correlates with an increase of the power consumption of the processor. Under the difficult environmental conditions where engine control systems need to operate a continuation of this process would lead to the need for active cooling of the device, increasing the costs considerably. Moreover, the increase on complexity caused by active cooling would bring the risk of increasing failure rates, which would be not acceptable for a safety critical system. An alternative to a further scaling of the processing speed is to use parallel execution by several CPU cores working on the same data and program memory.

As a consequence, the existing software which has been developed in the past for single-core processors has to be modified to be executed by such a concurrent system in a robust and efficient way. The theoretical performance of the processor is mainly determined by the number of CPUs integrated on the chip. Making use of the full performance of the processors is only possible if the application can be completely divided into parts which can be executed without any restriction in parallel [12]. Generally, this can be implemented by allocating executables dynamically or statically to cores. Dynamic allocation leads to high efficiency and a good handling of varying execution times. On the contrary, it results in some overhead as well as additional requirements for programming [23], which are not considered in most legacy applications.

In this paper we focus on allocating executables statically to cores, being the more appropriate approach for the migration from singlecore to multicore systems in the presence of legacy applications. For engine management systems, a common pragmatic idea of deployment is mapping time domain scheduled executables to one core and angle domain executables on a different core. Having a look on the result of this approach shows that the load balancing, the scheduling metrics and the resulting inter-core communication rates are not satisfying and not optimized. In addition, it is expected that the result will always depend on the integration scenario, different types of engines (e.g. gasoline or diesel engine), different number of cores, and different core affinity constraints.

Automotive software is divided into atomic software components. They typically contain several runnables [10], which represent the smallest granularity of executables. The executables are aggregated into tasks which are executed by the scheduler of the operating system. In this work, we only consider the mapping of such tasks to cores or the splitting of previously existing tasks into more parts. To ensure the initial execution order, a synchronization point is added for each splitting position. Consequently, the parts of a split task are always activated in the same order as on a singlecore system for each instance of the split task. As the runnables of practical automotive software strongly interact with each other [10], communication-based effects need to be taken carefully into account in order to harness the full computational potential of multicore processors. However, the underlying problem of runnable partitioning and task-to-core mapping is equal to the bin-packing problem, which is known to be NP-hard [7].

Consequently an exhaustive search, i.e. the evaluation of every possible solution, is not an option.

In summary, it can be stated that the described deployment step is a NP-hard multi-objective optimization problem. Evolutionary algorithms have been identified to be particularly suitable for such problems [11].

The main goal of this work is to support the integrator in solving the aforementioned problem. To significantly reduce the number of possible solutions, deployment guidelines shall be developed. First, an evolutionary algorithm is used to sample the design space. A subset of the resulting deployment solutions is analyzed regarding affinities between the runnables and tasks in a second step. Based on the analysis, deployment guidelines stating which tasks should or should not be mapped together on one core are derived in a final step. In addition, possible task splitting points are recommended.

The remainder of this paper is organized in the following way: The deployment step in the automotive domain will be thoroughly discussed in the next section. In section 3 we present the developed approach for deriving deployment guidelines. Subsequently, we demonstrate the derivation of deployment guidelines for a practical automotive engine management system in a case-study. We conclude by a discussion of the results and their relevance to the industry.

2   Model-Based Deployment

In this section, we present the meta model used to describe an automotive system and how to evaluate the performance of deployment solutions. Moreover, an excerpt of state-of-the art techniques regarding deployment is provided.

2.1   System Model

The meta model is compatible with AUTOSAR [1], the AUTomotive Open System ARchitecture [24] and comparable to the meta model developed within the AMALTHEA project [2]. It consists of the sub-models hardware, software, operating system, stimulation and mapping. Moreover, design constraints and requirements can be specified. The requirements sub-model will be discussed in Section 2.2 and the design constraints sub-model will be presented in Section 2.4.

- Hardware. The hardware sub-model contains all timing-relevant properties of a multicore processor. This includes the number of cores, their clock frequency, as well as the timing relevant memory architecture [25].
- Operating system. The operating system sub-model contains the list of schedulers used to manage software execution. For each scheduler, the scheduling algorithm (e.g. OSEK [16] or AUTOSAR and its respective scheduling parameters, the scheduling delay and the cores managed by a scheduler are described.

- Software. The software sub-model consists of a description of all tasks, runnables and signals (i.e. shared variables) in the system. Tasks are the entities which are managed by the schedulers and are described by their scheduling priority and scheduling deadline. Runnables denote atomic software functions. They execute in a specific order within the context of tasks. The signals are listed by name and bit size. Each runnable is described by the read and written signals and the number of instructions. Instructions quantify the computational power demand and can be modeled as a fixed number or by a statistical distribution, which for example takes alternative execution paths within the runnable into account.
- Stimulation. The stimulation sub-model allows the modeling of different task activation schemes. For automotive tasks for example, time-triggered (i.e. periodic with or without offset) and event-triggered activation is possible [15]. An example for event-triggered activation is modeling variable engine speeds by a clock-based stimulus. Moreover sporadic stimuli are described by a statistical distribution which denotes the deviation of the recurrence.
- Mapping. The mapping sub-model holds the information to which scheduler the tasks are assigned. It also contains the information which task is activated by which stimuli.

2.2 System Requirements

Embedded systems in the automotive domain belong to the class of hard real-time systems. Only when computational results are correct and produced in time, a hard real-time system functions according to specifications [13]. In order to evaluate if a task finishes in time, deadlines are defined. These denote the upper bound for the response time of the respective task. Consider a task set τ consisting of n tasks T_i as defined in the previous section. Multiple instances $J_{i,j}$ (also referred to as jobs) of each task exist in a certain time interval.

The response time $RT_{i,j}$ (Equation 1) of the j-th job of the i-th task $J_{i,j}$ calculates as the difference between its finishing time $FT_{i,j}$ and its activation time $AT_{i,j}$. The finishing time $FT_{i,j}$ is hereby determined relative to $AT_{i,j}$.

$$RT_{i,j} = FT_{i,j} - AT_{i,j} \tag{1}$$

The requirements sub-model consists of a list of deadline requirements for the tasks. A deadline requirement denotes the upper limit for the response time of a task according to the definition above. Similarly, another requirements can be defined. One example is an upper limit for the duration of a critical execution path. A critical execution path could be the processing chain starting with a specific stimuli followed by the calculation of the response to the availability of the response for a subsequent consumer.

2.3 Evaluation of Deployment Solutions

In order to ensure that the tasks meet their deadlines, the multicore scheduling problem has to be solved [14]. In case of partitioned multicore scheduling approach [26], it consists of the task-to-core mapping and the priority assignment problem. The latter deals with the question in what order the task jobs should execute on the cores. In this work, it is assumed that a fixed priority is assigned to each task according to the deadline monotonic scheme [5]. The highest priority is hereby assigned to the task with the shortest relative deadline. Moreover, we assume that each core is managed by a local OSEK [16] scheduler.

The runnables exchange data with each other by sharing global variables. To ensure data consistency when runnables concurrently access the same data, buffering is used [12]. This means when a task is activated, all the data required by its runnables is read from shared memory into the local memory of the core where the task is located. Before termination, all data produced by the runnables within a task is written back into shared memory. Consequently, data consistency is ensured for the complete execution of a task job. The decision which data accesses have to be buffered is hereby determined for each task based on the priorities of the allocated tasks. Read and write operations to and from the respective buffers are protected by a semaphore in order to guarantee data consistency. Moreover, a priority ceiling protocol [6] is used to prevent deadlocks.

In our work, we use the discrete, event-based simulation tool TA Tool Suite [4] to evaluate the performance of a deployment solution. The simulator operates on the aforementioned system model. State transitions of tasks like the activation, termination or preemption are recorded into a trace together with the respective time-stamps [1]. When statistical estimators are applied to the trace, different kinds of metrics can be obtained.

Consequently the response times for the tasks can be determined. In addition, the *BufferSize* metric can be calculated by model-based analysis of the system model. It denotes the size of the core-local memories required to perform buffering as introduced above for a specific deployment solution. Another metric that can be calculated from simulation results is the *CpuWaiting* metric. It denotes the fraction of simulation time a task remained in the state (active-)waiting for a resource.

Contrary to formal approaches like the real-time calculus [18] which yield hard upper bounds for task response times, timing simulation can only provide estimations. However, formal methods for practical embedded real-time systems with strongly interacting tasks and concurrent execution are computationally highly expensive and often lead to unacceptable pessimism due to an incomplete modeling of the system[2]. In the scope of deployment guideline derivation, however, a simulation-based evaluation approach provides satisfactory accuracy.

---

[1] The trace format BTF used by the simulation has been released open source to Eclipse Auto IWG within the scope of the AMALTHEA project [3].

[2] To the best of our knowledge, approaches for formal schedulability analysis are not yet available for the combination of mixed preemptive and cooperative scheduling, mixed periodic, sporadic and clock-dependent task activation pattern as well as state dependent runnable execution times and multicore shared and cached memory architectures.

2.4   Design Constraints

The design constraints sub-model contains a list of constraints which restrict the degrees of freedom when tasks are mapped to the cores. Similar to the approach of Mehiaoui et al. [8], we consider utilization constraints and allocation constraints. Utilization constraints restrict task to core mapping so that the load of the specified cores does not exceed the threshold defined by the constraints. Allocation constraints in our approach apply both to tasks and runnables. Some runnables for example must execute on different cores due to lock step execution. Allocation constraints also facilitate the consideration of preliminary analyses. One example is the work of Kienberger et al. [9]. They analyze the communication between runnables in AUTOSAR models and determine sub-sets of runnables which can execute independently. Constraining those identified sub-sets so that the runnables of each sub-set must execute on the same core obviates a grouping of runnables to tasks as described in Section 2.5. Consequently, the overall design space can be reduced significantly.

2.5   State-of-the-Art

In order to harness the full computational power of multicore processors, Scheidenmann et al. [12] identified three basic ways of conducting the deployment of automotive software to a multicore processor with regard to parallelization. The first way is to map runnables to cores without any restrictions. The second possibility is to re-group the runnables of previously defined tasks and map the newly created tasks to the cores. The re-grouping decision is based on the data flow between the runnables. The third possibility is to split previously defined tasks into explicitly synchronized individual tasks. Our approach is similar to the third possibility. We want to benefit from the computational power of multicore technology but at the same time facilitate the migration of legacy systems. Therefore, modifying fundamental properties like the execution order of runnables within a task is beyond scope.

Monot et al. [22] present how to deploy a set of runnables to a multicore ECU in the context of AUTOSAR [1] scheduling. First, inter-dependent runnables are clustered together. Runnables without dependencies on others denote a cluster of size one. If affinity constraints for runnables exist, those runnables are directly mapped to the respective cores. The remaining runnable clusters are mapped to the cores using the Worst-Fit Decreasing (WFD) bin-packing [7] heuristic. Finally the runnables are scheduled using one or more dispatcher tasks for each core. Different "least-loaded" heuristics are used for creating the respective dispatch tables.

3   Derivation of Deployment Guidelines

The derivation of deployment guidelines denotes the process of extracting common properties out of a set of best-ranked solutions. One example is the impact

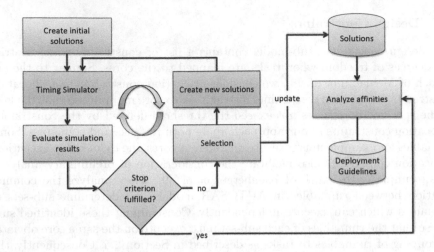

Fig. 1. Schematic overview of the proposed deployment guideline derivation approach

of communication between certain strongly inter-dependent runnables on timing. A deployment guideline in this case would suggest to map such runnables together to one core when this specific allocation is common to the majority of the respective best-ranked solutions.

3.1 Overview

Figure 1 provides an overview of the proposed deployment guideline derivation approach. The left part of the figure depicts how evolutionary algorithms work in general. They simulate natural selection and natural evolution in an iterative approach [20]. The iterations of the algorithm are called generations and in the first generation a set of initial solutions is created using an uniform distribution for randomly mapping tasks to cores. Solutions are evaluated as described in Section 2.3 and a fitness value is assigned to each solution in the subsequent step. The fitness quantifies the quality of a solution with respect to the system requirements. After the evaluation step the stop criterion is evaluated. It is fulfilled when a certain stagnation threshold or the maximum limit of generations has been reached. When the stop criterion has not yet been fulfilled, the parent solutions for the subsequent variation step are selected. In order to create new solutions for the population of the next generation, mutation and crossover techniques are used. While mutation changes one property of a parent solution to create a new one, crossover combines the properties of two or more parents to create new solutions. The algorithm then continues with the evaluation step.

After the optimization stops the resulting set of near to optimal solutions is analyzed. The analysis takes the best solutions into account and evaluates their common properties in terms of allocation. The identified affinities between runnables and tasks are finally used to derive deployment guidelines.

3.2   Evolutionary Optimization Algorithm

In this section, the specific properties of the evolutionary algorithm used in this work are discussed. The first property to be discussed is the fitness assignment step. Despite the fact that the problem at hand is multi-objective, we pursue a more traditional approach for fitness assignment. Instead of using a non-dominated ranking technique [19] for fitness assignment, we use a modified weighted sum approach to aggregate all objectives into one fitness value. One drawback of this approach is that certain regions of the design space may no longer be reached [21]. However, the reason for this choice is the requirement for a scalar fitness value which will be discussed in the next section. We use a modified euclidean norm [17] where each of the n metrics considered as optimization goal is normalized from its actual range to the range $[0.0, 1.0]$. The minimum value $m_i^{\min}$ as well as the maximum value $m_i^{\max}$ of the respective metric m_i are used for normalization.

$$\overline{m}_i = \frac{\left(m_i - m_i^{\min}\right)}{\left(m_i^{\max} - m_i^{\min}\right)}, i \in 1, ..., N \tag{2}$$

For fitness calculation, each normalized metric $\overline{m}_i$ is multiplied with a predefined weight factor w_i. The fitness f then calculates for each solution as denoted by:

$$f = \sqrt{\sum_{i=1}^{N} \left(w_i * \overline{m}_i\right)^4} \tag{3}$$

We create the solutions of the initial population by randomly assigning tasks to cores using a uniform distribution. The decision if a task should be split and on which core the second part of it should execute is also made randomly using a uniform distribution. For the creation of new solutions a bit-flip mutation technique is used. One task of a parent solution is selected randomly. The core the selected task is allocated to or the splitting property is modified to create a new solution. A change of the splitting property includes splitting a previously non-split task, undo the splitting for a task, choosing a different splitting position within the task or changing the allocation of the first or second part. Again, these choices are made randomly using a uniform distribution. To keep the search efficient, useless double-evaluation is prevented by a uniqueness check and impossible solutions with cores being loaded beyond 100% are eliminated directly from the population.

3.3   Derivation Approach

In this section we will present how we derive deployment guidelines from a set of best-ranked solutions.

Definition 1. *Let T_i and T_j be two different tasks of a task set τ of size N, with $i \neq j$ and $1 \leq i, j \leq N$. The affinity $a_{i,j}$ between those tasks is defined as:*

$$a_{i,j} = \begin{cases} 1 & \text{if } Allocation(T_i) = Allocation(T_j) \\ -1 & \text{if } Allocation(T_i) \neq Allocation(T_j) \end{cases} \tag{4}$$

$Allocation(T_i)$ hereby denotes to which core T_i is mapped. Note that the definition not only applies to tasks, but also to runnables.

Let the size of a solution set be M and consider that the K best solutions (according fitness), with $K < M$ and $K, M \in \mathbb{N}^+$, are considered.

Definition 2. *Let $a_{i,j}^k$ be the affinity between tasks T_i and T_j derived from the k-th best solution. The normalized affinity $\overline{a_{i,j}}$ between tasks T_i and T_j over all K best solutions then calculates as:*

$$\overline{a_{i,j}} = \frac{1}{K} \sum_{k=1}^{K} a_{i,j}^k \tag{5}$$

When $\overline{a_{i,j}} = 1$, tasks T_i and T_j were allocated to the same core in all of the K best solutions. On the contrary, when $\overline{a_{i,j}} = -1$, tasks T_i and T_j were allocated to different cores in all of the K best solutions.

Following Definition 2, the normalized affinities between all N tasks are calculated. These are the elements of the affinity matrix A_K for the K best solutions (Equation 6). Due to the fact that $a_{i,j} \equiv a_{j,i}$ for $i \neq j$, only the $\frac{N(N-1)}{2}$ elements of the upper triangular matrix of A_K have to be calculated.

$$A_K = \begin{pmatrix} \overline{a_{1,1}} & \overline{a_{1,2}} & \cdots & \overline{a_{1,j}} \\ \overline{a_{2,1}} & \overline{a_{2,2}} & \cdots & \overline{a_{2,j}} \\ \vdots & \vdots & \ddots & \vdots \\ \overline{a_{i,1}} & \overline{a_{i,2}} & \cdots & \overline{a_{i,j}} \end{pmatrix} \tag{6}$$

Algorithm 1. Deployment guideline extraction from an affinity matrix

---

Input: A_k, $t_{i,lower}$
Output: G
    $G \leftarrow \{\}$
    for $1 \leq i \leq N$ do
        for $1 \leq j \leq N$ do
            if $j > i$ then
                if $t_{i_{lower}} \leq |\overline{a_{i,j}}| \leq 1$ then
                    if $\overline{a_{i,j}} > 0$ then
                        $G \leftarrow G + \{i, j, 1\}$
                  else if $\overline{a_{i,j}} < 0$ then
                        $G \leftarrow G + \{i, j, -1\}$

Task #		1	2	2	2	3	3	3	3	4	5
	Runnable #	1	1	2	3	1	2	3	4	1	1
1	1		0.30	-0.28	-0.30	-0.30	-0.30	-0.30	-0.30	-0.30	-0.30
2	1			-0.78	0.20	-1.00	-1.00	-1.00	-0.95	-0.80	-0.70
2	2				0.78	0.78	0.78	0.78	0.78	0.78	0.78
2	3					-0.20	0.10	0.30	0.20	0.10	1.00
3	1						1.00	1.00	1.00	0.80	1.00
3	2							1.00	1.00	0.70	0.60
3	3								1.00	0.20	0.50
3	4									-0.35	0.35
4	1										-0.20
5	1										

Fig. 2. Example for an affinity matrix for a task set that consists of five tasks and 10 runnables in total

Algorithm 1 describes how the set of deployment guidelines G is derived from the affinity matrix A_K. For each element of the upper triangular matrix it is checked if the absolute value of the respective normalized affinity lies within the range $[t_{lower}, 1.0]$. t_{lower} hereby denotes the lower acceptance threshold to consider a normalized affinity as a guideline. If the check is successful, the tuple $\{i, j, A\}$, $A \in \{-1, 1\}$ is added to the set of guidelines. The tuple $\{1, 2, 1\}$ for example states that tasks T_1 and T_2 should be mapped to the same core. On the contrary, the tuple $\{1, 2, -1\}$ denotes that tasks T_1 and T_2 should be mapped to different cores.

3.4 Motivational Example

Consider a task set with five tasks. While Tasks 1, 4 and 5 contain one runnable, Task 2 contains three and Task 3 contains four runnables. Figure 2 shows an affinity matrix A_K for this task set. For example Runnable 2 of Task 3 in the figure denotes the second runnable of Task 3. For the derivation of deployment guidelines from the example affinity matrix, $t_{lower} = 0.95$ has been used. The respective cells of those normalized affinities considered for guideline derivation are colored in dark grey in Figure 2. In total 12 guidelines exist in this example. The guideline derived from the second row and the fifth column for example states that the first runnable of Task 2 should not execute together with the first runnable of Task 3.

4 Case Study

The goal of this case-study is to demonstrate the effectiveness of the presented deployment guideline derivation approach. In order to be able to quantify if near to optimal results can be achieved by the presented approach, we conducted an exhaustive search for a complex artificial task set. In order to conduct the exhaustive search in reasonable time, we evaluated only the BufferSize metric as defined in Section 2.3. Every solution in this case study thereby was evaluated using the model-based data consistency needs analysis included in the TA Tool Suite version 14.1.0.

The artificial task set which is comparable in terms of complexity to an automotive engine management system consists of 12 fully preemptive real-time tasks. Within the scope of the task set, 151 runnables are called which execute on a processor with three symmetric cores and a clock frequency of 360 Mhz for each core. Every core is managed by an independent instance of an OSEK scheduler. The runnables in total perform 20,178 accesses to 6,000 global variables with bit sizes in the range between 8 Bit and 256 Bit. This communication pattern has been generated randomly using an uniform distribution. The computational power demand of the different runnables has been modeled by a Weibull distribution in the system model [24].

The goal is to use the presented approach to produce near to optimal solutions with minimal BufferSize. Each of the tasks can be mapped to the cores individually and Tasks 1 and 12 can be split at two positions each. Tasks 1 and 12 are hereby divided into multiple execution phases where the runnables are called [10]. This results in over 8.6 million possible solutions which have been created and evaluated in an exhaustive search.

The deployment guidelines for BufferSize minimization have been derived in the following way: We performed an optimization run as described in Section 3.2 with an initial population size of 100. Moreover, the 50 best solutions were selected within each generation to create 50 new solutions. The optimization was configured to stop after the creation of 3,000 solutions. On the basis of these 3,000 solutions, the deployment guidelines have been derived.

Table 1. Configuration parameters A, B and C as well as sub-configuration parameters I – VI for guideline extraction

Configuration	Number of solutions [%]	K [%]	t_{lower}
A-I ... A-VI	10	{1, 3, 5}	{0.7, 0.9}
B-I ... B-VI	20	{1, 3, 5}	{0.7, 0.9}
C-I ... C-VI	30	{1, 3, 5}	{0.7, 0.9}

We selected 18 different parameter configurations for guideline derivation which are listed in Table 1. The parameter configurations consist of main configurations A, B and C as well as the respective sub-configurations I – VI. The main configuration denotes the percentage of the solutions from optimization in the order of creation which were used to derive the guidelines. The sub-configurations denote the K-best solutions and the lower acceptance threshold t_{lower}. Configuration A-I for instance denotes the following configuration: The first 10% of the solutions from optimization were used. The best 1% of those 10% were finally used for guideline extraction with a lower acceptance threshold $t_{lower} = 0.7$. For each configuration 3,000 solutions have been created. The tasks have hereby been randomly allocated to the cores while been compliant to the respective guideline.

Figure 3 denotes the comparison of the results of the exhaustive search and the deployment guideline derivation. The box plot for all BufferSize values from exhaustive search (ES) with a minimum of 111.17 kB and a maximum of 148.03 kB is shown in the left sub-figure. The right sub-figure shows the box plot for the BufferSize values from the solutions resulting from the application of the 18 different guideline derivation configurations. The best solution [3] yield a near to optimal minimum BufferSize of 112.6 kB. This is only 1.3% worse than the actual best solution. The worst solution created using the guidelines with a BufferSize of 137.12 kB is still 7.4% better than the actual worst solution. Moreover, the BufferSize of the worst solution created using the guidelines is 2.5% better than the median of all solutions from exhaustive search. The results indicate that deployment guidelines noticeably prevent the majority of worst solutions from being created. Moreover, only a small fraction (0.03% in this study) of all possible solutions have to be evaluated to find near to optimal solutions.

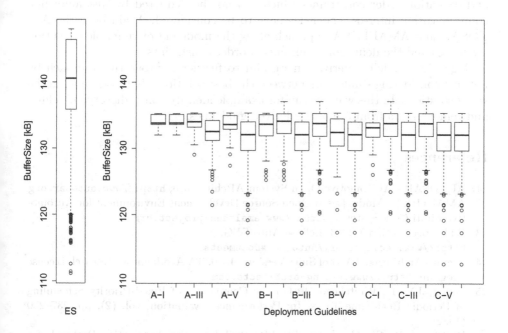

Fig. 3. Comparison of the BufferSize values from exhaustive search (ES) and BufferSize values from solutions produced by using the deployment guidelines

---

[3] The application of the deployment guidelines derived by using any of configurations A-VI, B-III, B-VI, C-III, C-V and C-VI lead to the best minimum Buffersize of 112.6 kB.

5 Conclusion

In this work we presented a model-based approach to derive deployment guidelines for the mapping of tasks to cores and for task splitting. The case study we conducted demonstrates that near to optimal results can be achieved with the presented approach which require the evaluation of only a small fraction of the overall design space. As the approach is compatible with AUTOSAR and the AMALTHEA meta-model, applicability for the industry is widely ensured. While the properties of a particular deployment solution can be exported to both formats, the AMALTHEA meta-model additionally allows the direct modeling of deployment guidelines as affinity constraints.

Future work in that field of research will include the extension of the deployment scope. Instead of splitting tasks with explicit synchronization to maintain the initial execution order of runnables, the runnables of a previously defined task are re-grouped and mapped to the cores. According to the proposal of Scheidenmann et al. [12], the decision base for this are the inter-dependencies between runnables. As a result, the execution sequence of runnables has to be optimized and execution order constraints which can not be deducted by just analyzing communication inter-dependencies have to be considered. Again both the AUTOSAR and AMALTHEA approach allow the modeling of runnable execution sequences and the definition of execution order constraints.

Regarding guideline derivation we aim to further improve the approach by not just considering similarities between the best solutions, but also between the worst solutions. In this way, we can for example identify contradictory guidelines and remove them from the set of derived guidelines.

References

1. AUTOSAR - AUTomotive Open System ARchitecture, http://www.autosar.org
2. AMALTHEA - Model Based Open Source Development Environment for Automotive Multi Core Systems, http://www.amalthea-project.org
3. BTF Specification V2.1.3, Eclipse Auto IWG,
   http://wiki.eclipse.org/Auto_IWG#Documents
4. Timing-Architects, TA Tool Suite Version 14.1.0. TA Academic & Research License Program, http://www.timing-architects.com
5. Leung, J.Y.-T., Whitehead, J.: On the Complexity of Fixed-Priority Scheduling of Periodic Real-Time Tasks. In: Performance Evaluation, vol. (2), pp. 237–250 (1982)
6. Rajkumar, R., Sha, L., Lehoczky, J.P.: Real-Time Synchronization Protocols for Multiprocessors. In: RTSS, vol. 88, pp. 259–269 (1988)
7. Coffman, E.G., Garey, M.R., Johnson, D.S.: Approximation algorithms for bin packing: A survey. In: Approximation Algorithms for NP-Hard Problems, pp. 46–93 (1996)
8. Mehiaoui, A., Tucci-Piergiovanni, S., Babau, J., Lemarchand, L.: Optimizing the Deployment of Distributed Real-Time Embedded Applications. In: 18th International Conference on Embedded and Real-Time Computing Systems and Applications (RTCSA). IEEE (2012)

9. Kienberger, J., Minnerup, P., Kuntz, S., Bauer, B.: Analysis and Validation of AUTOSAR Models. In: MODELSWARD (2014)
10. Claraz, D., Kuntz, S., Margull, U., Niemetz, M., Wirrer, G.: Deterministic Execution Sequence in Component Based Multi-Contributor Powertrain Control Systems. In: Proceedings of ERTS, Toulouse (2012)
11. Deb, K.: Multi-objective optimization. In: Search Methodologies, vol. 10 (2005)
12. Scheidenmann, K.D., Knapp, M., Stellwag, C.: Load Balancing in AUTOSAR-Multicore-Systemen. In: Elektroniknet, 3/2010, pp. 22–25 (2010)
13. Buttazzo, G.: Hard real-time computing systems: predictable scheduling algorithms and applications (2005)
14. Burns, A.: A survey of hard real-time scheduling algorithms and schedulability analysis techniques for multiprocessor systems. In: Techreport YCS-2009-443, University of York, Department of Computer Science (2009)
15. Scheickl, O., Rudorfer, M.: Automotive Real Rime Development Using a Timing-augmented AUTOSAR Specification. In: Proceedings of Embedded Real Time Software and Systems Conference, ERTS (2008)
16. Raab, P., Mottok, J., Meier, H.: OSEK-RTOS für Jedermann (Teil 1). In: Embedded Software Engineering Report, p. 14 (September 2009)
17. König, F., Boers, D., Slomka, F., Margull, U., Niemetz, M., Wirrer, G.: Application specific performance indicators for quantitative evaluation of the timing behavior for embedded real-time systems. In: Proceedings of the Conference on Design, Automation and Test in Europe (2009)
18. Chakraborty, S., Künzli, S., Thiele, L.: A general framework for analysing system properties in platform-based embedded system designs. In: Proceedings of the 6th Design, Automation and Test in Europe (DATE) Conference, pp. 190–195 (2003)
19. Deb, K., Pratap, A., Agarwal, S., Meyarivan, T.: A fast and elitist multiobjective genetic algorithm: NSGA-II. IEEE Transactions on Evolutionary Computation, 182–197 (April 2002)
20. Konak, A., Coit, D.W., Smith, A.E.: Multi-objective optimization using genetic algorithms: A tutorial. Reliability Engineering & System Safety 91(9), 992–1007 (2006)
21. Gries, M.: Methods for evaluating and covering the design space during early design development. Integration, the VLSI Journal 38(2), 131–183 (2004)
22. Monot, A., Navet, N.: Multicore scheduling in automotive ECUs. In: Proceedings of Embedded Real Time Software and Systems Conference, ERTS (2010)
23. Deubzer, M., Mottok, J., Margull, U., Niemetz, M., Wirrer, G.: Efficient Scheduling of Reliable Automotive Multi-core Systems with PD2 by Weakening PFAIR Tasksystem Requirements. In: Proceedings of the Automotive Safety & Security (2010)
24. Sailer, A., Schmidhuber, S., Deubzer, M., Alfranseder, M., Mucha, M., Mottok, J.: Optimizing the Task Allocation Step for Multi-Core Processors within AUTOSAR. In: Proceedings of the IEEE International Conference on Applied Electronics (2013)
25. Helm, C., Deubzer, M., Mottok, J.: Multicore Memory Architectures in Real-Time Systems. In: Proceedings of the Applied Research Conference (2013)
26. Carpenter, J., Funk, S., Holman, P., Srinivasan, A., Anderson, J., Baruah, S.: A categorization of real-time multiprocessor scheduling problems and algorithms. In: Handbook on Scheduling Algorithms, Methods, and Models (2004)

Adaptive Error and Sensor Management
for Autonomous Vehicles:
Model-Based Approach and Run-Time System

Jelena Frtunikj[1], Vladimir Rupanov[1], Michael Armbruster[2], and Alois Knoll[3]

[1] Fortiss GmbH, An-Institut Technische Universität München,
Guerickestraße 2. 25, 80805 München, Germany
{frtunikj,rupanov}@fortiss.org
[2] Siemens AG, Corporate Research and Technologies,
Otto-Hahn-Ring 6, 81730 München, Germany
michael.armbruster@siemens.com
[3] Fakultät für Informatik, Technische Universität München
Boltzmannstraße 3, 85748 Garching bei München, Germany
knoll@in.tum.de

Abstract. Over the past few years semi-autonomous driving functionality was introduced in the automotive market, and this trend continues towards fully autonomous cars. While in autonomous vehicles data from various types of sensors realize the new highly safety critical autonomous functionality, the already complex system architecture faces the challenge of designing highly reliable and safe autonomous driving system. Since sensors are prone to intermittent faults, using different sensors is better and more cost effective than duplicating the same sensor type because of diversity of reaction of different sensor typesto the same environmental condition. Specifying and validating sensors and providing technical means that enable usage of data from different sensors in case of failures is a challenging, time-consuming and error-prone task for engineers. Therefore, in this paper we present our model-based approach and a run-time system that improves the safety of autonomous driving systems by providing reusable framework managing different sensor setups in a vehicle in a case of a error. Moreover, the solution that we provide enables adaptive graceful degradation and reconfiguration by effective use of the system resources. At the end we explain in an example when and how the approach can be applied.

Keywords: safety, sensor models, autonomous driving systems, adaptive graceful degradation.

1 Introduction

Nowadays, the automotive industry faces the challenge to manage the electrics and electronics E/E-architecture's complexity [12] while in parallel more and more functionality (we will call each considered software-implemented function "system function" herein) is added within a vehicle. Moreover, a recent study [9]

F. Ortmeier and A. Rauzy (Eds.): IMBSA 2014, LNCS 8822, pp. 166–180, 2014.
© Springer International Publishing Switzerland 2014

shows that the E/E architecture faces the challenge of raising demand for vehicle automation up to fully automated driving. Therefore, the new E/E architecture must be scalable enough to support autonomous functionality, such as driving [10], parking or charging, and new driver assistance systems.

Due to high criticality and the requirement for fail-operational behavior of these functions, the E/E architecture must provide built-in mechanisms to achieve fault-tolerance. This means that systems should be able to resume affected functions without negligible interruption. Traditional fault tolerance techniques, such as installing multiple identical hardware backup systems, may be cost prohibitive for automotive systems. This introduces limits to the design effort and redundant resources that can be spent to make the system dependable. Graceful degradation mechanisms provide increased system dependability without need for providing redundant system resources. It enables, in case of a subsystem failure, resulting in the loss of some system resources, run-time evaluation of the system state and reconfiguration to be applied. The reconfiguration is required for efficient utilization of the remaining resources and different sensor/actuator modalities to execute the required functions.

A possible technical approach to enable graceful degradation consists of a formal framework for specifying degradation rules and a run-time system that ensures different non-functional qualities of interfaces and function behavior at run-time. The idea behind using a run-time system approach is to reuse the already developed safety measures for different systems and functions and save future development costs spent on non-functional aspects. This run-time system should implement technical means that can ensure fault-tolerance and enable adaptive graceful degradation of automotive system functions by effectively utilizing system resources and available data (supplied by different sources, e.g. sensors). However, the technical measures that enable the graceful degradation of functions must be generic, in order to be easily reused for all system functions in the vehicle.

The challenge considered in this paper is to provide a framework for generic (function-unspecific) graceful degradation applicable to all system functions that takes into consideration different types of data sources (sensors), their configuration and the available system resources. To do so, we consider each function as a composition of fault containment regions (FCR). Due to the fact that only the function developer has the knowledge which FCRs compose certain function and which system resources (e.g. CPU, memory etc.) are required by the function, the information has to be provided a priori as configuration parameters. Since the run-time system contains safety mechanisms that are capable of determining the "health" state of each FCR and has information about the available non-faulty system resources, it is able to identify/diagnose the "health" and degradation level of each function and to perform the necessary reconfigurations in order to provide the required functionalitiy in the system every moment. The reconfiguration is based on the available system resources, subsystems and their configuration, function criticality and function resource requirements. Our approach uses a formal function model and a set of formal constraints that describe the validity of possible function degradation. The approach (and the models that we use) allows to analyze at run-time if the desired system safety properties can be fulfilled and which set of functions should still be provided after one or multiple isolation FCRs or system resources.

This article is structured as follows. In Section 2, we first introduce the target scalable fault-tolerant E/E architecture and give a short overview of its main features. Afterwards we give a detailed description of the proposed concept, explaining the meta-model and the run-time environment in details. Section 4 presents an example explaining how this approach can be applied. Section 5 compares our approach against available solutions provided by industry and scientific community. The last section provides a brief conclusion and summarizes future steps.

2   RACE System Architecture and Safety Concept

As discussed in the introduction, future vehicles must support an increasing amount of new complex functionalities, such as predictive advanced driver assistance systems (ADAS) up to highly and fully automated driving and parking. Since, today's vehicle E/E architectures are very complex, extending the system with more hardware or software (which supports new functionalities) is not trivial at all. As a result, a new system architecture for modern cars is required.

Basic requirements for such an E/E architecture are to be scalable, open and thus easily expandable. Such architecture is proposed in the Robust and Reliant Automotive Computing Environment for Future eCars (RACE)[1] project [13]. The fail-operational centralized platform (Figure 1) consists of a redundant and reliable communication infrastructure based on a switched Ethernet topology, redundant power supply (blue and red lines in Figure 1) and redundant controllers. The centralized platform computer is composed from two or more duplex control-computers (DCC) and is responsible for executing all system functions. In order to guarantee fail-safe behavior, a DCC has two execution lanes that monitor input and output data mutually. In case an error occurs their results are discarded. Fail-operational behavior is guaranteed by a second DCC, which takes over the control tasks in case the first DCC has failed. The sensors and actuators used in the approach are smart and responsible for the low level control tasks. They are connected to the DCCs by a high-bandwidth Ethernet network.

A run-time system, together with the operating system, drivers, and components provides services, interconnects all system components. The run-time system facilitates generic safety mechanisms such as real-time deterministic scheduling, data exchange services, health monitoring and diagnosis, as well as an execution platform with time and space partitioning for applications running on the same HW and having different Automotive Safety Integrity Level (ASIL) classifications.

---

[1] Robust and Reliant Automotive Computing Environment for Future eCars, http://www.projekt-race.de/

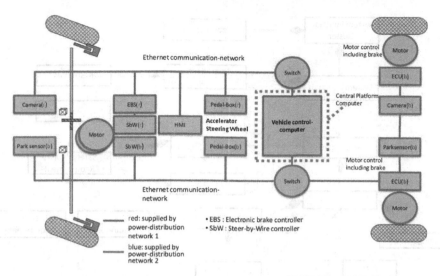

Fig. 1. System Architecture: fail-operational design

3 Proposed Approach

This section presents the proposed concept by giving insights in our modeling approach and the run-time system.

3.1 Domain-Specific Meta-model

In order to provide a generic approach dealing with system function degradation and dynamic resource reconfiguration, we need to introduce changes to the development process. We have to take into account the abstraction of functions from their former dedicated electronic control unit and the requirement, that functions can be integrated into a variety of architecture variants (we consider any combination of allocated functions to the control/computing units of the system as a variant). Therefore, data dependencies between functions, required sensor data and resource requirements (e.g., CPU and memory) need to be defined explicitly and in an unambiguous manner. To do so, at design time a domain-specific model is used. In Figure 2, a meta-model describing system functions, subsystems and their properties and dependencies, is depicted. This is the first step towards automated and uniform function description. The model enables composition of functions from different subsystems (HW and/or SW) and definition of degradation rules. The degradation rules represent specification of reduced functionality of a system function after occurrence of failures of the subsystems, from which the function is composed. The meta-model is used in a model-driven development tool, which allows modeling each function based on available data in the system and subsequent generation of data structures from this model for further run-time use by the run-time system. The resulting models are called models@run-time [2] since they contain information (e.g. required memory resources, degradation rules etc.) that is relevant at run-time.

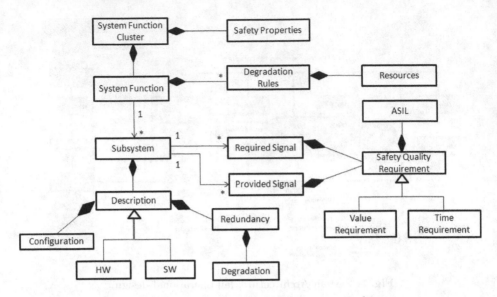

Fig. 2. Domain-specific meta-model defining function and its components

It is important to emphasize that each subsystem has a configuration description that expresses additional restrictions to be considered in the models. For example, if a subsystem is a sensor, the configuration description (Figure 3) contains such information as sensor position, viewing direction, maximum distance, type of target or collision objects w.r.t. geometry and material data, etc. [3]. The information is used to identify and validate allowed sensor configurations and check if data from one type of sensor in case of failure can be replaced by the data from another type of sensor.

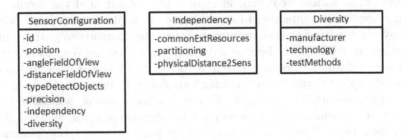

Fig. 3. Meta-Model defining sensor configuration

Moreover, each subsystem fulfills the assigned ASIL capability according to ISO 26262 [11]. In order to check if data from different sensors (considered and modeled as subsystems) can be fused to achieve certain higher ASIL level, properties such as diversity and independence have to be specified (Figure 3). Two subsystems are diverse in case they are produced by different manufacturers, use different technology and production processes, use different test methods etc. Independence property can be checked for example by checking partitions of functions or software elements, physical distance between hardware elements, common external resources, etc.

The information about the safety quality requirement is important for the health monitoring mechanisms that provide information required to determine the "health state" and degradation of the subsystem and thereby of a function.

3.2 Formal System Model

Below we present the formal foundation of the models used in our approach.

Definition 1. A vehicle $V = (F_a, SW_a, HW_a, D)$ is built up from a finite set of System Function Architecture F_a, a Software Architecture SW_a, a Hardware Architecture HW_a and a Deployment Configuration D.

Definition 2. System Function Architecture $F_a = (S_f, S_{fc})$ is composed by a finite set of System Functions S_f and a set of System Function Clusters S_{fc}.

Definition 3. A System Function set $S_f = \{sf_1, ...sf_n\}$ contains the system functions of the vehicle. A system function can be realized by one or more SW components and the required Sensors and Actuators.

Definition 4. System functions are grouped into a set of System Function Clusters $S_{fc} = \{sfc_1, ...sfc_k\}$, where $sfc_i \subseteq S_{fc}$ while $\forall i, j : sfc_i \cap sfc_j = \emptyset$. We define the mapping of $sf \in S_f$ to $sfc \in S_{fc}$ with $\epsilon(sfc) \rightarrow \{sf_i \in S_f | sf_i$ is mapped to $sfc\}$.

The grouping of sf is based on the safety properties of the functions such as: 1) criticality level of the function (ASIL); 2) performance requirements regarding fail-operational or fail-safe behavior. This way of grouping of the system functions reduces the system complexity with regard to the amount of combinations to be considered for deployment.

Definition 5. A Software Architecture is composed by a finite set of SW components $SW_a = \{s_1, ...s_m\}$ that belong to at least one system function $s \in SW_a$ to $sf \in S_f$ with $\alpha(s) \rightarrow \{s_i \in SW_a | s_i$ is mapped to $sf\}$.

Definition 6. A Hardware Architecture is composed by a finite set of HW components $HW_a = \{h_1, ...h_l\}$. The set is divided in set of execution nodes and set of peripheral actuator or sensor nodes $HW_a = HW_e \cup HW_p$.

Definition 7. The Deployment Configuration $D = (\delta(sfc))$ defines how the System Function Clusters and the corresponding SW components are deployed to the execution nodes HW_e. For $sfc \in S_{fc}$, we define to $\delta(sfc) \rightarrow \{h_i \in HW_e | sfc$ is executed to $h_i\}$.

The execution nodes represent the previously mentioned duplex control-computers (DCC). The set of the execution nodes is also called Central Platform Computer (CPC).

Definition 8. A fault is a physical defect, an imperfection or a flaw that occurs within some hardware or software component. An error is the manifestation of a fault and a failure occurs, when the component's behavior deviates from its specified behavior [1].

Depending on the level of abstraction, at which a system is explored, the occurrence of a malicious event may be classified as a fault, error or a failure. We define all malicious events that might occur within a subsystem as error.

Fault Tolerance deals with mechanisms (error and fault handling) in place. These mechanisms allow a system to deliver the required service in the presence of faults despite degraded level of that service.

Definition 9. A subsystem set is defined by the set of SW components and peripheral actuator or sensor nodes $SubS = SW_a \cup HW_p$.

Lemma 1. Following definitions 3, 5, 6 and 9, a system function is unambiguously defined by a set of logical subsystems $SF = \{subS_1, ...subS_k\}$.

The subsystems represent Fault-Containment Regions (FCR) which can be seen as black boxes w.r.t. safety and error handling. The FCRs have precisely specified interfaces in the domains of time and value, which are required to detect anomalies at run-time. This means, in a case of error the FCR and with that the subsystem is marked and handled as faulty. The alteration of subsystem state can be expressed formally by the definition of new state transition $subSState_{ok} \rightarrow subSState_{err}$. This definition and handling is required in order to be sure that the fault within the FCR will not be extended out of the defined subsystem borders.

Each subsystem $subS$ has a defined configuration $subSConfig$. The configuration information is taken into consideration when an evaluation about interchangeable subsystems is performed. In case of a failure of one $subS$, the data required from that $subS$ can be substituted by the before validated interchangeable subsystem.

Definition 10. Based on the subsystem $subS$ "health" state (error free or erroneous) and the redundancy information, different degradation level of the subsystem $subSDeg^0$, $subSDeg^1$, ..,$subSDeg^N$ can be defined.

The subsystem degradation level (also named only degradation) can take values form 0 to N. The zero degradation level is the lowest one and represent fully functionality, while the Nth level is the highest one and means no functionality available (the subsystem is in erroneous state s_{err}).

Definition 11. A system function sf degradation predicate $sfDeg^x$ is a boolean function over a set of degradation level states of the subsystems composing the function. The set of system function degradation predicates represents the specification of the function and system degradation w.r.t. safety. For each degradation predicate a set of attributes $A = \{memoryResources, runtimeResources\}$ are specified and are used by the reconfiguration mechanism that keeps system safety after a failure of execution component. A system function degradation predicate can also get values form 0 to N.

Reconfiguration Mechanism: In case of execution nodes scarce (due to a failure), a reconfiguration mechanism has to be activated in the system in order to make the decision about which system functions to be run in the system and which not. The decision criteria needs to take into consideration the available resources (execution and system resources e.g. different sensors) and the criticalites of the functions. As this is obviously a computationally complex multi-dimensional optimization problem that has to be solved at run-time, techniques that are not computationally extensive like greedy approximation algorithm should be used.

3.3   Run-Time System and Degradation Approach

Even though our approach is based on a formal foundation, here we explain the
approach in more details in an informal way for the sake of clarity.

As mentioned before, we consider a system function $sf \in S_f$ as a composition of subsystems. Since the subsystems have precisely specified interfaces
in the domains of time and value, that information is used for configuring the
safety mechanisms of the run-time system, which provide information and error
indications required to determine the "health" state of the corresponding subsystems. We define the following relevant FCRs/subsystems of a system function:
1) sensors or actuators and 2) application software components - SW functions
implementing the system function control algorithm, including respective partitions (in both time and space domains). The defined FCRs also include the
communication links, through which they send and/or receive data.

In order to enable calculation and appropriate determination of function
degradation level at run-time, a run-time system component named System
Function Manager (SFM) identifies the state of each subsystem belonging to
each system function. This means the SFM is able to determine the "health"
state (correct or faulty) and the degradation level of all subsystems based on the
system state and the error indications that result from diagnosis of these specific subsystems. More detailed explanation of the safety mechanisms that the
run-time system offers can be found in [5]. The process of fault detection (health
monitoring), consolidation of error indications, "health" state determination and
the mapping to run-time system components is depicted on Figure 4.

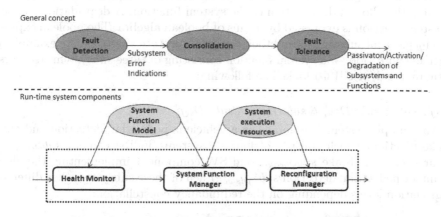

Fig. 4. Separation of fault detection from fault handling

Depending on the error indications that the health monitoring run-time system components generate and the redundancy type of the subsystem (e.g. single,
double, triple redundancy etc.), the SFM identifies the "health" state and the
degradation level of each subsystem at run-time. SFM is based on a developed
algorithm that evaluates the error indications, which are a result of detected
faults, and in that way it provides the required information that represents the

basis for error handling. The task of the System Function Manager is mainly focused on the phases of isolation, passivization and activation on of all subsystems $subS$ belonging to all system functions, based on their current "health" state. The System Function Manager together with the Reconfiguration Manager determine the next "health" state. In case of a permanent fault, the FCR and the corresponding $subS$ is isolated. In a case of transient fault, the FCR is passivated, and if no faults more are found, the FCR continues to be active. The mentioned "health" states can be applied to all types of subsystems (FCRs) that are defined in the system.

Based on the "health" states and the redundancy information, we have defined the following degradation level of the subsystems $subS$:

- degradation level 0 ($subSDeg^0$): data available (no fault detected and the subsystem is "active")
- degradation level 1 ($subSDeg^1$): data available but data coming via one network link in the previously mentioned system architecture are not available (and the subsystem is "active")
- degradation level 2 ($subSDeg^2$): data available but one redundant subsystem from same type is faulty (lost) (and the subsystem is "active")
- degradation level N ($subSDeg^N$): data are not available due to a fault (and the subsystem is "isolated")

The information about the degradation level of each subsystem is used to calculate the degradation of a system function $sfDeg$ at run-time. Since only the function developer has the knowledge and the expertise, which subsystems compose and are required for certain system function, he/she is responsible for defining the allowed degradation of the system function. A degradation rule for a system function is expressed by means of boolean algebra. The boolean expression includes all subsystems and their degradation state $subSDeg$. An example of such an expression for a system function consisting of three subsystems (sensors, actuators and/or SWC) looks like following:

$$sfDeg^1 = subSDeg_i^0 \wedge subSDeg_j^1 \wedge subSDeg_k^0$$

An example system function sf in a vehicle is pedestrian detection and auto brake function, which consists of four subsystems/FCRs: camera $subS_{camera}$, radar $subS_{radar}$, brake $subS_{brake}$, and SW component implementing the algorithm for pedestrian detection $subS_{pdswc}$. Each of these subsystems has different degradation levels depending on the redundancy constellation:

- camera: $subSDeg_{camera}^0$ and $subSDeg_{camera}^N$
- radar: $subSDeg_{radar}^0$, $subSDeg_{radar}^1$ and $subSDeg_{radar}^N$
- brake: $subSDeg_{brake}^0$ and $subSDeg_{brake}^N$
- pedestrian detection SW component: $subSDeg_{pdswc}^0$ and $subSDeg_{pdswc}^N$

The degradation rules specified by the predicates define the dependency between a specific function and the sensors or actuators and other applications, whose data is required in order the function to work. Based on the degradation rules and the actual degradation level $subSDeg_i^x$ of each subsystem, the boolean expressions are evaluated at run-time and the "best" system function degradation $sfDeg$ is calculated. For the pedestrian detection and auto brake function the system function developer has specified the following degradation rules:

$$sfDeg_{pedDet}^0 = subSDeg_{camera}^0 \wedge subSDeg_{radar}^0 \wedge subSDeg_{brake}^0 \wedge subSDeg_{pdswc}^0$$

$$sfDeg_{pedDet}^1 = subSDeg_{camera}^0 \wedge subSDeg_{radar}^1 \wedge subSDeg_{brake}^0 \wedge subSDeg_{pdswc}^0$$

$$sfDeg_{pedDet}^2 = subSDeg_{camera}^0 \wedge subSDeg_{radar}^N \wedge subSDeg_{brake}^0 \wedge subSDeg_{pdswc}^0$$

......

$$sfDeg_{pedDet}^N = \neg(sfDeg_{pedDet}^0 \vee sfDeg_{pedDet}^1 \vee sfDeg_{pedDet}^2 \vee sfDeg_{pedDet}^3 \cdots \vee sfDeg_{pedDet}^{N-1})$$

Based on the the degradation calculation algorithm shown in Algorithm 1, the actual system function degradation level is calculated at run-time for all active sf belonging to all active system function clusters sfc.

Algorithm 1. Degradation calculation

---
1. **for all** SFCluster sfc in SFClusterList $sfcList$ **do**
2.   **for all** SysFunction sf in SFCluster sfc **do**
3.   **for all** SubSystems $sbubS$ in SysFunction sf **do**
4.   calculateHealthStateAndDegLevel($subS$,$subS.Deg$)
5.   **end for**
6.   calculateSysFDegLevel(sf,$sf.degRules$,$sf.subSs$)
7.   **end for**
8. **end for**

As stated in [8], autonomous vehicles have various sensor types with different modalities. Since sensors are prone to intermittent faults, using a different sensor is better than duplicating the same type of sensors. Different types of sensors typically react to the same environmental condition in diverse ways. For example, in case a vehicle is equipped with radars for blind spot detection, if rear-looking radar does not work properly, a software algorithm detecting obstacles from images obtained via rear-looking camera can be used.

With the above in mind, our approach offers the possibility to define additional degradation rules including different types of sensors in cases when different types of sensors provide the same data/information. This is beneficial especially in the case of a failure of one or more data sources. In such a situation, a possibility to switch to a different source providing the same information (that has correct configuration w.r.t. position, viewing direction etc.) exists and the system function still remains fully available in the system. The correct configuration of two interchangeable sensor subsystems is validated in our model-driven development tool and the information is available at run-time. For example, properties like angle of view ais checked:

$$subSConfig_{lidar}.angleFOV >= subSConfig_{radar}.angleFOV$$

$$subSConfig_{lidar}.distanceFOV >= subSConfig_{radar}.distanceFOV$$

An example of such a case for the previously described pedestrian detection and auto brake function, is when data from Radar $subS_{radar}$ sensor can be "substituted" by data produced by a LiDAR (Light detection and ranging) $subS_{lidar}$ sensor. We have to mention that the different sensor might require different monitoring functions that help at run-time the "health" state of the sunsystem to be calculated. Additional degradation rules for the pedestrian detection and auto brake functionality like the one below can be specified. Having this opportunity is useful and important since various algorithms using different types of sensors even for a common goal may consume significantly different amount of resources.

$$sfDeg^0_{pedDet} = subSDeg^0_{camera} \wedge subSDeg^0_{lidar} \wedge subSDeg^0_{brake} \wedge subSDeg^0_{pdswc}$$

The approach also offers the possibility to model data redundancy not only from same types of units but also from diverse ones. Different degradation levels of the units, are supported in case of diverse units and additional degradation rules for the function can be specified. The advantage of using data from both types of units lies in the possibility for data fusion and obtaining more thereby accurate information. With that also a higher ASIL level can be achieved. In case of the above example, both radar $subSDeg_{radar}$ and LiDAR $subSDeg_{lidar}$ degradation can be included in the degradation rules of the function:

$$sfDeg^0_{pedDet} = subSDeg^0_{camera} \wedge (subSDeg^0_{radar} \vee subSDeg^0_{lidar}) \wedge subSDeg^0_{brake} \wedge subSDeg^0_{pdswc}$$

Based on the fact that the function developer also specifies the required resources for each degradation level and the criticality level of the functions (as shown in the meta-model Figure 2), the run-time system has the possibility to react appropriately in case of resource scarce. For example, if not enough system resources are available, the run-time system can deploy and run all high criticality functions in the full functionality, but the less critical ones in a degraded mode in which they require fewer resources. The mentioned decision is done by the Reconfiguration Manager (RM) component that dynamically decides if and at which degradation level to execute each function. An Execution Manager component, which manages the scheduling and execution of functions, performs the required schedule changes.

3.4   Approach Benefits

To sum up, we enable adaptive graceful degradation for all system function in a generic and uniform manner. Our degradation specifications have several advantages. The specifications: 1) are high-level, ensuring that the user is not overwhelmed by implementation details. Our specifications require users only to describe desired behavior, not implement techniques for achieving it; 2) are concerned only with describing functional behavior, yet they provide a natural interface to the models used to describe the failures and degradation. Since the system function developer only has to focus on the description of each function instead of developing technical measures that manage graceful degradation, we save his efforts and time, by providing a run-time system that does that automatically for him. Furthermore, the formalized specification and the usage of generated models@run-time guarantee consistency and completeness in the critical transition from the requirements engineering to software design, where lot of errors can be introduced into the system by using conventional, non-formal techniques.

4   Example

This section presents how the previously explained concept can be used in a scenario, where pedestrian detection and auto brake system function in a vehicle is composed from data coming from different sensors.

The pedestrian detection and auto brake technology usually relies on data that come from camera, radar and/or LiDAR subsystems. Depending on the available data sources the function requires different amount of resources to detect pedestrians in the nearby environment of the vehicle. With the help of the model-based development tool, the developer of the function specifies the degradation rules for the different subsystem combinations and the different resource requirements for each degradation level of the function. In our case, the degradation rules stated in the previous section reflect the different possibilities for describing the function. The function has a $sfDeg^0_{pedDet}$ when all subsystems are fully available ($subSDeg^0_i$). The function degrades to second level $sfDeg^2_{pedDet}$ when the radar subsystem is not available any more $subSDeg^N_{radar}$. However, since in the system the data coming from the LiDAR sensor (whose configuration has been validated before) can substitute the data from the radar sensor the pedestrian detection and auto brake function can be run again at $sfDeg^0_{pedDet}$. This is important for autonomous vehicles where this functionality is very essential and contributes to the overall system safety.

In addition to the rules, for each of them the requirements regarding the run-time execution resources (worst-case execution time- WCET) and the RAM and ROM are stated in ms and $MBytes$ respectively. For example, for $sfDeg^0_{pedDet}$ where we have the full functionality the resource requirements are the following ones: $WCET = 800ms$, $RAM = 10MBytes$ and $ROM = 10MBytes$. In comparison to that for $sfDeg^2_{pedDet}$ the $WCET = 500ms$, $RAM = 5MBytes$ and $ROM = 5MBytes$. This information is useful in case of computing resources scarce, since a function can be executed in a degraded mode where it (normally) requires less resources.

5   Related Work

In this section, we discuss the related work and we present ones that are most relevant to our work and state the differences between the approaches.

Tichy [7], suggest an approach that includes formal visual specification technique to describe known standard fault tolerance solutions. They propose fault tolerance patterns (similar to our degradation rules) which capture the essential structure and relevant deployment restrictions of these solutions. In contrast to our approach, they do not aim at self-reconfiguration of the system at run-time and do not offer any solution for sensor management.

A MDE approach for managing different sensor setups in a cyber-physical system development environment to leverage automated model verification, support system testing, and enable code generation is presented in [4]. The models are used as the single point of truth to configure and generate sensor setups for system validations in a 3D simulation environment. This approach only focuses on the validation process and the verification of possible pin assignments for connecting the required sensors and does not offers a run-time system that enables usage of the data from different sensors and a possibility for degradation.

Authors in [14] aim at graceful degradation by adapting the functionality of a system to the driving situation and the available resources. Since adaptation significantly complicates the development of embedded systems, they present an approach to the model-based design of adaptive embedded systems that allows coping with the increased complexity posed by adaptation. Furthermore, they show how the obtained models can be formally verified by a model checker. This approach is similar to ours, but in our opinion it is applicable at design time.

The industrial automotive AUTOSAR standard [15] describes a platform which allows implementing future vehicle applications and minimizes the current barriers between functional domains. One of the main objectives of AUTOSAR version 4 release is to support safety related applications by implementing features to comply with the safety ISO 26262 standard requirements. The AUTOSAR execution environment safety capabilities focus on the correct execution of software components only, and the monitoring of functional behavior of the system functions is neglected. Currently 3 levels of statically pre-configured mode managers that allow degradation are supported by AUTOSAR. However they lead to a cluttered and complex implementation. In comparison to this with our framework we enable easy and reusable system and function degradation by specifying intuitive degradation rules, so our approach can be seen as an extension and improvement to AUTOSAR.

6   Conclusion and Future Work

Motivated by new challenges that automotive architectures face, we presented a domain-specific meta-model that enables to compose different high-level functions from different components, define their dependencies and their required resources. Furthermore, we specified run-time system components that, based on this information. are able to calculate the available degradation level of all system functions at run-time, and based on the resources and the information about the criticality of the functions, perform appropriate reconfiguration (self-repair in case of failures).

Acknowledgment. The work presented in this paper is partially funded by the German Federal Ministry for Economic Affairs and Energy (BMWi) through the project Robust and Reliant Automotive Computing Environment for Future eCars.

References

1. Laprie, J.C.C., Avizienis, A., Kopetz, H.: Dependability: Basic Concepts and Terminology. Springer-Verlag New York, Inc. (1992)
2. Lehmann, G., Blumendorf, M., Trollmann, F., Albayrak, S.: Meta-modeling Runtime Models. In: MoDELS Workshops (2010)
3. Roth, E., Dirndorfer, T., von Neumann-Cosel, K., Fischer, M.-O., Ganslmeier, T., Kern, A., Knoll, A.: Analysis and Validation of Perception Sensor Models in an Integrated Vehicle and Environment Simulation. In: Proceedings of the 22nd Enhanced Safety of Vehicles Conference (2011)
4. Mamun, M., Berger, C., Hansson, J.: MDE-based Sensor Management and Verification for a Self-Driving Miniature Vehicle. In: Proceedings of the 13th Workshop on Domain-Specific Modeling (2013)
5. Frtunikj, J., Rupanov, V., Camek, A., Buckl, C., Knoll, A.: A Safety Aware Run-Time Environment for Adaptive Automotive Control Systems. In: Embedded Real-Time Software and Systems, ERTS2 (2014)
6. Shelton, C.P., Koopman, P., Nace, W.: A framework for scalable analysis and design of system-wide graceful degradation in distributed embedded systems. In: Proceedings of the Eighth International Workshop on Object-Oriented Real-Time Dependable Systems (2003)
7. Tichy, M., Giese, H.: Extending Fault Tolerance Patterns by Visual Degradation Rules. In: Proceedings of the Workshop on Visual Modeling for Software Intensive Systems, VMSIS (2005)
8. Urmson, C., et al.: Autonomous driving in urban environments: Boss and the Urban Challenge. Journal of Field Robotics Special Issue on the 2007 DARPA Urban Challenge, Part I (2008)
9. Bernhard, M., et al.: The Software Car: Information and Communication Technology (ICT) as an Engine for the Electromobility of the Future, Summary of results of the "eCar ICT System Architecture for Electromobility" research project sponsored by the Federal Ministry of Economics and Technology (2011)
10. Dmitri, D., et al.: Path Planning for Autonomous Vehicles in Unknown Semi-structured Environments. Sage Publications, Inc. (2010)
11. International Organization for Standardization: ISO/DIS 26262 - Road vehicles. Functional safety. Technical Committee 22, ISO/TC 22 (2011)
12. Broy, M., Kruger, I.H., Pretschner, A., Salzmann, C.: Engineering Automotive Software. Proceedings of the IEEE (2007)

13. Sommer, S., et al.: RACE: A Centralized Platform Computer Based Architecture for Automotive Applications. In: Vehicular Electronics Conference (VEC) and the International Electric Vehicle Conference, IEVC (2013)
14. Adler, R., Schaefer, I., Schuele, T.: Model-Based Development of an Adaptive Vehicle Stability Control System, Modellbasierte Entwicklung von eingebetteten Fahrzeugfunktionen, MBEFF (2008)
15. AUTOSAR Group: AUTomotive Open System ARchitecture (AUTOSAR) Release 4.1 (2013)

Safety Assessment of an Electrical System with AltaRica 3.0

Hala Mortada[1], Tatiana Prosvirnova[1], and Antoine Rauzy[2]

[1] Computer Science Lab, Ecole Polytechnique, Route de Saclay, Palaiseau, France
{Hala.Mortada,Prosvirnova}@lix.polytechnique.fr
[2] Chaire Blériot Fabre, LGI Ecole Centrale de Paris Grande voie des vignes,
92295 Châtenay-Malabry, France
Antoine.Rauzy@ecp.fr

Abstract. This article presents the high level, modeling language AltaRica 3.0 through the safety assessment of an electrical system. It shows how, starting from a purely structural model, several variants can be derived.Two of them target a compilation into Fault Trees and two others target a compilation into Markov chains. Experimental results are reported to show that each of these variants has its own interest. It also advocates that this approach made of successive derivation of variants is a solid ground to build a modeling methodology onto.

Keywords: AltaRica3.0, Complex systems, Reliability, Modeling, Safety.

1 Introduction

The increasing complexity of industrial systems calls for the development of sophisticated engineering tools. This is indeed true for all engineering disciplines, but especially for safety and reliability engineering. Experience shows that traditional modeling formalisms such as Fault Trees, Petri nets or Markov processes do not allow a smooth integration of risk analysis within the overall development process. These analysis require both considerable time and expertise. The specialization and the lack of model's structures make it difficult to share models amongst stakeholders, to maintain them throughout the life-cycle of the systems, and to reuse them from one project to another.

The AltaRica modeling language ([1],[2]) has been created at the end of the nineties to tackle these problems. AltaRica makes it possible to design high-level models with a structure that is very close to the functional or the physical architecture of the system under study. Its constructions allow models to be structured into a hierarchy of reusable components. It is also possible to associate graphical representations to these components in order to make models visually close to Process and Instrumentation Diagrams. The formal semantics of AltaRica allowed the development of a versatile set of processing tools such as compilers into Fault Trees ([2]), model-checkers ([3]) or stochastic simulators ([4]). A large number of successful industrial experiments with the language have been reported (see e.g. [5], [6], [7], [8] and [9]). Despite its quality, AltaRica faced

F. Ortmeier and A. Rauzy (Eds.): IMBSA 2014, LNCS 8822, pp. 181–194, 2014.

two issues of very different natures. First, systems with instant feedback's loops turned out to be hard to handle. Second, constructs of model's structuring were not fully satisfying.

AltaRica 3.0 [10] is a new version of the language that has been designed to tackle these two issues. Regarding model structuring, AltaRica 3.0 implements the prototype-oriented paradigm [11]. This paradigm fits well with the level of abstraction reliability and safety analysis stand at. Regarding mathematical foundations, AltaRica 3.0 is based on Guarded Transition Systems (GTS) [12]. GTS combine the advantages of state/event formalisms such as Petri nets and combinatorial formalisms such as block diagrams. This combination is necessary to model system patterns namely cold redundancies, cascading failures or remote interactions.

AltaRica 3.0 comes with a variety of assessment tools. In this article, we show how, starting from the same root model, different variants can be obtained by successive refinements: a first series targeting a compilation into Fault Trees and a second one targeting a compilation into Markov chains. Each of these variants capture a particular aspect of the system under study. We advocate that this approach made of successive derivation of variants is a solid ground to build a modeling methodology onto.

The remainder of this article is organized as follows. Section 2 presents the electrical system that is used as a red-wire example throughout the paper. Section 3 discusses how to describe the architecture of the system with a purely structural model. Section 4 proposes a first variant of this structural model which targets a compilation into Fault Trees. Section 5 presents a second variant which targets a compilation into Markov Chains. Finally, section 6 concludes this article.

2   Red Wire Example

Figure 1 shows a simple electrical system with cascade redundancies borrowed from [13] (we present it here with some additional complexity).

In a normal operating mode, the busbar BB is powered by the grid GR either through line 1 or through line 2. Each line is made of an upper circuit breaker CBUi, a transformer TRi and a lower circuit breaker CBDi. The two lines are in cold redundancy: Let's assume for instance that line 1 was working and that it failed either because one of the circuit breakers CBU1 or CBD1 failed, or because the transformer failed. In this case, the line 2 is attempted to start. This requires opening the circuit breaker CBD1 (if possible/necessary) and closing the circuit breakers of line 2. Since line 2 was out of service, the circuit breaker CBD2 was necessarily open.

If both lines fail, the diesel generator DG is expected to function, which requires closing the circuit breaker CB3. Circuit breakers may fail to open and to close on demand. The diesel generator may fail on demand as well. The grid GR may be lost either because of an internal failure or because of a short circuit in the transformer TRi followed by a failure to open the corresponding circuit breaker CBUi.

The two transformers are subject to a common cause failure.

There is a limited repair crew that can work on only two components at a time. After maintenance, the components are as good as new, but may be badly reconfigured.

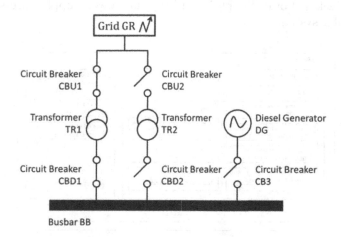

Fig. 1. A small electrical system

The problem is to estimate the reliability and the availability of this system. This example is small but concentrates on a number of modeling difficulties (warm redundancies, on demand failures, short-circuit propagation, common cause failures, limited resources), due to its multi-domains aspects.

3   Describing the Architecture of the System

The first step in analyzing a system consists of describing its functional and physical architecture. Figure 1 describes a possible decomposition of our electrical system. This decomposition deserves three important remarks.

First, it mixes functional and physical aspects. In fact, due to the small size of the example, only basic blocks (leaves of the decomposition) represent physical components. The others represent functions. We could consider functional and physical architectures separately. However, considering both in the same diagram simplifies things here. Moreover, it matches better with the usual way of designing models for safety and dependability analysis. Note also that at this step, we do not consider interactions between components.

Second, the underlying structure of this decomposition is not a tree, but a directed acyclic graph for the external power supply is shared between Line 1 and Line 2. As we shall see, this has very important consequences in terms of structuring constructs.

Third, the system embeds five circuit breakers and two transformers. We can assume that the circuit breakers on the one hand, the transformers on the other hand are all the same. From a modeling point of view, it means that we need to be able to define generic components and to instantiate them in different places in our model. On the contrary, components like "Primary Power Supply", "Backup Power Supply" and "Busbar Power Supply" are specific to that particular system.

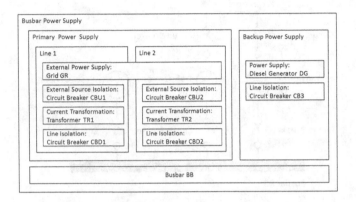

Fig. 2. Architecture of the Busbar Power Supply System

The structure of the AltaRica 3.0 model that reflects this architecture is sketched in Figure 2. In AltaRica 3.0, components are represented by means of blocks. Blocks contain variables, events, transitions, and everything necessary to describe their behavior. At this step, the behavioral part is still empty. Blocks can also contain other blocks and form hierarchies. The block "BusbarPowerSupply" contains two blocks: "PrimaryPowerSupply" and "BackupPowerSupply". "BusbarPowerSupply" is the parent block of "PrimaryPowerSupply" and an ancestor of "CBU1". Objects defined in a block are visible in all its ancestors. For instance, if the class "CircuitBreaker" defines an event "failToOpen", the instantiation of this event in "CBU1" is visible in the block "BusbarPowerSupply" through the dot notation, i.e. "PrimaryPowerSupply.Line1.CBU1.failToOpen".

An instance "GR" of the class "Grid" is declared in the block "PrimaryPowerSupply". It is convenient to be able to refer to it as "GR" as if it was declared in "Line1". This is the purpose of the "embeds" clause. This clause makes it clear that "GR" is part of "Line1", even if it is probably shared with some sibling blocks.

Classes in AltaRica 3.0 are similar to classes in object-oriented programming languages (see e.g. [14], [15] for conceptual presentations of the object-oriented paradigm). A class is a block that can be instantiated, i.e. copied, elsewhere in the model. There are several differences however between blocks and classes. AltaRica 3.0 makes a clear distinction between "on-the-shelf", stabilized knowledge, for which classes are used, from the model itself, i.e. the implicit main block and all its descendants. Such a distinction has been conceptualized in C-K-theory ([16]). The implicit main block can be seen as the sandbox in which the analyst is designing his model. Declaring a class is in some sense creating another sandbox. Amongst other consequences, this means that it is neither possible to refer in a class to an object which is declared outside of the class, nor to declare a class inside another one or in a block. A class may of course contain blocks and instances of other classes up to the condition that this introduces no circular definition (recursive data types are not allowed in AltaRica 3.0). To summarize, AltaRica 3.0 borrows concepts to both object-oriented programming and prototype-oriented programming [11] - blocks can be seen as prototypes - so to provide the analyst with powerful structuring constructs that are well suited for the level of abstraction of safety analysis.

```
block BusbarPowerSupply
  block PrimaryPowerSupply
    Grid GR;
    block Line1
      embeds GR;
      CircuitBreaker CBU1, CBD1;
      Transformer TR1;
    end
    block Line2
      embeds GR;
      CircuitBreaker CBU2, CBD2;
      Transformer TR2;
    end
  end
  block BackupPowerSupply
    DieselGenerator DG;
    CircuitBreaker CB3;
  end
end
class Grid
end
...
```

Fig. 3. Structure of the AltaRica 3.0 Model for the Electrical System (partial view)

4 Targeting Compilation into Fault Trees

4.1 A Simple Block-Diagram like Model

We shall consider first a very simple model, close to a block diagram, in which basic blocks have a (Boolean) input, a (Boolean) output and an internal state (WORKING or FAILED). This basic block changes its state, from WORKING

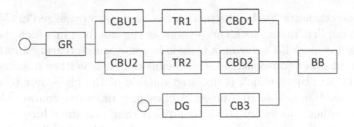

Fig. 4. A Block Diagram for the electric supply system

to FAILED, when the event "failure" occurs. The diagram for the whole system is pictured in Figure 4.

The AltaRica code for the diagram (with the architecture defined in the previous section) is sketched in Figure 5. The class "NonRepairableComponent" declares a state variable "s" and two Boolean flow variables: "inFlow" and "outFlow". "s" takes its value in the domain "ComponentState" and is initially set to WORKING. "inFlow" and "outFlow" are (at least conceptually) reset to false after each transition firing. Their default value is false. The class also declares the event "failure" which is associated with an exponential probability distribution of parameter "lambda". This parameter has the value "1.0e-4" unless stated otherwise.

After the declaration part, which consists in declaring flow and state variables, events and parameters, comes the behavioral part. This behavioral part itself includes transitions and assertions. In our example, there is only one transition and one assertion. The transition is labeled with the event "failure" and can be read as follows. The event "failure" can occur when the condition "s == WORKING" is satisfied. The firing of the transition gives the value FAILED to the variable "s".

The assertion describes the action to be performed to stabilize the system after each transition firing (and in the initial state). In our example, the variable "outFlow" takes the value true if "s" is equal to WORKING and "inFlow" is true, and false otherwise. In the initial state, all components are working, so the value true propagates from the input flow of the grid "GR" to the output flow of the system. If the circuit breaker "CBU2" fails, then the value false propagates from the output flow of "CBU2" to the output flow of the Line 2.

It would be possible to copy-paste the declaration of "NonRepairableComponent" in the declaration of the basic components of our model ("Grid", "CircuitBreaker", etc.). However, AltaRica 3.0 is an object-oriented language and thus provides a much more elegant way to obtain the same result: inheritance. It suffices to declare that the class "Grid" inherits from class "NonRepairableComponent". This is done in the code of Figure 5. In the class "Grid" the default value of the input flow is set to "true". This change makes the grid a source block. The remainder of the model consists in plugging inputs and outputs of the components in order to build the system. Note that the resulting model is

```
domain ComponentState { WORKING, FAILED }
class NonRepairableComponent
  Boolean s (init = WORKING);
  Boolean inFlow, outFlow (reset = false);
  event failure (delay = exponential(lambda));
  parameter Real lambda = 0.0001;
  transition
    failure: s == WORKING -> s := FAILED;
  assertion
    outFlow := s == WORKING and inFlow;
end
class Grid extends NonRepairableComponent(inFlow.reset = true);
end
...
block BusbarPowerSupply
  Boolean outFlow(reset = false);
  Grid GR;
  block PrimaryPowerSupply
    Boolean outFlow (reset = false);
    block Line1
      Boolean outFlow (reset = false);
      embeds GR;
      CircuitBreaker CBU1, CBD1;
      Transformer TR1;
      assertion
        CBU1.inFlow := GR.outFlow;
        ...
    end
    block Line2
    ... // similar to Line1
    end
    assertion
      outFlow := Line1.outFlow or Line2.outFlow;
  end
  ...
  assertion
    outFlow := PrimaryPowerSupply.outFlow or BackupPowerSupply.outFlow;
end
```

Fig. 5. A simple model targeting a compilation into Fault Trees (partial view)

not just a flat block diagram, but a hierarchical one. The compilation of this model into Fault Trees is performed according to the principle defined in [2]. The idea is to build a Fault Tree such that:

- The basic events of this Fault Tree are the events of the AltaRica model.
- There is (at least) an intermediate event for each pair (variable, value) of the AltaRica model.

- For each minimal cutset of the Fault Tree rooted by an intermediate event (variable, value), there exists at least one sequence of transitions in the AltaRica model labeled with events of the cutset that ends up in a state where this variable takes this value. Moreover, this sequence is minimal in the sense that no strict subset of the minimal cutsets can label a sequence of transitions ending up in a state where this variable takes this value.

For technical reasons, the Fault Trees generated by the AltaRica compiler are quite different from those an analyst would write by hand. The minimal cutsets are however the expected ones. For instance, the minimal cutsets for the target "(BusbarPowerSupply.outFlow, false)", i.e. the busbar is not powered, with our first model are as follows.

GR.failure DG.failure   GR.failure CB3.failure
CBU1.failure CBU2.failure DG.failure   CBU1.failure TR2.failure DG.failure
CBU1.failure CBU2.failure CB3.failure   TR1.failure CBD2.failure DG.failure
CBU1.failure CBD2.failure CB3.failure   TR1.failure CBU2.failure DG.failure
CBU1.failure CBD2.failure DG.failure   TR1.failure CBU2.failure CB3.failure
CBD1.failure CBU2.failure DG.failure   TR1.failure TR2.failure CB3.failure
CBU1.failure TR2.failure CB3.failure   TR1.failure CBD2.failure CB3.failure
CBD1.failure CBU2.failure CB3.failure   TR1.failure TR2.failure DG.failure
CBD1.failure CBD2.failure DG.failure   CBD1.failure TR2.failure CB3.failure
CBD1.failure CBD2.failure CB3.failure   CBD1.failure TR2.failure DG.failure

4.2   Taking into Account Common Cause Failures

We shall now design a second model in order to take into account the common cause failure of the two transformers (due for instance to fire propagation). To do so, we have to model that transformers fail simultaneously when the common cause failure occurs. AltaRica provides powerful synchronization mechanisms to make transitions simultaneous. The idea is to create an event "CCF" and a transition at the first common ancestor of the two transformers, i.e. "PrimaryPowerSupply". The new code for the "PrimaryPowerSupply" is sketched in Figure 6. The operator & synchronizes the transitions "failure" defined for each transformer. The operator & is associative and commutative. Any number of transitions can be thus synchronized. To fire the synchronizing transition, at least one of the synchronized transitions must be fireable. If the synchronizing transition is fired, then all the possible synchronized transitions are fired simultaneously. The modality ? indicates that the corresponding synchronized transition is not mandatory to fire the synchronizing transition. The modality ! indicates that the corresponding transition is mandatory.

Note that the synchronized transitions continue to exist independently of the synchronizing transition. It is possible to hide transitions by means of a special clause "hide". Our second model has the following two additional minimal cutsets.

PrimaryPowerSupply.CCF, BackupPowerSupply.DG.failure
PrimaryPowerSupply.CCF, BackupPowerSupply.CB3.failure

```
block PrimaryPowerSupply
  ...
  event CCF (delay = exponential(lambdaCCF));
  parameter Real lambdaCCF = 1.0e-5;
  ...
  transition
    CCF: ?Line1.TR1.failure & ?Line2.TR2.failure;
  assertion
  ...
end
```

Fig. 6. Synchronization mechanism to model the Common Cause Failures

5 Targeting Compilation into Markov Chains

In this section we consider repairs of components, reconfigurations and limited resources. First, we assume that there is an unlimited number of repairers. Then, we refine our model to take into account a limited number of repairers. Both models are compiled into Markov chains.

5.1 Unlimited Number of Repairers

All components are repairable. The AltaRica code in this case is similar to the one of the "NonRepairableComponent" (see Figure 5), except that a new event "repair", the corresponding parameter mu and the corresponding transition are added to the previous model. Instead of the "NonRepairableComponent", the classes "Transformer" and "Grid" of this model, will inherit from a "Repairable-Component".

The on demand failures of the circuit breakers and the diesel generator are also considered. The automata describing the behavior of the diesel generator, the transformer, the grid and the circuit breakers are figured in 7 and 8. The solid lines correspond to the stochastic transitions, whereas the dashes correspond to the immediate ones.

Figure 9 represents the AltaRica 3.0 model of the spare component corresponding to the left automaton depicted in Figure 7. Transitions "stop", "start" and "failureOnDemand" are immediate (their delays are equal to 0). When the state variable "s" is equal to STANDBY and the flow variable "demanded" is true, the event "start" may occur with the probability "1-gamma" and the event "failureOnDemand" may occur with the probability "gamma". The values of the probabilities are given through the attribute "expectation".

In this example, we also take into consideration the short circuit case (see the automaton in the right hand side of the Figure 8). For the transformer, the event failure is considered as a short circuit, that will propagate into the whole line and make it instantly fail. If the short circuit is in the "Grid", the whole "Primary Power Supply" system will eventually fail, inducing the spare block (the "Backup Power Supply" system) to take over. The structure of the whole

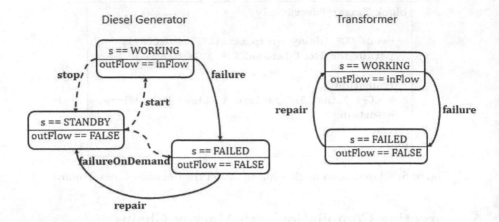

Fig. 7. Two automata describing the behavior of the Diesel Generator and the Transformer

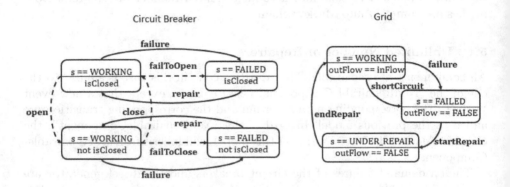

Fig. 8. Two automata describing the behavior of the Circuit Breaker and the Grid

model remains the same as in Figure 3. Some additional assertions are added in order to represent the propagation of the short circuit from the transformers to the grid and the reconfigurations (orders to open/close circuit breakers, to start/stop the diesel generator).

The semantics of AltaRica 3.0 are a Kripke structure (a reachability graph) with nodes defined by variable assignments (i.e. variables and their values) and edges defined by transitions and labeled by events. If the delays associated to the events are exponentially distributed, then the reachability graph can be interpreted as a continuous time Markov chain. In the case when the graph contains immediate transitions, they are just collapsed using the fact that an exponential delay with rate λ followed by an immediate transition of probability p is equivalent to a transition with an exponential delay of rate $p\lambda$.

```
domain SpareComponentState { STANDBY, WORKING, FAILED }
class SpareComponent
  Boolean s (init = WORKING);
  Boolean demanded, inFlow, outFlow (reset = false);
  event failure (delay = exponential(lambda));
  event repair (delay = exponential(mu));
  event start (delay = 0, expectation = 1 - gamma);
  event failureOnDemand (delay = 0, expectation = gamma);
  event stop(delay = 0);
  parameter Real lambda = 0.0001;
  parameter Real mu = 0.1;
  parameter Real gamma = 0.001;
  transition
    failure: s == WORKING -> s := FAILED;
    repair: s == FAILED -> s := STANDBY;
    start: s == STANDBY and demanded -> s := WORKING;
    failureOnDemand: s == STANDBY and demanded -> s := FAILED;
    stop: s == WORKING and not demanded -> s := STANDBY;
  assertion
    outFlow := s == WORKING and inFlow;
end
```

Fig. 9. AltaRica 3.0 model of a spare component (Diesel generator)

The generated Markov Chain contains 7270 states and 24679 transitions. The tool XMRK calculates the unavailability for different mission times. For $\lambda = 10^{-4}$, $\gamma = 10^{-3}$ and $\mu = 10^{-1}$, the probabilities are represented in Figure 12.

5.2 Limited Number of Repairers

In this part, we consider the case of a limited number of repairers, namely lower than the number of failures. Counter to the previous model, in order for a repair to take place, the repairer should be available and not used by another component. In this case, some changes in the behavior of the system take place. We will not only be interested in the "repair" transition, but also in the time it starts and ends at. Therefore, the "repair" transition is replaced by a whole set of transitions: startRepair and endRepair (see for example the automaton in the right hand side of the Figure 8). Besides, a new class called "RepairCrew" that defines when a job can start is added to the previous model (see Figure 10).

The transitions "startRepair" and "startJob", as well as "endRepair" and "endJob" are synchronized using the operator & as shown in Figure 11.

Compared to the definition of the common cause failure (see Figure 6), here the modality ! is used in the synchronization, which means that both synchronized events should be fireable to be able to fire the synchronizing transitions. In this example, the synchronized events are hidden explicitly using the clause "hide".

```
class RepairCrew
  Integer numberOfBusyRep (init = 0);
  parameter Integer totalNumberOfRepairers = 1;
  event startJob, endJob;
transition
  startJob: numberOfBusyRep < totalNumberOfRep ->
      numberOfBusyRep := numberOfBusyRep + 1;
  endJob: numberOfBusyRep > 0 ->
      numberOfBusyRep := numberOfBusyRep - 1;
end
```

Fig. 10. AltaRica model of the Repair Crew

```
block BusbarPowerSupply
  RepairCrew R;
  block PrimaryPowerSupply
    ...
  end
  block BackupPowerSupplySystem
    ...
  end
  event PPS_GR_startRepair, PPS_GR_endRepair;
  ...
transition
  PPS_GR_startRepair: !R.startJob & !PrimaryPowerSupply.GR.startRepair;
  PPS_GR_endRepair: !R.endJob & !PrimaryPowerSupply.GR.endRepair;
  hide R.startJob, PrimaryPowerSupply.GR.startRepair;
  hide R.endJob, PrimaryPowerSupply.GR.endRepair;
  ...
end
```

Fig. 11. A model targeting a compilation into Markov Chains (partial view)

In order to make the results more interesting, two numbers of repairers $n = 1$ and $n = 3$ are considered. This will allow us to compare the two graphs of unavailability. The same parameters mentioned in the first subsection are used here as well. The Markov Chain consists of 29332 states and 98010 transitions. The graph in Figure 12 shows indeed that the unavailability is lower when the number of repairers is bigger, and even lower when it is unlimited.

6 Conclusion

In this paper we showed, using an electrical system as a red-wire example, how AltaRica 3.0 can be used to model complex phenomena. A purely structural model was designed. Then, we derived four variants from it: two of them targeting a compilation into Fault Trees and two others targeting a compilation into

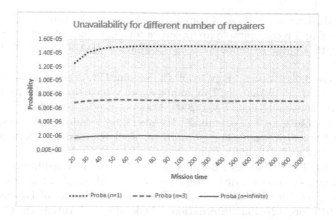

Fig. 12. Unavailability for a different number of repairers

Markov chains. Each variant, or subset of variants, was tailored for a particular assessment tool, i.e. to capture a particular aspect of the system under study. Based on this experience (and several others we have performed), we are convinced that this approach, consisting of deriving models by means of successive refinements, is a solid ground to build a modeling methodology. The calculations to be performed are actually very resource consuming. Therefore, a model is always a trade-off between the accuracy of the description and the ability to perform calculations. Refining a model in successive variants is a good way to seek a good trade-off. Moreover, the trade-off depends on the characteristics of the system to be observed. Therefore, different tools must be applied. As a consequence, the refinement process should not be linear, but rather have a tree-like structure.

References

1. Arnold, A., Griffault, A., Point, G., Rauzy, A.: The altarica formalism for describing concurrent systems. Fundamenta Informaticae 34, 109–124 (2000)
2. Rauzy, A.: Modes automata and their compilation into fault trees. Reliability Engneering and System Safety (2002)
3. Griffault, A., Vincent, A.: The mec 5 model-checker. In: Alur, R., Peled, D.A. (eds.) CAV 2004. LNCS, vol. 3114, pp. 488–491. Springer, Heidelberg (2004)
4. Khuu, M.: Contribution à l'accélération de la simulation stochastique sur des modèles AltaRica Data Flow. PhD thesis, Université de la Mèditerranée, Aix-Marscille II (2008)
5. Humbert, S., Seguin, C., Castel, C., Bosc, J.-M.: Deriving safety software requirements from an altarica system model. In: Harrison, M.D., Sujan, M.-A. (eds.) SAFECOMP 2008. LNCS, vol. 5219, pp. 320–331. Springer, Heidelberg (2008)
6. Quayzin, X., Arbaretier, E.: Performance modeling of a surveillance mission. In: Proceedings of the Annual Reliability and Maintainability Symposium, RAMS 2009, Fort Worth, Texas USA, pp. 206–211 (2009) ISBN 978-1-4244-2508-2

7. Sghairi, M., De-Bonneval, A., Crouzet, Y., Aubert, J.J., Brot, P., Laarouchi, Y.: Distributed and reconfigurable architecture for flight control system. In: Proceedings of 28th Digital Avionics Systems Conference (DASC 2009), Orlando, USA (2009)

8. Chaudemar, J.C., Bensana, E., Castel, C., Seguin, C.: Altarica and event-b models for operational safety analysis: Unmanned aerial vehicle case study. In: Proceedings Formal Methods and Tools, FMT 2009, London, England (2009)

9. Adeline, R., Cardoso, J., Darfeuil, P., Humbert, S., Seguin, C.: Toward a methodology for the altarica modelling of multi-physical systems. In: Proceedings of European Safety and Reliability Conference, ESREL 2010, Rhodes, Greece (2010)

10. Prosvirnova, T., Batteux, M., Brameret, P.A., Cherfi, A., Friedlhuber, T., Roussel, J.M., Rauzy, A.: The altarica 3.0 project for model-based safety assessment. In: Proceedings of 4th IFAC Workshop on Dependable Control of Discrete Systems, DCDS 2013, pp. 127–132. International Federation of Automatic Control, York (2013) ISBN: 978-3-902823-49-6, ISSN: 1474-6670

11. Noble, J., Taivalsaari, A., Moore, I.: Prototype-Based Programming: Concepts, Languages and Applications. Springer, Heidelberg (1999) ISBN-10: 9814021253. ISBN-13: 978-9814021258

12. Rauzy, A.: Guarded transition systems: A new states/events formalism for reliability studies. Journal of Risk and Reliability 222, 495–505 (2008)

13. Bouissou, M., Bon, J.L.: A new formalism that combines advantages of fault-trees and markov models: Boolean logic-driven markov processes. Reliability Engineering and System Safety 82, 149–163 (2003)

14. Meyer, B.: Object-Oriented Software Construction. Prentice Hall (1988) ISBN-10: 0136290493. ISBN-13: 978-0136290490

15. Abadi, M., Cardelli, L.: A Theory of Objects. Monographs in Computer Science. Springer-Verlag. New York Inc. (1998) ISBN-10: 0387947752. ISBN-13: 978-0387947754

16. Hatchuel, A., Weil, B.: C-k design theory: An advanced formulation. research in engineering design. Research in Engineering Design 19, 181–192 (2009)

Applying Formal Methods
into Safety-Critical Health Applications

Mohammad-Reza Gholami and Hanifa Boucheneb

VeriForm Lab,
Department of Computer and Software Engineering
Ecole Polytechnique of Montreal, Canada
{reza.gholami,hanifa.boucheneb}@polymtl.ca

Abstract. Software performs a critical role in almost every aspect of
our daily life specially in the embedded systems of medical equipments.
A key goal of software engineering is to make it possible for developers to
construct systems that operate reliably regardless of their complexity. In
this paper, by employing Model-Based Design for large and safety-related
applications and applying formal verification techniques, we define specific properties to ensure that a software system satisfies its correctness
criteria. We use the formal approach to study and verify the properties of
a medical device known as Endotracheal intubation. We present how the
system is modeled in the Simulink and Stateflow and present a functionality formalization. In order to formally prove some critical properties,
we employ Simulink Design Verifier toolset.

1 Introduction

The increasing complexity of embedded systems (e.g. avionics, health and automotive systems) conveys the producers of safety-critical applications to use
more systematic processes for development. Traditional design processes are not
fast enough in discovering the errors in requirements; hence, the whole process
would be longer and more expensive.

A key goal of software engineering is to construct systems that operate reliably regardless of their complexity. A promising approach to achieve this goal
is to use formal methods, which are mathematically based languages, tools and
techniques for specifying and verifying such systems. Formal methods can significantly increase our understanding of a system by disclosing inconsistencies,
ambiguities, and incompleteness in the early design phase so that they can be
eliminated in order to ensure the appropriate behavior of the system.

Software vendors typically spend large amounts of time of their total development time and resources on software testing. The severity of the defects also
increases the detection time and the cost of total development budget for a
software product. So there is a need for a sophisticated discipline of software
engineering to ensure that all the expected requirements were satisfied by means
of the specified software. In other words, software verification refers to the process that can determine whether the artifacts of one software-development phase
fulfill the specified requirements produced during the previous phase.

F. Ortmeier and A. Rauzy (Eds.): IMBSA 2014, LNCS 8822, pp. 195–208, 2014.

In a safety critical system, even a single error in the source code and an associated malfunction of the system can cause high costs and could even endanger the health of people. In critical real-time embedded systems, verification and validation activities are becoming huge and quite costly when the complexity and size of the systems grows.

Formal verification can be performed by employing Model-Based Design [9] in order to specify formal model of the system. Model-Based design facilitates the addressing of difficulties and complexities existing in control system design by providing an executable specification which implies that the model exists as more than just a document, but as a functional part of the design process [15]. It also provides a single design environment that enables developers to use a single model of their entire system for data analysis, model visualization, testing and validation, and ultimately product deployment, with or without automatic code generation [14]. Furthermore, model-based design creates a structure for software reuse that permits established designs to be effectively and reliably upgraded in a more simplistic and cost effective manner.

In this paper we are using the formal approach to study and verify the properties of an Endotracheal intubation which is a specific type of tracheal tube that is inserted through the patient's mouth to maintain an open airway [1]. This medical device is illustrated in Figure 1. Using Simulink/Stateflow, we come up with a model with parallel components, where event passing and synchronization is efficiently provided.

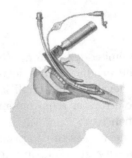

Fig. 1. Endotracheal intubation

The rest of the paper is organized as follows: Section 2 presents some background and previous work related to this research topic. Employed tools are described in Section 3. We present our case study in Section 4 which consists of definition, properties, and implementation of the model. The outcomes of our implementation are analyzed in Section 5. Finally, Section 6 concludes our paper.

2   Background and Related Work

Formal methods enhance verification process by using formal notations and concepts in writing requirements and specifications. In formal methods, mathematical and logical techniques are used to express, investigate, and analyze the specification, design, documentation, and behavior of both hardware and software. The word *formal* in formal methods derives from *formal logic* and means "to do with form" [19]. In formal logic, dependence on human intuition and judgment is avoided in evaluating the arguments. In order to constitute an acceptable statement or a valid proof, formal logic employs a restricted language with very precise rules for writing assumptions, theorems, and proofs. In formal methods for computer science, languages are enriched with some of the ideas from programming languages and are called *specification languages*, but their underlying interpretation is usually based on a standard logic.

Formal verification in the field of software means the automated proof of specified properties on the code without executing the program. Also, it ensures that a design conforms to some precisely expressed notion of functional correctness [6]. The main benefits of formal verification in comparison to testing (dynamic verification), are its soundness and exhaustiveness. Specifications in formal methods are *well-formed* mathematical statements which are used to specify a property that needs to be verified in the system [4].

Many projects currently use MathWorks Simulink and Simulink Coder [3] which formerly known as Real-Time Workshop for at least some of their modeling and code development [7]. This kind of Design focuses on using executable system models as the foundation for the specification, design, implementation, test, and verification [5]. The executable specification in Model-based design, replaces parts or all of the paper format of the system specification and requirements as the main deliverable between design stages. It consists of an executable model of the application algorithm that can be simulated. The next step of Model-Based Design is known as model elaboration which consists of transforming the executable specification into a more design based form [17]. In Section 3, we briefly explain how to build an executable model by using Simulink and Stateflow.

Recently, some efforts have been made in order to employ formal methods in designing critical systems. In particular, Jiang *et al.* [13] developed a real-time Virtual Heart Model (VHM) for modeling the electro-physiological operation of proper functioning and malfunctioning. They introduced a timed-automaton model to define the timing properties of the heart and used Simulink Design Verifier as the main tool for designing their model.

Simulink/Stateflow has also been used in [8] to model a train tracking function for an automatic train protection system. The model was implemented based on the requirements specification document in which safety and functional properties were originally written in natural language. The authors of [8] used Simulink Design Verifier for verification and validation. They also had a positive experience when they used this tool for the safety-critical function in the railway transportation domain.

Another case example for a medical device has been presented in [16] where an iterative approach is applied for system verification based on software architectural model. They employed Simulink/Stateflow for describing the component

level behavior of the model and used Simulink Design Verifier for proving the
system level properties to establish component-level properties.

In our work, we also use Simulink/Stateflow to model and simulate the system. For the formal analysis, we use Simulink Design Verifier, which intensively
employs the BMC and K-Induction features of the PROVER[2] engine to establish the satisfiability of the proof objectives. We also employ this tool to verify
Integer overflow, Division by zero, Assertions and Violations of design properties
as a part of our work.

3   Simulink and Stateflow

The executable model can be built by Simulink which is an environment for
multi-domain simulation and Model-based Design for dynamic and embedded
systems. Mode logic in Simulink models is described in terms of hierarchical
state machines specified in a variant of Statecharts called Stateflow [3].

Stateflow is a widespread model-based development environment is Matlab/Simulink toolset, which is used in several industries, such as aerospace,
medical, and automotive. It uses a variant of the finite state machine notation established by Harel [11] and provides the language elements required to
describe complex logic in a natural, readable, and understandable form. Since
it is tightly integrated with MATLAB and Simulink, it can provide an efficient
environment for designing embedded systems that contain control and supervisory. In particular, Stateflow diagram enables the graphical representation of
hierarchical and parallel states as well as transitions between them and inherits
all simulation and code generation capabilities from Matlab toolset.

A state is called as *superstate* when it contains other states and a state is called
substate when it is contained by a supersate. When a state consists of one or more
substates, it has *decomposition* that can be either parallel (AND) or exclusive
(OR) decomposition. All substates at a particular level in the hierarchy of the
stateflow must have the same decomposition.

In parallel (AND) decomposition, states can be active at the same time and
the activity of each parallel state is essentially independent of other states.

We can use our defined *Events* to trigger actions in parallel states of a Stateflow chart. Broadcasting of an event can trigger a transition and/or an action.
The *Actions* can be executed either as part of a transition from one state to
another or based on the activity status of a state which can be entry, during,
exit, and on event actions.

The general form of a transition in Stateflow is presented in Figure 2. It
shows the behavior of a simple event, condition and transition action specified
on a transition from one exclusive (OR) state to another. Initially, state *Start* is
active and *Entry* action is executed. When the event *eFill* is received, the chart
root detects that there is a valid transition to state *Fill* as a result of the event
eFill, so it validates the condition and if the result is true, the *Condition Action*
immediately gets executed and completed. The state *Start* is marked as inactive
and the *Transition Action* is executed and completed when the transition destination *Fill* has been determined to be valid. States can have different actions

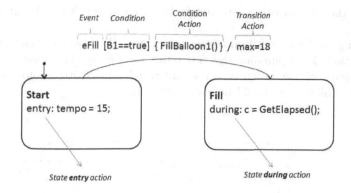

Fig. 2. Stateflow Semantic

such as: *entry, during, exit,* and *on event-name* which are being executed based on the current status of the active state.

4   Case Study

This case study aims to show and familiarize how a system works with a framework where time aspects are combined with multi task programming. In this case study, we are modeling and verifying the properties of a Filling system of balloons of an intubation probe. An intubation probe is placed to ensure continuous passage of air to the lungs and introduce oxygen sensors, aspiration probes to the lung for patient treatment. This system consists of two balloons, two access valves for manual inflation, two pressure sensors, a power distributor, a pump and an air tank. The pump is actuated by a gear motor and a transmission by a cylinder rack. The pumped air is propelled through the power distributor (B and D) to one of the balloons or outside. The probe has several buttons (*Start, Stop, Duration, Pressure, StopAlarm*) and LEDs (*L1, L2, Alarm*). The Alarm LED reports the anomalies. L1 and L2 are witnesses indicating the inflated balloons, and the button *StopAlarm* allows the user to stop the alarm. The system controlled by a Programmable Controller who is responsible for controlling the commands and messages which are sent to or received by other components. We are using Simulink and Stateflow as an integrated tool environment for modeling, and Simulink Design Verifier for verification of some properties.

4.1   The Model

A model is known as abstract representation of a system. Software model is actually the ways of expressing a software design, and in order to express the software design some kind of abstract language or pictures are usually used. Software modeling need to deal with the entire software design, including interfaces, interactions with other software, and all the software methods [10]. Engineers can model the system using a modeling language which it can be graphical or textual [12].

According to the description of the case study, the first step when modeling the Intubation, is to pinpoint the superstates in the system. One of the most important parts of the design is to find out which superstates should be parallel (AND) and which ones should be exclusive (OR).

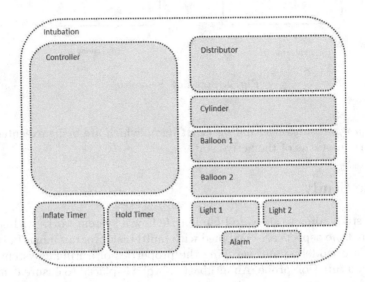

Fig. 3. Components of the Endotracheal Intubation

In the Intubation statechart there are ten distinguished blocks which are illustrated in Figure 3. All of these blocks are working in a parallel execution order. These blocks are represented with ten different superstates in the model. In every moment of running the model, at least one state has to be active in each superstate. The superstates are: *Controller, Distributor, Cylinder, Balloons, Alarm, Lights* and *Timers*. These superstates are designed to be parallel(AND) because a change in these states is allowed at every time step.

The superstates interact together through sending direct broadcast event and one simplified function to make the model smaller, initializing the variables and status. Direct event broadcasting is used to prevent receiving an error pertaining to recursion in the Stateflow chart. In our figures, we remove some functions are removed to simplicity. To explain and describe the model, this section is divided into three different parts as follow:

- Inputs & Local variables, ranges and default values
- Events
- Components (Parallel (AND) States)

In the following we will give a short description of the components. We included some screenshots taken from Simulink to complement the description of the statecharts.

Variables:
We maintain the current state and values of the processes using local variables. For simplification, we used integer values to represent the corresponding physical step of the components. The range of variables, their steps and default values are defined and set in declaration of the stateflow, for example, for the cylider:
$int\ nCylPos = -1$

For this specific variable, the value can be set to either -1, 0 or 1 which respectively correspond to the position of the cylinder as: *Back*, *Center* and *Forward*. Some input and output variables for the Stateflow diagram listed in Table 1.

Table 1. Variables

Name	Type	Values
nCylPos	Output	-1, 0, 1, 2
nBallonState	Output	-1, 0, 1
bLightState	Output	true, false
bAlarm	Output	true, false
nDuration	Input	10, 20, 30 mins
nPressure	Input	12, 18, 24
bStopAlarm	Input	true, false
bStart	Input	true, false

Events:
Different events were defined to model the communication between different components of the system. According to their usage, they are defined in the statechart as *Directed Event Broadcast*. Their relationship with each section is listed in the Table 2.

Table 2. Events

Component	Events
Alarms	eStartAlarm, eStopAlarm
Lights	eLight1On, eLight1Off, eLight2On, eLight2Off
Distributor	eFill, eEmpty
Cylinder	vPlus, vMinus

Statechart
This section describes each component that we have modeled as superstates. We explain the nature and the interaction of each one of them.

Controller. The model of the controller was realized from the specification based on the provided Grafcet [18]. In order to model the controller some local variables representing the steps, transitions and actions and some local variables representing the channels and reflecting the value of local actions in the system were also defined. The local variables B and D are defined as *boolean*, and being used to set the channels and activate them.

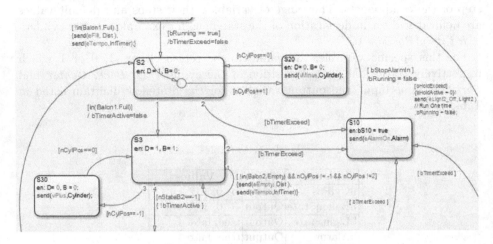

Fig. 4. Part of Controller State

The entire controller is included in a single superstate. In order to do a specific action, the controller set the values for the channels and send the event to the Distributor state. Table 3 presents events and channels used by the controller for specific actions.

Instead of modeling the user's interaction with the system. We use local variables to simulate the choice of target pressure and the targeted cycle time (*nPressure* and *nDuration*). Those values are set at the beginning and are left untouched during the simulation. Our model assumes that at the beginning the cylinder is in the position *Back* and both balloons are considered *Empty*.

One of the major building blocks of our controller which is responsible to fill and empty the balloons is illustrated in Figure 4. In this figure, in order to inflate the first balloon, on the entry action of the state *S2* corresponded values for B and D are set then the event *eFill* is sent to the *Distributor*.

Cylinder. The cylinder has three substates: *Back, Center* and *Forward.* This state is constantly waiting to receive the events *vPlus* or *vMinus* from the controller to change its position. To model the 2 seconds delay for each position transition, we included an in-between location, and used an *after* temporal operator between each position. Once the delay is exhausted, the cylinder position changes. We use a local variable *nCylPos* (*Back* = -1, *Center* = 0, *Forward* = 1 and *In-between* = 2) to store the current position of the cylinder. Initially, the state *Back* is active. We set this variable to 2 when the cylinder is in transition between two positions. The controller has guards using the transitional value to ensure the cylinder has completed its movement.

Pressure Distributor. This state receives the specified event from the controller in order to launch the selected action for filling or emptying the desired balloon. The selected action is relevant to the current value of the local variables *B* and *D* which are set to *true* or *false* by the controller before sending the event *eFill* or *eEmpty*. In addition, to complete the entire function, it also sends specific events to states *Cylinder* and *Balloon* for their relevant actions. Table 3 shows the events and variables used for specific functions.

Table 3. Actions

Distributor Channel	Event	Function
B=0, D=1	vPlus	Inflate ballon 1
B=1, D=0	vPlus	Inflate ballon 2
D=0 or B=0, D=0	vPlus	Move cylinder forward
B=0, D=1	vMinus	Deflate ballon 1
B=1, D=1	vMinus	Deflate ballon 2
D=0 or B=0, D=0	vMinus	Move cylinder backward

Initially, the state *Init* is active and waits to receive a specific event from *Controller* to complete the selected function. The state on the rightmost side of Figure 5 has to run iteratively until the destined balloon is filled. Similarly, the emptiness of the balloon is ensured by running the state on the leftmost side of this figure.

Balloons. The state balloon has three substates: *Empty*, *NotFull* and *Full*. In this model, we consider two different superstates corresponding to each balloon. Initially, the state *Empty* is active in both balloons. The transition between substates has a guard; so, the movement is done when one of the events *eFill* or *eEmpty* is received from the state *Distributor*. We use a local variable *nBalloon-State* (*Empty* = -1, *NotFull* = 0, *Full* = 1) to store the current status of the balloon.

Timers. In our model, timers are designed as two different components: The *InflateTimer* which is responsible for the inflation time of a balloon, and the *HoldTimer* which is the time that a balloon should maintain the status *Full*.

The state *InflateTimer* contains two substates: State *Off* which is initially active, and the state *On* which is activated by the controller while requesting for a *Fill* function. The *InflateTimer* is illustrated in Figure 6:

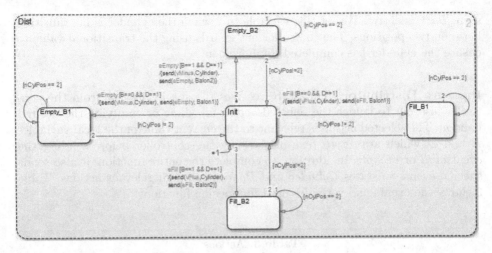

Fig. 5. Pressure distributor

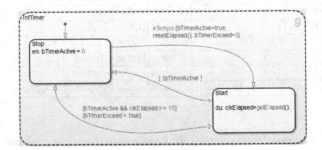

Fig. 6. Timer State

Alarm. The alert state contains two substates: *Off* and *On*. Initially, the state *Off* is active. When the timer exceeds from the specified threshold or if any anomaly happens, the controller stops the system operation and sends the event *eAlarm*. Once the event received, the state *On* will be activated and remains in this state until the user stops the alarm.

5   Results and Analysis

This section describes our method and results of formal verification using Design Verifier with Simulink and Stateflow. Before verification, we run the simulation for our provided model using predefined input parameters in order to ensure that the model can be executed properly. Figure 7 illustrates an execution snapshot of our Simulink implementation for one of the system properties which states that two lights should not be turned on at the same time. Similarly, Figure 8 validates the emptiness property of each balloon, meaning that a balloon's light is *off* when the balloon is completely empty.

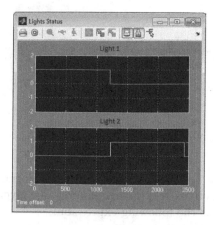

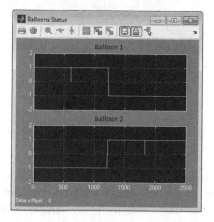

Fig. 7. Lights status   **Fig. 8.** Balloons status

5.1 Properties

The term property refers to a logical expression of signal values in a model. For example, we can specify that a signal in a model should attain a particular value during simulation. The Simulink Design Verifier software can then prove the validity of such properties. This is done by performing a formal analysis of the model to prove or disprove the specified properties. If the software disproves a property, it provides a counterexample that demonstrates a property violation. Our design model consists of the following properties:

1. Balloons should not be inflated simultaneously for more than five time steps.
2. The pressure in each balloon never exceeds a predetermined value.
3. Any anomaly is followed by alarm activation.
4. The lights *L1* and *L2* are never illuminated simultaneously.
5. There must be no anomaly alarm (False alarms).
6. If a light is *ON* then the corresponding balloon is inflated.

The following section details each property and the results obtained by Simulink Design Verifier:

Property I: The goal of this property is to ensure that two balloons are not inflated simultaneously more than the accepted time. Although the controller sends appropriate commands to inflate a balloon and deflate another, but the functionality also depends to the position of the cylinder and current state of each balloons. So, verifying this property ensures this time will not exceed the expected time steps. As illustrated in Figure 9, we use a temporal operator *Detector* in formalization of this property. This property is proven *Valid* with values greater than 5, and is proven *Falsified* with values between 1 and 5.

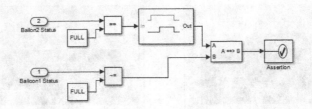

Fig. 9. Formalization of property I

Property II: The goal of this property is to validate that the model do not permit the pressure within the two balloons to exceed the maximum value given by the user. This property can be defined as the following expression:

$$A[\ ](nPressB1 <= nPressure \\ \&\& \ nPressB2 <= nPressure) \tag{1}$$

We have modeled this property by doing a simple comparison between the balloon pressure and the target pressure using our variables $nPressB1$ and $nPressB2$ which contains the current pressure within the balloons 1 and 2, and by using $nPressure$ which represents the target pressure given by the user. We validate both pressures by using the same property statement.

Property III: The goal of this property is to make sure our model does not skip any alarms. Therefore all possible anomaly should be followed by an alarm activation. In our model, the alarm is triggered by the event $eAlarmOn$. It automatically lights the Alarm indicator. We have modeled this property by using the light 'On' location and the controller's anomaly location 'S10' which is a location where all anomaly detections are directed.

$$A[\ ]((bRunning == true \&\& in(Controller.S10)) \\ \Rightarrow Alarm.On\ ) \tag{2}$$

This property validates that our model is running and then makes sure that all paths that goes through 'S10' are followed by the 'Alarm.On' location.

Property IV: The goal of this property is to make sure that both balloon's status light are not both lighted at the same moment.

$$A[\ ]((Light1.On + Light2.On) <= 1) \tag{3}$$

Since this property is a safety property, all paths needs to validate it. As we saw in property I, we may have both balloons inflated for a short period of time. Therefore, in order to validate this property, we have to make sure the controller have control over the lights. The controller always starts by closing a light, and then opens another. This is validated by making the sum of values in states 'Light1.On' and 'Light2.On' which should not exceed 1.

Property V: The goal of this property is to make sure our model does not generate false alarms. To address this property we have designed a statement that validates the opposite condition and applied a *'not'* to it.

$$A[\,](not\ (bRunning == true \\ \&\&\ bAlarmDetected == false \\ \&\&\ Alarm.On)) \tag{4}$$

This invariant property makes sure that we never end up in a state where we have *'bRunning == true'* (which means the process is undergoing) and we have the alarm light on without having detected any anomaly. The anomaly detection always sets the variable *'bAlarmDetected'* to *true*. Hence, if *'bAlarmDetected'* is set to *false* we have no anomaly and 'Alarm.Off' is valid.

Property VI: The goal of this property is to ensure that when a light for a balloon is on the corresponding balloon's pressure has reached the target pressure.

$$A[\,]((Light1.On \Rightarrow nPressB1 == nPressure) \\ and\ (Light2.On \Rightarrow nPressB2 == nPressure)) \tag{5}$$

We have included both balloons in the same property, where they both need to be *true*. This statement validates that when the state 'Light1.On' is active, we have reached the target pressure in the first balloon. It does the same validation for the second balloon and ensures that both condition are always valid.

6 Conclusion

In this paper, we used formal approach and model-based design in order to specify and formally verify the functionalities of a medical device The system is modeled with parallel components in Simulink/Stateflow, where event passing/handling and synchronization is efficiently provided. We also employed Simulink Design Verifier toolset to prove correctness of the model as well as some important properties from different components of the system. Initially, total property proving time was about ten hours on a Core 2 Due machine with 4GB of RAM. After removing some dead logic in some states like *Distributer* and specifying the precise proof assumptions to inputs, we could significantly reduce it to seven hours and sixteen minutes.

References

1. Intensive care hotline, intubation, http://intensivecarehotline.com/intubation/
2. Prover plug-in, prover, http://www.prover.com/products/
3. User's guide, the mathworks, http://www.mathworks.com/products/
4. Alagar, V.S., Periyasamy, K.: Specification of software systems. Springer-Verlag New York Inc. (2011)

5. Behboodian, A.: Model-based design. DSP Magazine (May 2006)
6. Bjesse, P.: What is formal verification? ACM SIGDA Newsletter 35(24), 1 (2005)
7. Denney, E., Trac, S.: A software safety certification tool for automatically generated guidance, navigation and control code. In: IEEE Aerospace Conference, pp. 1–11. IEEE (2008)
8. Etienne, J.F., Fechter, S., Juppeaux, E.: Using simulink design verifier for proving behavioral properties on a complex safety critical system in the ground transportation domain. In: Complex Systems Design & Management, pp. 61–72 (2010)
9. Fey, I., Mller, J., Conrad, M.: Model-based design for safety-related applications. In: Proceedings of SAE Convergence (2008)
10. Fowler, M.: UML distilled: A brief guide to the standard object modeling language. Addison-Wesley Professional (2004)
11. Harel, D.: Statecharts: A visual formalism for complex systems. Science of Computer Programming 8(3), 231–274 (1987)
12. He, X., Ma, Z., Shao, W., Li, G.: A metamodel for the notation of graphical modeling languages. In: 31st Annual International Computer Software and Applications Conference, COMPSAC 2007, vol. 1, pp. 219–224. IEEE (2007)
13. Jiang, Z., Pajic, M., Connolly, A., Dixit, S., Mangharam, R.: Real-time heart model for implantable cardiac device validation and verification. In: 2010 22nd Euromicro Conference on Real-Time Systems (ECRTS), pp. 239–248. IEEE (2010)
14. Krasner, J.: Model-based design and beyond: Solutions for todays embedded systems requirements. Technical report, Mathworks (2004)
15. Friedman, J., Anthony, M.: Model-based design for large safety-critical systems: A discussion regarding model architecture. Technical report, Mathworks
16. Murugesan, A., Whalen, M.W., Rayadurgam, S., Heimdahl M.P.E.: Compositional verification of a medical device system. In: Proceedings of the 2013 ACM SIGAda Annual Conference on High Integrity Language Technology, pp. 51–64. ACM (2013)
17. Popovici, K., Lalo, M.: Formal model and code verification in model-based design. In: Joint IEEE North-East Workshop on Circuits and Systems and TAISA Conference, NEWCAS-TAISA 2009, pp. 1–4. IEEE (2009)
18. Portugal, P., Carvalho, A.: The grafcet specification (2005)
19. Rushby, J.: Formal methods and the certification of critical systems. SRI International, Computer Science Laboratory (1993)

Author Index